on track ...
Steely
Dan

the music of Walter Becker & Donald Fagen

every album, every song

Jez Rowden

sonicbondpublishing.com

on track ...
Steely Dan

the music of Walter Becker & Donald Fagen

every album, every song

Jez Rowden

sonicbondpublishing.com

Sonicbond Publishing Limited
www.sonicbondpublishing.co.uk
Email: info@sonicbondpublishing.co.uk

First Published in the United Kingdom 2020
First Published in the United States 2020

British Library Cataloguing in Publication Data:
A Catalogue record for this book is available from the British Library

Copyright Jez Rowden 2019

ISBN 978-1-78952-043-9

Typeset in ITC Garamond & ITC Avant Garde
Printed and bound in England

Graphic design and typesetting: Full Moon Media

Acknowledgements

Firstly, I must extend a huge thank you to Stephen Lambe and all at Sonicbond for giving me the opportunity to write this book and more fully familiarise myself with a band that has resonated deeply with me for many years. It has been a fascinating journey, learning more about these wonderful songs and getting closer to the wickedly devious minds of the perpetrators. To that end, I must also offer my deepest appreciation to Donald Fagen and Walter Becker themselves, for going the extra mile and making these songs as good as they could be – the results achieved speak for themselves and are often extraordinary.

Big thanks to Roger Trenwith and Mel Allen for their insights on the draft manuscript, allowing for significant improvements to be made to the finished item you now hold, also to Kevan Furbank for his support.

Last – but certainly not least – to my long-suffering wife Paula ('Dan-widow' over many months) I offer my heartfelt love and thanks. During a particularly testing period for us, writing this book – for good or ill – has helped to keep me going, and I would never have got anywhere near finishing it without you.
Love you lots x

This book is dedicated to Walter Carl Becker (1950-2017)

on track ...

Steely Dan

the music of Walter Becker & Donald Fagen

Contents

1. Foreword 9
2. Donald and Walter – The Early Years 11
3. The Birth of The Dan 13
4. Can't Buy a Thrill (1972) 15
5. Countdown to Ecstasy (1973) 26
6. Pretzel Logic (1974) 33
7. Katy Lied (1975) 42
8. The Royal Scam (1976) 51
9. Aja (1977) 59
10. Gaucho (1980) 68
11. The Nightfly (Donald Fagen solo) (1982) 79
12. Interregnum (1982 – 1993) 86
13. Kamakiriad (Donald Fagen solo) (1993) 88
14. 11 Tracks of Whack (Walter Becker solo) (1994) 94
15. Alive in America (1995) 100
16. Two Against Nature (2000) 102
17. Plush TV Jazz-Rock Party (2000) 111
18. Everything Must Go (2003) 112
19. Morph the Cat (Donald Fagen solo) (2006) 118
20. Circus Money (Walter Becker solo) (2008) 124
21. Sunken Condos (Donald Fagen solo) (2012) 130
22. Live 2013 – 2017, Becker's Death & Beyond 136
23. Postscript 138
Appendices:
24. Becker & Fagen's Early Recordings: 1968-1971 139
25. You've Got to Walk It Like You Talk It or You'll Lose That Beat
    (OST) (1971) 146
26. Official Compilations 148
27. 20 Dan Deep Cuts 150
28. Bibliography & References 151

Foreword
'Any major dude will tell you...'

It's true. Anyone with a decent knowledge of popular music should be able to tell you that Steely Dan is one of the finest bands to emerge in the 1970s – or indeed at any time.

But is it a band? Yes. No.

Yes and No?

Initially at least, starting out as a traditional rock band, but always under the control of arch songwriting savants Walter Becker and Donald Fagen, as an outlet for their idiosyncratic songs. Despite having other band members on board in the early days, the weirdly dynamic and deviously 'other' nature of the duo's songs were always at the heart of the matter. Becker and Fagen perpetually sought ways to present them in the best light, ultimately backing away from live performance to hone their studio work, with the help of some of the best session musicians around.

Band or not, I'll often refer to Steely Dan as such within the body of this text. But if these things need to be sorted out at all, Steely Dan is an aesthetic, a way of doing things, a standard of excellence, a world view, a knowing wink and a muffled chuckle at the situations people continue to get themselves involved in. It is a trademark and one that has the word 'Quality' woven into it in immaculate stitching.

After several years of working to get their songs heard in their native New York, a series of fortunate breaks led Becker and Fagen to California and the formation of the band that was to become Steely Dan in 1972. The lucky breaks continued to make the band a massive hit with listeners – even if most of them were unaware of the depravity going on within the darkly comic yet smoothly upbeat songs.

The songs sparkled and fizzed, but with their penchant for jazz, R'n'B, soul and doo-wop, the pop songs they wrote were always going to be different; pop songs played by a rock band underpinned with jazz. The Groove was always where it was at for them, Fagen confirming that 'when you get a groove going, time flies.' Nothing interfered with The Groove, the result being some of the most rhythmically catchy songs ever written. Crucial to the success of the band were producer Gary Katz, who understood what they were trying to do, and engineer Roger Nichols, who added the fairy dust that made Dan albums sound like no one else, becoming legendary in the world of engineering.

There's a quote in the booklet of the *Citizen Steely Dan* boxed collection that says that Steely Dan 'were busy being the band of the '90s way back in the '70s'. I'd go further; Steely Dan is a band for all time, with a catalogue of songs that rank right up there with anyone – and I include the Beatles in that – a timeless body of work that will hopefully mesmerise and seduce for generations to come. If you're unsure of the quality inherent within the Dan discography, I think it's fair to say that you can drop the proverbial needle at any point within it and come up with gold. A remarkable achievement.

This book endeavours to look at the careers of rock 'n' roll's most successful outsiders, with specific consideration to the songs, not in an academic sense but with the unexcused enthusiasm of a fan, in the hope that it encourages more people to listen, or for those who know the songs to listen a little more deeply. You won't regret it. We'll look at all the Steely Dan albums and all the officially released songs, plus many unreleased recordings (available to hear online and well worth seeking out as they underline the quality even in songs they chose to discard). We'll look at the early demo material recorded by Walter and Donald prior to forming Steely Dan, official live releases and solo albums (but not unreleased solo tracks). Compilations are covered briefly, but unofficial live recordings are omitted, as are cover versions played by the reconvened touring band in recent years.

The lyrics of Becker and Fagen are often inscrutable and open to interpretation – and many interpretations are available. The ones included here are the ones I favour; they are not meant to be in any way definitive so feel free to come up with your own.

With over 40 million album sales, numerous hit singles and an induction into the Rock and Roll Hall of Fame, from humble beginnings many of the songs of Walter Becker and Donald Fagen have entered the wider consciousness, the single-minded determination of the pair and their wilful belief in their output helping them to achieve greater success than they could ever have imagined. However, I wonder how many listeners realise the depth of the intricate beauty and detail with which these songs are imbued? The hardcore Dan fanatics know, drawn into a bizarre world of lowlifes, scoundrels and illicit deeds, sharply at odds with the shining smoothness of the music.

Walter Becker and Donald Fagen: the coolest, baddest, funkiest mofos ever to surf The Groove.

Donald and Walter – The Early Years

Donald Jay Fagen was born in Passaic, New Jersey on 10 January 1948, moving to the suburb of Fair Lawn in 1958 and then to South Brunswick. 'I think I lost faith in my parents' judgment', he said of his distaste for the suburbs, 'it was probably the first time I realised I had my own view of life.'

He became interested in rock and R&B at around ten years old, his first record was Chuck Berry's 'Reelin' and Rockin'', quickly moving on to jazz via late-night radio stations. Fagen later stated that he liked the music, but even at that early stage, he saw jazz as an appealing 'cultural alternative'. During the early 1960s, he saw and was inspired by many of the luminaries of the genre, including Count Basie's band at Birdland: 'When the whole band pumped out one of those thirteenth chords, you could feel the breeze on your face.' He learnt piano, largely self-taught, but never wanted to be a singer. A few years later he became drawn to funk, soul, and Motown, all influences on his later work.

Fagen studied English Literature at the liberal Bard College in Annandale-on-Hudson from 1965, meeting Walter Becker in 1967 after overhearing him playing guitar at a campus café and liking what he heard – 'an authentic blues touch and feel, and a convincing vibrato'.

Walter Carl Becker was born on 20 February 1950 in Queens, New York. His parents separated when he was young, his mother moving back to her native England, and he lived with his father and grandmother in Eastchester. He started learning saxophone but moved to guitar under the influence of neighbour and future Spirit guitarist Randy California, whose mother taught Walter his first chords. He graduated from high school in 1967 before moving on to Bard College.

Becker and Fagen discovered mutual literary, cinematic and musical influences, and immediately began writing songs together. From the limited pool of musicians available at Bard they formed various bands, including The Leather Canary with fellow student Chevy Chase on drums (who later described the group as 'a bad jazz band'), and enjoyed the beatnik lifestyle.

Becker flunked out of college in 1968 and they moved to Brooklyn to begin building a career as songwriters, prior to Fagen graduating in 1969. Hawking their wares around the Brill Building, starting at the top floor and working their way down, knocking on doors as they went, they had little initial success but eventually arrived at the fourth-floor office of Jay and the Americans, a pop band who had achieved success in the early '60s, including opening for both the Beatles and the Rolling Stones at their first US shows. There they met band founder Kenny Vance, who recalled that 'Fagen was basically a nonentity in terms of social interaction. Walter was the front man, more of the spokesperson for the two of them.' They didn't have a tape so played some songs with Fagen at the office piano. Vance didn't hear pop potential, but he knew there was something there – 'It was like aliens had landed in the Brill Building'; the songs were different, quirky. He signed them to a publishing deal and hired them as sidemen for Jay and the Americans.

They arranged horns and strings for the Americans and spent about 18 months touring as bassist and keyboard man (under the pseudonyms Gus Mahler and Tristan Fabriani), amusing themselves by subtly mocking their employers whenever possible, and played on the group's last Top 20 hit, 'Walkin' in the Rain'. Singer Jay Black dubbed them 'the Manson and Starkweather of rock 'n' roll' (after Charles Manson and spree-killer Charles Starkweather) and later remembered them as 'cocksuckers who I may kick in the ass next time I see them', although he admired their skills – 'There are no finer songwriters in the country ... If they don't blow it by being assholes, they'll be around for a long time.'

Becker shared Fagen's jazz and soul influences and the pair also drew inspiration from Bob Dylan and The Band's *Music from Big Pink*. Describing their influences, Becker later said, 'I think we were trying to be as musically sophisticated as we could, and that wasn't really a priority for a lot of people, and still isn't. A lot of people want things to be as rootsy and gutsy as possible, which is very valid too ... I think a lot of people were influenced by the same things we were. Old jazz records, classical ideas...'

Between 1968 and 1971 they wrote dozens of songs, 28 of which are known to have been recorded as lo-fi demos to promote their songwriting, a handful of these later reappearing in completed form on Steely Dan albums. In 1989, Becker noted that there were some 'very very strange things and people didn't react as favourably to them as we had hoped at the time. So, this gradually showed us that we perhaps had to tone down certain elements of what we were doing. And I think it was a maturing process, too. We were wise-ass college kids writing bizarre, somewhat grotesque things and gradually we moved away from that.'

In 1970, they achieved some success when Barbra Streisand recorded their 'I Mean to Shine' for her *Barbra Joan Streisand* album, released in August 1971. Producer Richard Perry changed the arrangement and some of the words, but it was their first professionally recorded song, Fagen playing Hammond organ for the session. You can certainly hear elements of Steely Dan in the chording, Fagen later saying, 'Not a good song, but at least she recorded it.'

Also in 1970, in a deal orchestrated by Kenny Vance, Becker and Fagen were contracted to compose music for the soundtrack of low-budget comedy-drama film *You've Got to Walk It Like You Talk It or You'll Lose That Beat*, written and directed by Peter Locke and featuring Richard Pryor in one of his earliest roles. Fagen and Becker had little good to say about these songs, considering them to be basic and underdeveloped. Becker confirmed, in typically direct fashion, 'we did it for the money', recording 'however many minutes' worth of dog meat is on the album' for $250 each. Fagen has called their work for the soundtrack 'nothing to be proud of.'

The early demo recordings and film soundtrack are important in the development of Becker and Fagen's writing and are considered in the Appendices section of this book.

The Birth of The Dan

In 1971, Walter and Donald's fortunes began to change. Gary Katz, a friend of Kenny Vance, took a producer job with ABC Dunhill Records in Los Angeles and insisted to his new employers that the duo be hired as staff songwriters. Based on the demos they'd recorded in New York, they were. In 1974, Katz told *Rolling Stone*, 'for the first year after I heard their songs, I just couldn't *hear* them. Then one day they hit me – wow.' Becker and Fagen flew to California in November 1971; the trust in Katz would prove to be wise as he would produce all of their 1970s albums.

Growing up in Brooklyn, Katz also started in the music business via friends in Jay and the Americans. He got a job with Bobby Darin and then Avco, before a friend suggested that he write to Jay Lasker at ABC, who subsequently hired him. Katz worked with The Mamas & the Papas, Steppenwolf and Three Dog Night, and as an A&R man signed Jim Croce, Rufus (with Chaka Khan) and Jimmy Buffett.

Becker and Fagen were still under contract to Kenny Vance but, frustrated at the lack of progress, they starting insulting him at every opportunity, and it became obvious to Vance that the relationship could not continue. He, therefore, agreed to tear up the contract in exchange for half of the royalties from their first album. Becker and Fagen readily agreed.

As staff writers, Donald and Walter's songs were never going to be a good fit for the artists on ABC's roster. They secretly began to put together their own band, with Gary Katz as producer. They enlisted Denny Dias, who they had met in New York in 1970. They had also encountered Jeff Baxter, agreeing that if there was ever the opportunity to work together, they should get in touch. Baxter had worked with drummer Jim Hodder and recommended him.

A native New Yorker, guitarist Dias had placed an ad in *The Village Voice* in the summer of 1970: 'Looking for keyboardist and bassist. Must have jazz chops! Assholes need not apply.' Fagen and Becker responded, joined Dias' band and ultimately took it over, starting to play their own songs and firing the rest of the band in the process. Jeff Baxter was born in Washington, DC, joining his first band at 11. In 1966 he met Jimi Hendrix and for a short period played bass in Hendrix's Jimmy James and the Blue Flames, which also included Randy California. He subsequently played guitar in numerous bands, including Ultimate Spinach, picking up the 'Skunk' nickname during this period, the origin of which may have something to do with a friend's front door and a burning need to urinate whilst intoxicated. New Yorker Jim Hodder played drums and sang with The Bead Game in Boston, where he got to know Baxter.

With Baxter, Hodder and Dias all relocating to Los Angeles, the band was nearly complete with Donald on keyboards and vocals and Walter on bass, but Fagen was not comfortable being lead singer. They struggled to find anyone else with the right feel for the music, at one point asking their new LA buddy

Loudon Wainwright III to join (as Fagen noted in 2011, 'because he's smirky'), but he declined.

The new band signed to ABC Dunhill and David Palmer was hired as a second lead vocalist, mostly because of Fagen's occasional stage fright and reluctance to sing in front of an audience, but also because the label believed that Fagen's voice was not commercial enough. Originally from New Jersey, Palmer had been singing in bands since 1964 and was an acquaintance of Jim Hodder, who recommended him for the role.

Now all that was needed was a name. After going through long lists of possibilities, they eventually came up with Steely Dan. Fans of Beat Generation literature, Fagen and Becker sourced the name from a steam-powered dildo ('Steely Dan III from Yokohama') mentioned in William S. Burroughs' *Naked Lunch*. The name had first appeared in one of their early demos, 'Soul Ram', and they didn't consider that it would last, as none of the other names they had come up with had. However, it stuck, much to their embarrassment in future years, although Walter ultimately conceded that they liked 'the suggestion of a big guy named Steely Dan.'

Can't Buy a Thrill (1972)

Personnel:
David Palmer: Lead & Backing Vocals
Donald Fagen: Keyboards, Lead & Backing Vocals
Walter Becker: Bass, Lead & Backing Vocals
Jeff "Skunk" Baxter: Guitar, Pedal Steel Guitar, Spoken Word
Denny Dias: Guitar, Electric Sitar
Jim Hodder: Drums & Percussion, Lead & Backing Vocals
Elliott Randall: Guitar
Jerome Richardson: Tenor Saxophone
Snooky Young: Flugelhorn
Victor Feldman: Percussion
Venetta Fields, Clydie King, Sherlie Matthews: Backing Vocals
Producer: Gary Katz
Engineer: Roger Nichols
Released: Oct. 1972 (Jan. 1973 UK)
Record Label: ABC Records (Probe Records in the UK)
Recorded: Village Recorders (Los Angeles), Apr. to Oct. 1972
Running Time: 40:58
Highest chart place: US: 17, UK: 38

After initially working with them on a demo session in 1971 – and only because no one else was available – Becker, Fagen and Katz discovered that they had a lot in common with engineer Roger Nichols. They were determined to have him work on the debut album, but this conflicted with a holiday Nichols had planned, so it was decided to hold up the recording until his return, much to the annoyance of ABC.

Californian Nichols attended school with Frank Zappa, recording him on his first reel-to-reel tape machine. He studied nuclear physics and from 1965 to 1968 worked in the nuclear industry. Creating Quantum Studios with friends in 1965 to record high school bands, he went on to produce commercials, Richard and Karen Carpenter and guitarist Larry Carlton performing on some, before being hired as an engineer by ABC in 1970. Nichols worked with Steely Dan for the next decade and beyond: 'We're all perfectionists. It wasn't a drag for me to do things over and over until it was perfect. It would have driven a lot of other engineers up the wall. In my own way, I'm just as crazy as they are.' Nichols won six of his eight Grammys for his work with Steely Dan and is highlighted in liner notes with the soubriquet 'the Immortal'.

The recording process took longer than was usual at the time, Nichols later saying, 'We finished it in six months, which was quick for them. But even then, their acceptance level was way above everyone else's. They never had the attitude of "It's getting late that's good enough", or "No-one else will notice". Everything had to be as near perfect as technically and humanly possible.' The attention to detail immediately paid off.

From the outset, the band's style and direction came from the songs, all of which were of course written by Becker and Fagen. David Palmer sang most of the lead vocals on the band's first tour, getting a couple of leads on the album as well as doubling parts of Fagen's vocals on three others, mainly to reach the higher notes.

The first release for the band was the 1972 single 'Dallas', backed with 'Sail the Waterway', followed by their first live show in October, just prior to the release of *Can't Buy a Thrill*, in Glendale, California at a venue called Under the Ice House. The band's East Coast debut came at Max's Kansas City in New York in November, but they didn't play their first headline shows until 1973.

In the band's first interview, conducted after the debut gig, Becker and Fagen thought that the group was gelling well and that it was 'a sure thing that these six people will stay together', acknowledging that they would continue to write the songs, but everyone would have a hand in the arranging. Fagen also commented that Palmer was a better singer than himself and would be doing most of the singing in the future. Fortunately – and with no disrespect to Palmer's performances – this did not pan out as planned.

Can't Buy a Thrill is a strong album, tightly played and fully formed, that outperforms the 'debut album' tag, laying out the Steely Dan stall of sharp, efficient and well-played numbers with striking lyrics, generally between 3 and 5 and a half minutes long. The songwriting had matured, not only since the early demos but also since the 'Dallas' single. Those songs would have changed the balance of the album considerably, so it was probably wise that they were not included.

Guest players were already being brought in, to expand the palette and add different textures to augment the sound, such as with horns and backing singers, but also to add extra firepower to instruments that the band already covered. With three guitarists in the band (including Walter) it would seem unnecessary to bring in another, but Elliott Randall, who had met Donald and Walter while they were all playing in Jay and the Americans' backing band, adds an extra layer to an already detailed setup.

It's very definitely a rock'n'roll band, the drums are in the rock realm, but unfussy, as will always be the Dan way, here lacking the jazz and R'n'B sensibilities of later releases. Becker's basslines are inventive, and the twin guitars mesh nicely, with Fagen's keyboards already at the centre of the sound. It feels like a band, they work well together, and the results speak for themselves. The other members may fade away over time, leaving Donald and Walter to sail the waterway alone, but to me, the beauty of Steely Dan is that it ALWAYS feels like a band. That is the sound that they continually strove for, and this is where it all began.

A cheeky subversiveness is already on display, each track receiving a subtitle on the back of the original sleeve, which also included an introductory essay under the familiar name of Tristan Fabriani, a collective persona for Donald and Walter, intended to amuse and 'cast an oblique light on the music'. When later asked about it, Fagen said, 'You shouldn't believe anything it says on a Steely Dan record, it's just a bunch of lies and bullshit that we write to confuse the listener.' Lying became a favourite way of dealing with interviewers, the lines between reality and the band's fictional world continually being blurred, Fagen advising the other band members to say what they liked in interviews, 'just don't say anything that's true.'

Becker and Fagen have described the cover art, by Robert Lockart, as 'the most hideous album cover of the seventies, bar none'. They are not entirely wrong; the Day-Glo colours, massive lips, bananas, naked people and a line of expectant hookers being something of a mishmash, to say the least. The thick-set chap at the front is particularly disturbing! The 'Steely Dan' logo is attractively curvy, but the overall look isn't great.

With a distinct counter-culture feel, the hangover from Walter and Donald's college years remains evident on this and subsequent albums, it's a great debut that emerges fully realised (the effort in the studio already paying dividends), bridging the gap between late '60s psychedelia and the real-world traumas of Vietnam in the early '70s. It's not perfect but upon its release *Can't Buy a Thrill* was deservedly successful, spawning two hit singles in 'Do It Again' and 'Reelin' In the Years', both of which continue to be played regularly on radio, alongside 'Dirty Work'. This was like 'a dream come true', Becker explained later, 'we had zero expectations.'

Can't Buy a Thrill is an anomaly in the Dan catalogue. It's a fine album in its own right, there's no doubting that, but the band dynamic sets it at odds with later albums. David Palmer's contribution is very good, but not really fitting, and he isn't missed on subsequent albums, nor are Jim Hodder's lead vocals as Donald's confidence grew, and his brilliantly idiosyncratic delivery of the songs became the essence of Steely Dan.

The Songs:

'Do It Again' (Becker / Fagen) (5:56)
In the first verse of the first song on the debut album, there's heinous crime and retribution ('In the mornin' you go gunnin' / For the man who stole your water / And you fire till he's done in / But they catch you at the border'), but justice of the most terminal kind remains unserved as 'the hangman isn't hangin'', thus leading to a cycle of criminality being allowed to continue. This song of addiction and compulsive losers who allow their weaknesses to repeat is a fine statement of intent, showing the unique characteristics of Becker and Fagen's writing. The murdering outlaw of the first verse is followed in the second by a man at the mercy of a love cheat, continually coming back for more despite the pain it brings, and a gambler who denies his obsession in the third. There's a cinematic feel to the words, easily conjuring images in the mind's eye, a trait that continues throughout their work.

Humorously subtitled as 'Traditional' on the back of the album, the vocal from Fagen is immediately commanding, with congas and other percussion from ex-Miles Davis sideman Victor Feldman giving a jazzy feel, particularly when set against the phased electric piano and deep bass in the intro which gives it a dream-like desert quality. Feldman would go on to contribute to every Steely Dan album up to and including *Gaucho* in 1980.

Ultimately, at its heart there's a straight rock track with Latin elements, lifted higher by colourful additions, including electric sitar by Denny Dias – the only time he ever played the instrument – that brings a psychedelic, Eastern vibe, and a cheap 'plastic' organ, 'competently fingered' (as per the liner notes!) by Fagen. Jim Hodder keeps a steady pace and the band sound well-drilled and together, Becker adding some funky bass parts.

It's forthright, confident and epically hummable, a wonderful song delivered with a laid-back groove. The only compromise on the vision was to allow an edited version to be released as the first single, shortening the intro and outro and omitting the organ solo to fit with radio formatting requirements and get airplay. It reached number six in the US charts in 1973, making it Steely Dan's second-highest charting single – a fine way to start. Becker's favourite song on *Can't Buy a Thrill*, he described it as 'a good blend of commercial potential without being silly.'

Kenny Vance remembers hearing it for the first time on the radio: 'It was like they had figured their way out of a puzzle. They took the song and dumbed it down to three simple chords. But inside the three chords, all the jazz-based countermelodies that they had done early on were going on. Initially, it was these countermelodies that had kept their work from commercial acceptance. But here, they masked that element to allow the three basic chords to take the lead and create the repetition that made the song memorable and palatable to the mainstream audience they needed to make it a hit. They had flipped it – subdued the aspect that they had previously featured.'

'Dirty Work' (Becker / Fagen) (3:08)

Almost a follow on from 'Do It Again', this time the protagonist knows that he's being taken advantage of and expecting a bad outcome ahead, but he can't help himself and remains at his married lover's beck and call: 'I foresee terrible trouble, and I stay here just the same.'

David Palmer sings this one, his higher-pitched voice a good fit and he's clearly a great singer, but it's obvious why Fagen better suits the material, he has the sardonic bite to deliver the words to much greater effect. It's a more commercial sound here, which is what ABC had looked to Palmer to provide, but ultimately the arch cynicism and knowing winks of Becker and Fagen's songs require a voice of more character and guile. It has been suggested that Becker and Fagen did not want 'Dirty Work' on the album, which is the reason Fagen wouldn't sing it, but it works well, a truly memorable song and worthy of its place, the feel of innocence inherent in Palmer's voice set against the sordid nature of the words.

The organ intro is followed by a mournful brass section, underlining the doubt before Palmer sings, his voice providing a truly emotional edge. The harmony vocals in the chorus give an indication of the band's future sound, and a sax solo from Jerome Richardson adds a different colour. The 'Like the castle in its corner in a medieval game' lines in the second verse reference Walter's enjoyment of chess.

The following year, after Palmer left the band, they stopped playing 'Dirty Work' live, finally rehabilitating it in 2006 with the backing singers presenting it from the perspective of a woman having an affair with a married man, this reworking still featuring in the set in 2019.

'Kings' (Becker / Fagen) (3:45)
The King is Dead – Long Live the King! But which one? Is it an ode to mob bosses and the need to suck up to them while they're still around to potentially whack you? Or maybe it concerns the lead up to Magna Carta, Richard the Lionheart being succeeded by his weaker brother John, from whom the barons were able to extract such things as the origins of habeas corpus? Alternatively, given the times in 1972, it could chronicle the imminent re-election of Richard Nixon ('King Richard'), with a call for a return to the perceived better times of John F. Kennedy ('King John') on the eve of the 10th Anniversary of his assassination. The sleeve notes contain a 'no political significance' disclaimer, so it almost certainly did, however, it is also described as a 'vacuous historical romance.' Hmmm…

Whatever the inspiration, with lines like 'While he plundered far and wide / All his starving children cried / And though we sung his fame / We all went hungry just the same', you can't go too far wrong. There's a killer opening with some lovely piano, the chorus coming out of nowhere with feisty female backing vocals. This song has a harder edge, classic Becker and Fagen, again with distinctive congas. The chorus is strong, and the brief guitar solo from Elliott Randall is a winner, but it's the song itself that is the star of the show, great stuff with Fagen's lack of confidence nowhere to be heard, his phrasing hitting the song square on. I love this song, one of my favourites from an album packed with winners. The melody is dynamic, the playing is rich with the expected diamond-sharp edge.

'Midnite Cruiser' (Becker / Fagen) (4:07)
Four songs in and it's the third lead vocalist as drummer Jim Hodder steps up to the mic, and he does a fine job. There's real depth in the band in the vocal area, serving them well when it comes to harmonies.

Taking the theme of time passing, to the point where you realise that you haven't actually achieved much ('The time of our time has come and gone / I fear we been waiting too long'), or possibly it's a wish to relive past glories ('So glad that you're here again / For one more time / Let your madness run with mine'), it's an anthem for the lost, as can be heard in the laid-back, world-weary, sorrowfulness of the approach, exemplified in the slight fragility of

Jim's vocals. There's a lyrical piano in the verses, which becomes more strident for the chorus, and tasty bass additions, Baxter and Dias duetting nicely with the former adding the solo. The chorus is again strong, the quality of the supporting vocals pointing to a signature area for the band's future sound, the setting suggesting New York, although the sound itself takes on a West Coast feel.

The use of the name 'Felonius' in the first line is a reference to legendary jazz pianist Thelonius Monk, a hero of Fagen's, who wrote the standard 'Round Midnight', another potential basis for the song. Monk virtually disappeared from performance and recording after 1971, hence possibly the nostalgic tone yearning for what once was.

'Only a Fool Would Say That' (Becker / Fagen) (2:57)
Prime territory for Donald and Walter again, the snarky vocal with that Latin edge familiar from their later work. It's a sunny and upbeat toe-tapper that belies its theme, which seems to be a repudiation of the hippy dream of 1968. This is particularly true of the chorus, where talk of 'a world where all is free' is deemed foolish and appears to be a dig at the likes of John Lennon, salad days of kids playing cowboys and Indians turning to the anti-war sentiments of young adulthood at the height of Vietnam, all of this at odds with the 'nine to five' necessity of the working man.

Possibly an unusual choice as the B-side for the 'Reelin' In the Years' single, although take the music on face value and it oozes positivity. The bridge is gorgeous, and there's a distinct Wes Montgomery influence in the guitar playing, probably from Baxter, a brief but tasty solo capping it off before the final chorus. Fagen stretches his range with the high parts, and his unusual phrasing again makes the song. The line of Spanish at the end, from Jeff Baxter, is a rough translation of the song's title.

Thank you Side One – you've been a blast. Five serious home runs, straight off the bat. How could they carry that on …?

'Reelin' In the Years' (Becker / Fagen) (4:37)
… Only with a monster hit, that's how!

The sliding opening guitar run immediately puts you on notice, this is a dyed in the wool classic. 'Reelin' In the Years' has one of those sublime chugging choruses that just gets under your skin, memorable and easy to sing along with, but the verse is a different matter in that there are an unusually large number of words to cram into each line, giving it an unorthodox flow, subtly supported by delicate piano flavourings. It appears unwieldy, but in Fagen's hands it just works, a testament to the creativity in the writing but also the talent he had as a vocalist, even at this early stage.

A rip-snorter of a song, it soars on the upbeat rhythm yet remains quirky as Fagen works hard to fit all the words in. The vocal harmonies are lovely, and there are more duelling guitars, plus another solo from Elliott Randall, reportedly Jimmy Page's favourite of all time, which was a happy accident as he just happened to be in the studio at the time while Baxter was struggling to produce one that worked. Despite the long fade, they cram a lot into a little over 4 minutes.

The words come over as a bitter song about love lost, a girl, thinking her youth is fading, latching onto someone who she thinks will do for her in the long term, rather than the singer (the 'diamond') who she is overlooking in favour of stability, foregoing the fun and adventures that they enjoyed together.

Alternatively, 'Reelin' In the Years' could be a cynical look at the music industry of the day, the 'Summer of Love' bubble bursting into a rash of experimental music-making, but by the early '70s, tastes were moving towards more 'throwaway' forms of musical expression. The labels were keen to pander to these trends, thus 'You wouldn't even know a diamond if you held it in your hand / The things you think are precious I can't understand'. Are Becker and Fagen writing about their own trip to Hollywood?

The song also alludes to the story behind 'My Old School' ('The weekend at the college didn't turn out like you planned'), which would appear on *Countdown to Ecstasy* the following year, so this could be one of the seeds for that song. Whatever the meaning, it contains some wonderful lines that you could only imagine Becker and Fagen writing, such as the biting 'You been tellin' me you're a genius since you were seventeen / In all the time I've known you I still don't know what you mean'.

It has pace and drive, singalong choruses, wicked soloing and pointy words, all wrapped up with a big quirky bow. This is songwriting straight out of the top drawer. In typical fashion Fagen later referred to the song as 'dumb but effective'.

The second single from the album, it reached number eleven in the US charts and has become Steely Dan's biggest hit, breaking out into a wider popularity, as evidenced in 1978 when it was used as a saccharine and smiley introductory number to a Donnie and Marie Osmond's TV variety spectacular – on ice. That version is jaw-dropping in its inability to comprehend the subtleties of the song, simply taking the nostalgic element of the title as its raison d'être.

There is also a quadraphonic mix of the song with additional lead guitar fills not heard in the more common stereo version.

'Fire in the Hole' (Becker / Fagen) (3:28)

Another winner, the title coming from a phrase used by soldiers in Vietnam, when deploying grenades into bunkers or tunnels. Piano-led, Fagen shows a good deal of dexterity, the verses sliding into a fine, if brief, chorus. It's a quite beautiful song, the yearning melody streaked through with minor chord melancholy to underline the divisive nature of the lyric, which alludes to draft evasion at the height of the Vietnam War, as Becker and Fagen managed to do: 'A woman's voice reminds me / To serve and not to speak. / Am I myself or just another freak?'

The B-side of the 'Do It Again' single, a staccato piano intro leads into a wonderfully heartfelt Fagen vocal, wringing out every drop of emotion and underlining what a great interpretive singer he is. The extended off-kilter piano section is a nice diversion and shows Fagen's jazz inclinations, while Baxter 'displays the cunning of the insane on steel guitar' (thank you again, Mr Fabriani!), initially in a supporting role and then via an emotive and very well delivered solo to the fade.

This is another song that would most likely be just so much fluff in other people's hands. In the years of songwriting since college, Becker and Fagen had honed their craft beautifully, ready to emerge as an almost finished article on this debut album. But this is just the start, complacency is never going to be a factor and to Donald and Walter the songs, and how to deliver them in the best light, are always all that matters.

'Brooklyn (Owes the Charmer Under Me)' (Becker / Fagen) (4:21)
After a bright opening guitar riff, David Palmer takes the lead again in a smooth and languid song, Baxter's extended use of pedal steel giving it a country twang, at odds with the NYC sentiment. Both of the songs that feature Palmer's lead vocals match his style nicely, this one soaring majestically to his upper limits in the late stages – which is probably why it hasn't been played live since 1974. It's beautifully paced, and a relaxed listen that hits the spot, the soul inflexions of the female backing to the chorus adding depth.

Even the title is distinctively unusual, as it it doesn't seem quite right, but it fits the sentiment of a song that takes a cynical jab at the downstairs neighbours from Becker and Fagen's time living in an apartment block in Brooklyn. These are the kind of people who moan about the indignities that they suffer having to live in a city that they seem to think owes them something: 'She daily preaches on where she wants to be / An evening with a movie queen, a face we all have seen.'

Both Fagen and Becker have said that it is simply based on overheard conversations coming up from the apartment below and is one of the most literal lyrics they ever wrote, but it works a treat. It is important to note that Nichol's work is already putting the icing on a particularly tasty cake.

'Change of the Guard' (Becker / Fagen) (3:39)
A rock stomp with strong verses and chorus, electric piano to the fore, but perhaps lacking some of the flair of the other tracks on the album. There's a fine guitar solo though from Jeff Baxter, and Fagen gives it his all in the vocal department.

Could it be a lyric of positivity? It seems so, possibly being a call to arms in support of the growing counter-culture and the anti-Vietnam movement of the time ('Take your guns off if you're willin' / And you know we're on your side'), a march of the masses leading to a move away from the status quo. 'If you live in this world / You're feelin' the change of the guard.' As with all of Becker and

Fagen's work, brevity is the key, it's succinct and to the point, even with space for soloing.

'Turn That Heartbeat Over Again' (Becker / Fagen) (4:58)

Becker co-leads on this one, with Palmer and Fagen, in a twisted lyric that's a tricky one to pin down. Initially it looks like a stick-up at a liquor store that goes wrong; with his accomplice shot, the protagonist vows to give up his wicked ways, calling on Jesus to 'turn that heartbeat over again' and let his stricken friend live, the bright and breezy nature of the music again at odds with the bleakness of the scene described. It's another of those songs that just slides over you as you tap your feet or cruise along with the top down, but when you get down to the words, it's a very different kettle of kippers.

The liner note subtitle calls it 'a solemn prayer for peace', but from whose perspective, the robber or the robbed? The second and third verses are more obscure, possibly referencing 'Sam' as a stereotypical bartender, and a William Wright, who might be the poet of that name, but it isn't obvious how that fits in. Either way, they're intriguing words: 'We warned the corpse of William Wright / Not to cuss and drink all night / Ticket in hand we saw him laid to rest / But zombie see and zombie do / He's here with me and you'. The 'jag' in the chorus phrase 'cry a jag on me' is slang for an uncontrollable outburst, so in this sense, probably refers to the sadness of Michael's relatives at his imminent passing.

The intro jumps straight into the lyric and is perhaps slightly underdeveloped. The rhythms are bright and decidedly bouncy and the harmony vocals in the chorus are as tight as you like, the last line sounding like it could have come from a Beach Boys record. There's some nice uncredited banjo picking, but the country feel of the twin guitar solo isn't a great fit. There's a hint of Frank Zappa influence in the keyboard section before the third verse, but despite the attempt at a big finish, overall, it's a bit of a light way to end the album, the song finishing as abruptly as it started.

Related Tracks:

'Dallas' (Becker / Fagen) (3:15)

Originally written in New York as 'Bye, Bye, Dallas' and sung by Fagen, Jim Hodder was brought in to sing the recorded version, released as a single prior to *Can't Buy a Thrill* in 1972. The band was as the album but without Denny Dias, who had not yet arrived in California, and with Tim Moore adding backing vocals alongside Palmer. From electric piano to start, Fagen's keys expand into melodic verse and harmony chorus, and there's a pedal steel and bongo flavoured instrumental section with a well-realised solo from Baxter.

Save for a vague reference to a 'Grand Hotel' in the opening line, there's nothing to specifically place 'Dallas' in its namesake city – probably chosen as the title to rhyme with 'palace' in the chorus! The song would later be covered by Poco on their 1975 album *Head Over Heels*.

Steely Dan were under contract to release a single before the album and 'Dallas' is a good song with a country feel and an excellent chorus, but ABC decided that it wasn't representative of the band, and as it wasn't receiving much radio airplay or positive reviews, it was quietly pushed aside. In fact, distribution was so limited that today promotional copies are easier to come by than general release copies.

Neither song from the single appeared on the debut album and remain the only officially released Steely Dan tracks that have not been reissued. It's strange discovering these songs from the debut single after all the albums, they sit aside from the rest of the catalogue, overlooked curios, and it is a shame that Donald and Walter retained such ambivalence towards them (Becker describing 'Dallas' as 'Stinko' in 1995); they have a charm of their own and deserve rehabilitation.

The songs are no doubt indicative of the progress Donald and Walter were making, transitioning from being staff songwriters at ABC to helming their own band. They sit somewhere between the early demos and the more rounded songs of the albums. Aimed squarely at the pop radio of the time, they're more than pleasant but seem lacking in sophistication compared to later work. With more promotion, they may have done well, but as it is, they're an anomaly in the catalogue.

'Sail the Waterway' (Becker / Fagen) (3:05)
The B-side of 'Dallas', it works in that context but is again not representative of the band at the time of their first album, lacking the depth of the other songs that made it onto the debut. But, as with 'Dallas', it's a shame that a space hasn't been found for it on a compilation or reissue (other than in Japan).

Fagen takes the vocal, stabbing piano leading into a nice chorus, which in style is reminiscent of other songs popular at the time, it's quite catchy, but overall a little insubstantial. There's some tasty blues guitar work with piano adding a different texture, and despite their humble place in the catalogue, these two songs are certainly not without merit.

'Runnin' Child' (Becker / Fagen) (4:22) [unreleased]
An unreleased song, it deserves hearing as it is of real quality with a lovely Fagen vocal. It would no doubt have worked on *Can't Buy a Thrill*, the chorus is very strong, and it is toe-tappingly catchy, a bright and breezy number that suits cruising the freeway. There's a brief guitar solo, presumably by Baxter, towards the end that fits well before the final chorus, which is repeated into the fade. It seems that 'Running Child' was recorded in late 1971 or early 1972 with Baxter, Hodder, Becker and Fagen, but probably again before Dias' arrival.

'Sacajawea' (Becker / Fagen) [unreleased]
This is going to be short – I've never heard it. It turned up on a tape reel a few years ago on eBay but has not yet found its way into general circulation, as

far as I'm aware. Based on the balance of probability, it's going to be great – however reports I've seen suggest otherwise.

'Gullywater' (Becker / Fagen) (3:08) [unreleased]

From the bongo infused intro, it's a strange song with some odd sound effects that throw you off balance, but it's very interesting, and Fagen's vocal is strong, supported by his piano. It's unlike anything else in the Dan catalogue, but good and catchy with nice lead guitar work, probably from Dias.

The brief lyric is fun, likening jealous love to the muddy water you find at the bottom of a dry well or the smile on the face of a dog hiding in your soul. Odd but fun.

'Everyone's Gone to the Movies' (Demo) (Becker / Fagen) (3:57)

Finally released in 1993 as the only previously unreleased track on the *Citizen Steely Dan* box set, it features the original band with Mark Volman and Howard Kaylan (Flo and Eddie) of the Turtles on backing vocals with percussion from Victor Feldman. The box set notes suggest that Donald and Walter only included it to add legitimacy to the tale told by Volman and Kaylan that they did in fact record with Steely Dan in the early days. The final version would appear on *Katy Lied* in 1975.

Countdown to Ecstasy (1973)

Personnel:
Donald Fagen: Acoustic & Electric Pianos, Synthesizer, Lead & Backing Vocals
Walter Becker: Electric Bass, Harmonica, Backing Vocals
Denny Dias: Guitar
Jeff "Skunk" Baxter: Electric & Pedal Steel Guitars
Jim Hodder: Drums & Percussion, Backing Vocals
Ray Brown: String Bass
Ben Benay: Acoustic Guitar
Rick Derringer: Slide Guitar
Victor Feldman: Vibraphone, Marimba, Percussion
Ernie Watts, Johnny Rotella, Lanny Morgan, Bill Perkins: Saxophones
Sherlie Matthews, Myrna Matthews, Patricia Hall, David Palmer, Royce Jones, James
Rolleston, Michael Fennelly: Backing Vocals
Producer: Gary Katz
Engineer: Roger Nichols
Released: July 1973
Record Label: ABC Records (Probe Records in the UK)
Recorded: Village Recorders (Los Angeles), Jan. to June 1973
Running Time: 41:04
Highest chart place: US: 35, UK: –

The next two years were mostly spent touring, recording as and when they could between shows. Gary Katz remembered the shows being some of the best he'd ever seen, 'then I'd go backstage and Donald and Walter would be sitting there with their heads in their hands complaining about how rotten they'd been.'

Becker and Fagen were not suited to the rock 'n' roll lifestyle and hated touring – the often poor hotels, the incessant travelling, the inappropriate pairings with bands and audiences of different musical taste. The band had no image – one critic going so far as to call them 'the ugliest band in the world' – which was fine as all they wanted was to get their songs out there to be heard. After the first few albums their photos did not appear on the covers, an 'anti-image' stance that increased the air of mystery – 'We wanted [the music] to stand for itself', said Fagen.

Fagen was still reluctant to sing live, but Katz and Becker decided that they preferred his interpretations of the songs, eventually persuading him to take over from Palmer. As Fagen said, 'I think we knew we weren't going to find anybody who could convey the attitude, which was really the most important thing.' David Palmer quietly left the group in April 1973 during the recording of *Countdown to Ecstasy*, contributing only some backing vocals to the finished album. He went on to write the words for Carole King's hit 'Jazzman' and later formed the band Wha-Koo, releasing three albums between 1977 and 1979. He also contributed a song to the 1985 film *Teen Wolf* but left singing in 2002 for a career in digital photography. In 2014, he sued Steely Dan for unpaid royalties.

The schedule of recording during the week and touring widely across the US at weekends was exhausting, and not conducive to songwriting, with lyrics often being written at the last minute, but a mere 9 months after *Can't Buy a Thrill*, *Countdown to Ecstasy* arrived in July 1973, the title a jibe at attempts to rationalise a state of spirituality. The cynical lyrical approach was now bedded in, delivered within beautifully packaged music.

A critical success, *Countdown to Ecstasy* lacked a hit single, and that stalled its chart progress. Becker and Fagen were unhappy with some of the performances on the record and believed that it sold poorly because it had been recorded hastily while the band continued to tour.

At just over 40 minutes, it's another compact album. The jazz content is higher, and the overall feel much more polished, a marked step forward from *Can't Buy a Thrill*. This was the only album written specifically for a live band. At the time the influence of *Countdown to Ecstasy* was far-reaching, Joe Jackson describing it as a revelation that bridged the gap between 'pure pop' and his jazz-rock and progressive influences, encouraging him to develop his attempts at songwriting.

It's a wide-ranging listen delivered as a unified whole that works a treat. There's the kick-ass opener 'Bodhisattva', college nostalgia (kinda) in 'My Old School', a gorgeous countrified song of lost love in 'Pearl of the Quarter', and much more besides.

The cover artwork, featuring three humanoid creatures sat in chairs in a seemingly blank space, two looking quizzically at some white spots higher on the sleeve, the other staring out at us with an odd smirk, was painted by Fagen's girlfriend Dorothy White ('Dotty of Hollywood'), Jay Lasker wasn't happy: 'That's no good. On the back cover, you've got a photo of five guys, and on the front, you have only three guys. People are going to ask, 'Where's the other two guys?' You've got to put two more guys on the front.' Dotty told him that it was just a painting, not a portrait of the band, but Lasker was adamant. The pressure was on but she found a way to put in two more figures without wrecking the design, taking the form of smaller, ghostlike figures in an upper corner. The album's back cover showed Steely Dan in the recording studio with Roger Nichols' disembodied hand on the mixing console as he hid beneath it.

One critic said that Fagen and Becker's lyrics on the album portray America as 'one big Las Vegas, with gangsters and gurus hustling for souls to steal', while another called it a 'dossier of literate lowlifes.' Becker and Fagen addressed the plaudits often showered on *Countdown to Ecstasy* in the liner for the remastered reissue: '… there is a substantial body of opinion which holds that Countdown was the best Steely Dan album, bar none. Generally speaking, the type of person who typically holds this position is not the sort of individual you want sitting across the table from you at a dinner party, especially one where alcoholic beverages are being served.'

The liner also described the label executive's initial reaction to hearing the record: 'They listened in silence and at the end offered up some tepid congratulations. The confusion and disappointment that filled the room was thick and nasty as a horny mother. Coming on the heels of the commercially successful first album, the company had been hoping for a second album blockbuster that would zoom to the top of the charts and stay there for weeks, months, years. Instead, they found themselves with what must have sounded to them like some sort of weird German art music, or worse. Later, when they found out that we have fired our suave Daltrey-esque lead singer, stolen the proofs for the album cover during a dispute over the final layout, and perversely insisted on choosing for a single a tune whose lyrics contained the word "fuck", they were not surprised.'

The Songs:

'Bodhisattva' (Becker / Fagen) (5:18)

Snarling out of the traps with a clipped drum beat and harsh guitar chords, a deft piano line and soaring twin lead guitars take it skyward. Handclaps and what sounds like strummed of piano strings introduce the vocals, walking guitar figures colouring the background. The bookended quirkiness of the pseudo orientalism in the lines 'Can you show me / The shine of your Japan / The sparkle of your China / Can you show me' immediately make an impact before the guitar solo.

Written by Fagen alone (but credited to the duo as usual), the title is a Buddhist term for someone able to reach nirvana but who delays doing so through compassion for the suffering of others. Fagan does not hold with such things, mocking that he too will sell his 'house in town' to join the search for enlightenment. A swipe at the Western view of Eastern religion, it's a strong opener that references a love of doo-wop. The guitars duet nicely, but it's the snappy vocals that take the day. There's room for jazzy soloing from both Dias and Baxter, duelling keys and guitar and some nice synth work over driving bluesy rhythms, culminating with a guitar crescendo and ringing piano chord.

It's a striking song with a ton of energy that seems a big step up from *Can't Buy a Thrill* and sets out the *Countdown to Ecstasy* stall very nicely. They cram a hell of a lot into 5 minutes, all of it sparkling like your china.

'Razor Boy' (Becker / Fagen) (3:11)

This song is the first real indication of the band's future direction, the Latin vibe coupled with close harmonies over Victor Feldman's congas in the chorus. Chorded piano carries the verse, Baxter's pedal steel subtly adding textures in the background before coming to the fore for a beautifully laid-back solo. String bass, courtesy of Ray Brown, and Feldman's vibraphone throw in some jazzy and exotic extra layers as the lyric takes a poke at materialism. Particular reference is given to the drugs and prostitution that are often drawn into that world, with a stark warning that the 'Razor Boy', or Grim Reaper to you and me, can deprive you of it all without a thought: 'Will you still have a song to sing / When the razor boy comes / And takes your fancy things away?'

Used as the B-side of the 'Show Biz Kids' single, the enigmatic verses set against the swooning beauty of the music help to make this a real winner, the uplifting nature shrouding a much darker message.

'The Boston Rag' (Becker / Fagen) (5:40)

Guitar, piano, bass and drums combine in a strident yet beautiful opening section that bears many a repeated hearing, giving way to a calling guitar. The verse is soft, supported by acoustic guitar from Ben Benay, moving into a much more 'in your face' chorus, again with harmony vocals and an edge to the guitar. The falling piano chords at the end of the chorus reset things for the second verse, which is sung with harmony vocals, sounding much as Steely Dan should. The tango section is an unexpected diversion, piano and cymbals counting out the rhythm while Baxter's enigmatic and echoey slide additions turn into a powerfully dirty solo, with strong support from Becker's bass, ramping up to a tough and hard-edged finish. As the liner notes point out; 'Enervated after an attack of unrelieved nostalgia, Jeff "Skunk" Baxter sheds his outer skin and stands revealed as a Wild Boy.'

At nearly 6 minutes, there's plenty of room to stretch out in an opaque song with an elusive meaning. Lonnie was Fagen's roommate at Bard in 1965, a guy who drank heavily and took a lot of drugs, passing out most nights, so there's a clear reference there, but also the song seems to ache for older, simpler times. Fagen spent a summer in Boston at the Berklee College of Music, that might be featured in the chorus, which Fagen confirmed he wrote, Becker writing the verses, Bayside being near where he used to live in Queens, he liked the sound of it.

A situation occurred during recording, the like of which would become all too frequent in subsequent years: no matter how many times they tried, the same three notes of Denny's intro melody would not record. The defective piece of tape was returned to the manufacturer for analysis and it turned out that there was a tiny blister on the tape containing a drop of mustard. A worker must have been eating a sandwich in the plant when the tape was being made.

'Your Gold Teeth' (Becker / Fagen) (7:02)

A tale of danger, chance and life on the road for a jaded female grifter, told from the perspective of both her and her intended target. The longest song recorded by the band so far, it again gave plenty of space to stretch with congas driving the rhythm and elements of jazz seeping into the tight instrumentation. There's an unusual amount of jamming, which adds to the song, but this will shortly become a thing of the past in Dan circles as things become stripped down, in terms of both song length and band members. Fagen adds a dexterous electric piano solo, and you can hear that the band have really gelled now. The more primitive sounds of *Can't Buy a Thrill* seem a long time ago, even though it was released less than a year previously.

The reference to mezzo-soprano Cathy Berberian is typical of Becker and Fagen's love of the obscure, her dextrous avant-garde interpretations of popular songs and contemporary experimental works showing a rare talent, but even she knew that some embellishments were beyond her prodigious capabilities, likewise the grifter – don't stretch yourself too far or you'll be caught out...

'Dumb luck my friend / Won't suck me in this time', and after the game of chance, the golden teeth have been rolled and Fagen gives quite a display of his keyboard talents in the outro. The line 'There ain't nothing in Chicago for a monkey woman to do' is adapted from Count Basie's 'Going to Chicago Blues'.

'Show Biz Kids' (Becker / Fagen) (5:26)

Sweeping in on furious slide guitar from Rick Derringer, this song turns into a funky strut, the backing singers weaving around Fagen's voice in the repeated refrain 'You go to Lost Wages', being a comedic twist on Las Vegas, inspired by Lenny Bruce, in a tale of gambling and a satirical look at the privileged LA lifestyle. The song shames consumerism and the 'have it all' movie stars when contrasted with the more down to earth life of the general populace: 'While the poor people sleepin' / All the stars come out at night'. The irony seeps through with a wink in the affirmation that all the bright young things will ultimately be wearing Steely Dan t-shirts on their 'shapely bods', but there's real bite at the heart of this one.

Becker and Fagen were uncomfortable Californians and remained solidly New York at heart, missing the artistic vitality and cultural familiarity, feeling like fish out of water. Becker described LA as being like 'living in a morgue', hence the song's album annotation, 'The Dan moves to LA and is forced to give an oral report.'

Unusual and effective, Derringer's scything slide hits the spot, but it's all about the vocals, Fagen carrying the syncopated words and dropping an unexpected 'F' bomb. Walter adds harmonica to the ending, but as the first single from the album, it was shortened and edited with that pesky expletive removed, only reaching 61 in the US charts, clearly too clever for the mass market and the last time that Becker, Fagen and Katz made the decision on which songs should be the singles.

Becker and Fagen were frustrated by the difficulties of getting every instrument in sync, and Roger Nichols was forced to improvise: 'There were no drum machines in those days, so we made a 24-track, eight-bar tape loop ... trailed it out through the door into the studio, around a little idler which was set up on a camera tripod, back into the studio and then copied that to a second 24-track machine. Everything was on tape except the lead vocal and the lead guitar. It worked like a dream.' Listening to it now, you can tell why this song was always going to be a nightmare to get properly in time.

'My Old School' (Becker / Fagen) (5:48)

A nostalgic tale of youth – and a 1969 drug bust at Bard College involving Donald, along with his girlfriend Dorothy White and Walter, who were just visiting. The college was complicit in the bust but posted bail for the students rounded up in the swoop, including Walter as an alumnus. However, Dorothy ended up 'with the working girls in the county jail' when Daddy (actually Donald's father) arrived to buy her out. Fagen was so upset with the college that he boycotted his own graduation ('I hear the whistle, but I can't go') and in the song he vows never to return there until 'California tumbles into the sea', although he obviously changed his mind and went back to receive an honorary doctorate in 1985.

The 'thirty-five sweet goodbyes' are said to derive from the farewell blowjob Fagen received before boarding the New York to Boston 'Wolverine' train service that would take him to Annandale – about half of a '69'! – and the girl who Donald couldn't believe could be so cruel wasn't Dorothy but the dean at Bard who was instrumental in the bust.

There are plenty of knowing phrases: Bard was often referred to as 'the William and Mary of the North' in reference to the college of that name in Virginia, and 'Daddy Gee' is assistant district attorney and future Watergate burglar G. Gordon Liddy.

Piano driven, sax and backing vocals give it an upbeat lift, again with a doo-wop twist, another fine chorus marking the writing partnership as being highly adept at working in hooks. The reggae inflexion in the rhythm became more prominent in later songs, as do the saxophones, of which four appear here to fine effect. The sharply delivered guitar solo comes from Baxter, and the horn section falling down the stairs effect as 'California tumbles into the sea' is just great.

The second single from the album, it did slightly worse than 'Show Biz Kids' reaching only number 63. it really should have been number 35...

'Pearl of the Quarter' (Becker / Fagen) (3:50)

The B-side of the 'My Old School' single gives a very different feel, laid-back with the essence of New Orleans, featuring such local landmarks as Tulane Avenue (the 'Miracle Mile'). The chord changes into the chorus are great, and Jeff gets his pedal steel out again to fine effect. It's an elegant piece, Fagen ringing every ounce of emotion from the chorus.

The focus of the love interest in this seemingly sweet and innocent song is Louise, a beguiling prostitute of French descent who works the dockside. Falling in love with a working girl has never been so sweetly emotional, but then she's on her way, possibly to another town. There's a room for her if she ever comes back, but she won't.

The song didn't get a live debut until 2011 and has only been played a handful of times since, which is probably unsurprising as there is no doubt that it is Baxter who makes it fly, including some perfect harmonics. The rest of the instrumentation is quite low-key, but the arrangement is superb and it's a lovely song, at odds with much of the rest of the album but well-realised and with a delicate beauty all its own.

'King of the World' (Becker / Fagen) (5:04)

From the pulse drums, wah-wah guitar and harmonic bass over skittering snare and echoed guitar flurries, the rampaging funk of the beautifully realised intro is one of the highlights of the album.

It leads into the words, a tale of life in a world after nuclear conflagration, a lonely survivor broadcasting into the void on his ham radio, but there are no rights, wrongs or self-pity, a 'just get on with it' vibe permeating a song packed with intent. The elegant rising electric piano chords support the vocals in the verse, exploding with energy in a great harmony chorus: 'No marigolds in the promised land / There's a hole in the ground where they used to grow. / Any man left on the Rio Grande / Is the king of the world / As far as I know.' No nostalgia or regret – the marigolds are gone; things have to move on.

But there's a real humanity to it. The survivor doesn't want to resort to savagery ('Assassins, cons and rapers / Might as well die') and is merely looking for some company to kick back in the afterglow of the devastation, making the most of whatever time is left, cruising the ruins of Santa Fe and watching the sun go down. The pay-off is an awareness that 'If I stay inside I might live 'til Saturday', so ultimately he might be better off dead already.

Inspired by the 1962 film *Panic In The Year Zero*, there's a headlong drive from start to finish, Jim Hodder doing a fine job and the band sounding particularly tight. A neat synth solo line, doubled on the repeat, leads into an unusual and odd keyboard breakdown with ham radio backing, then we're off again, a country edge from the guitar and some lovely picked soloing at the end.

Overall, it's a fantastic song, brimming with enthusiasm and interesting additions, all brought together in a wonderfully rounded whole (or 'hole', as in where the marigolds used to grow...?).

Pretzel Logic (1974)

Personnel:
Donald Fagen: Keyboards, Saxophone, Lead & Background Vocals
Walter Becker: Bass, Guitar, Background Vocals
Jeff Baxter: Lead Guitar, Pedal Steel Guitar
Denny Dias: Guitar
Michael Omartian, David Paich: Piano, Keyboards
Ben Benay: Guitar
Dean Parks: Guitar, Banjo
Wilton Felder, Chuck Rainey: Bass
Jim Gordon, Jeff Porcaro: Drums
Victor Feldman, Roger Nichols: Percussion
Plas Johnson, Jerome Richardson, Ernie Watts: Saxophones
Ollie Mitchell: Trumpet
Lew McCreary: Trombone
Timothy B. Schmit, Jim Hodder: Background Vocals
Producer: Gary Katz
Engineer: Roger Nichols
Record Label: ABC Records
Recorded: Village Recorders (Los Angeles), Oct. 1973 to Jan. 1974
Released: 2 March 1974
Running Time: 34:02
Highest chart place: US: 8, UK: 37

This is the starting point for classic Steely Dan, but after the lack of commercial success with *Countdown to Ecstasy*, the pressure was on to deliver high chart placings while retaining an uncompromising protectiveness of their art.

Jeff Baxter and Denny Dias were still aboard, but Jim Hodder contributes only some backing vocals to one track, the drum stool going to Jim Gordon, with future Toto man Jeff Porcaro on a couple of songs. He had joined the touring band, along with vocalist-percussionist Royce Jones and vocalist-keyboardist Michael McDonald, but was the only one to feature on *Pretzel Logic*. The album reflected Steely Dan's increasing reliance on top LA session musicians, like former Aretha Franklin bassman Chuck Rainey, *Pretzel Logic* being the first album to feature Becker on guitar: 'Once I met Chuck Rainey I felt there really was no need for me to be bringing my bass guitar to the studio anymore.' Striving for perfection, Becker and Fagen sometimes asked the musicians to record as many as forty takes of each track.

Becker and Fagen are cooking now; it's the third album release in only 18 months, and they're improving all the time. There was perhaps less overt experimentation than with the previous albums, the duo having a clearer idea beforehand of what they wanted and the abilities of the band members. Succinct, punchy and varied, it's a whizzing rollercoaster of a record, and by the end, you just don't know what to expect next. Brevity is a key attribute of

Steely Dan, and at 34 minutes this is the shortest album in the catalogue. Only a few of the other '70s albums breach the 40-minute mark, but this one has not an ounce of flab on it with fewer instrumental jams than previously. They never fell for self-indulgence or the grand concept, and this habit of keeping the albums efficiently to the point and reliant on quality is what made Steely Dan the revered act they became, and from here on in it's a run of albums to die for.

'I like composition', Fagen told an interviewer in 1974, 'I like arrangement. And Walter and I have always felt there was a place for intelligent lyrics in well-played music. We happen to write in a short, three-to-five-minute mode. In a sense we're miniaturists. We're fortunate because that happens to be a length that radio stations will program', the influence coming from classic jazz: 'In my opinion, Duke Ellington never wrote anything worthwhile over five minutes long.'

Despite the above, in many ways, *Pretzel Logic* feels like a taking stock of sorts, based on a foundation comprising three tracks originally demoed back in New York, plus an unexpected – and surprisingly straight – cover of Duke Ellington's 'East St. Louis Toodle-oo'. 'Barrytown', 'Parker's Band' and 'Charlie Freak' are all very different but key components of the sound that developed for this release, however, their inclusion was also down to expediency due to the pressures on writing time imposed by the rigorous touring schedule. The other tracks include their most successful single, 'Rikki Don't Lose That Number', and Dan classics 'Night by Night', 'Any Major Dude Will Tell You' and the title track.

With a title suggested by twisted and circular reasoning that ultimately proves fallible, the cover features a photo of a New York pretzel seller in winter, taken by Raeanne Rubenstein, it couldn't be more at odds with the sunny West Coast nature of the recording. The rear of the cover features a snowy park-scape, taken at the same time, while the inside of the gatefold sleeve shows the band posing at a large carved eagle in LA.

The opening trio of songs set the scene superbly, wonderful pieces that spark the imagination, but they don't prepare you for the left-field shunt into beautiful strangeness provided by the middle section of the album. Becker and Fagen considered this their attempt at complete musical statements within the three-minute pop format, the music characterised by harmonies, countermelodies and jazz phrasing mixed with more straightforward pop influences. Some songs incorporate additional instrumentation, including exotic percussion, a string section, bells and horns, but it is the basic band at the centre of it all.

They widely used the so-called 'Mu' chord, a long-time feature of Bebop and free jazz, that added an additional tone to enrich major chords. Becker said, 'it was kind of a joke, that name. In the late sixties when we first started writing together, we would write or play very simple tunes and the way that we came up with hopping up major triads was to add a second, usually right under the third. This was one of the few alterations that you could do to a major chord and still have it sound like a major chord and not a jazz chord.'

This use of harmony blurred the lines between pop and jazz, complex arrangements delivering crisp and catchy hooks with an uncanny knack of sounding both East and West Coast at the same time. Blues and country elements sat alongside Fagen's decidedly NYC delivery, his idiosyncratic voice, which after Palmer left became ubiquitous, a key part of the band's appeal, his inflexions, mannerisms and way with rhythm are absolutely essential in giving the songs their cool and knowing vibe. 'I'm not interested in a rock/jazz fusion', said Becker, 'that kind of marriage has so far only come up with ponderous results. We play rock and roll, but we swing when we play. We want that ongoing flow, that lightness, that forward rush of jazz.' In a 1989 interview, Becker spoke of 'sugar-coating' the jazz elements: 'in the rock audience, if they were aware they were hearing something that sounded like jazz, they weren't too happy about it. This is something that Donald and I always had to struggle with, to incorporate some harmonic elements that were more sophisticated than rock and roll and still have it sound like rock and roll.'

Pretzel Logic achieved high sales on the back of 'Rikki Don't Lose That Number'. The typical ambiguity of the lyrics added to the growing mystique, *Down Beat* asserting that 'there are no better rock recording groups in America, and damn few worldwide ... the lyrics baffle me; maybe they know what they're talking about, but I can't get a clue.' Frank Zappa came out as a fan in 1974: 'They're one of my favourite groups, I like their modality, their melodicism. Their lyrics aren't bad in that vein they're working, that downer surrealism.'

'I'll tell you what I like about our group,' said Fagen. 'What I like about us, outside of our technical accomplishments, is that our music scares me more than anybody else's. The combination of the words with the music—like a cheerful lyric and a sad or a menacing melody, or vice versa—I find that irony frightening. The idea is frightening, the idea that somebody would think of recording that ... I am attracted to music that frightens me. Like Coltrane's tone on the saxophone. It used to tear me to shreds.' But what really frightened him was 'mediocrity. The mediocrity of everyday life, the mediocrity we see around us. That frightens me.'

The band finally made it to the UK in 1974, their only shows outside the US in the '70s, but the tour was curtailed after five dates when Fagen became ill. With Becker and Fagen monopolising the writing, the rest of the band wanted to play live and pushed for more touring, a rift soon developing. Despite Baxter remembering Fagen as a natural performer who gave his all to deliver to the audience, Donald and Walter retained an extreme dislike for touring and a parting of the ways was inevitable. There was no falling out as such, Becker and Fagen had encouraged Baxter and Hodder to play with other artists, and as a way out of the touring and that element of their contract with ABC it seemed that the simplest way to do it was to not have a band to tour with. Baxter and McDonald went on to join The Doobie Brothers, while Denny Dias remained with the group until 1977's *Aja*. Steely Dan's last live performance of the '70s was on 5 July 1974 at the Santa Monica Civic Auditorium in California.

The Songs:

'Rikki Don't Lose That Number' (Becker / Fagen) (4:32)

If you can start an album with a complete classic, why not do it? The first single from the album, it reached number four in the US charts, but it has echoed down the years and sounds as fresh now as it must have done then, classic Steely Dan driven by the superb chorus.

Speculation has been rife for decades that the 'number' in question was a 'jazz' cigarette ('send it off in a letter to yourself' supposedly being a safe way to transport your stash back home), but Becker clearly stated in a 1985 interview for Musician magazine that this was not the case.

Typically, the over-analysis of Becker and Fagen's love of the obscure has come up with many alternative possibilities. However, Fagen revealed that Rikki was a woman he had a crush on in college, nothing more. But is he to be trusted? Well, whatever, it works as a beautiful song of lost love and Fagen delivers it with confidence and maturity, his vocals continuing to develop all the time.

It is far more accessible than most of their songs, so there is no real surprise that it scored well with a wider audience, but again, the detail in the arrangement and the interesting additions deployed give it the legs, and it sits well within the catalogue. A very well-deserved success.

After the burbling flapamba – a kind of marimba – intro from Victor Feldman (an odd choice which was dropped from the single version, although it can be heard in the background later on), the syncopated piano opening develops into the melody. Supplied by Michael Omartian and not Fagen, it's simple but highly effective with a wistful resonance that's hard to beat. There are distinct similarities in the intro piano and bass to Horace Silver's 1965 'Song for My Father', a piece that Donald and Walter would no doubt have been familiar with, but otherwise, the two songs follow different paths, and you can't blame them for usurping such a fitting device.

Jeff Baxter supplies a supple guitar solo alongside Becker's bass, but otherwise it's all session guys, Omartian and drummer Jim Gordon (whose subtle and restrained rimshots in the verses and first half of the chorus give way to a full-on rhythm in the second), with acoustic guitar from Dean Parks and Feldman's percussion. Future Eagle Timothy B. Schmit is on hand to help Fagen with the backing vocals.

Oddly, the single version of the song was included in original pressings of the *Citizen Steely Dan* box set, but this was rectified for later editions.

'Night by Night' (Becker / Fagen) (3:40)

A trumpet fanfare leads into scratchy street funk as a hustler does whatever he can to get by 'night by night', while envying the legitimate lifestyle. It's short but beautifully to the point, the horn arrangement just right, sparse where it needs to be, adding accents and countermelodies when called upon. Jeff Porcaro takes the drum stool from Jim Gordon for this one and there's some searing guitar.

Fagen excels on the lines 'When the joker tried to tell me / I could cut it in this rube town / When he tried to hang that sign on me / I said "Take it down"', you can feel the grime under the smoothness of the arrangement. People have to do what they have to do, but they aren't necessarily enjoying it.

I love this song, the enigmatic lyrics fitting perfectly the dense city-scape in the music – '"It's a beggar's life", said the Queen of Spain, but don't tell it to a poor man 'cause he's got to kill for every thrill the best he can.'

'Any Major Dude Will Tell You' (Becker / Fagen) 3:05

It's at this point that you start to realise what a magnificent album *Pretzel Logic* is turning into.

From the delicate strummed acoustic guitar intro and Fagen's strangely effective delivery over the warmth of the electric piano, this is a winner. There's a laid-back twang to the music and the words, bringing in street slang that doesn't feel contrived and is easily at home, like a pair of comfy slippers: 'I never seen you looking so bad my funky one / You tell me that your superfine mind has come undone.'

The whole song is effortless, a cloud of uplifting loveliness, devoid of the cynicism that Steely Dan became renowned for, a perfect B-side for the 'Rikki Don't Lose That Number' single, reassuring a friend that the bad times won't last forever. It doesn't downplay the unknown source of the distress and comes across like a warm and heartfelt hug.

The minor-key melody is achingly sad, but with a comforting arm around the shoulder in the uplifting message it is certainly one of the Dan's most underrated songs, the chorus of 'Any major dude with half a heart surely will tell you my friend / Any minor world that breaks apart falls together again' is just brilliant.

There's a reference to a squonk's tears, a couple of years before Genesis brought the mythical beast, who when cornered could dissolve itself into a pool of its own tears, out of their toy box. Chuck Rainey adds soulful bass, and Denny Dias gets a solo, although Jeff Baxter played the last five notes as vibrato was needed, which was not part of Dias' technique. The delayed final phrase is a masterstroke.

'Barrytown' (Becker / Fagen) (3:17)

Not played live since 1974, this song, predominantly written by Fagen, dates from the New York period in the late '60s where it was recorded as a demo. This version is, as you might expect, far more clearly defined and polished.

A moderate, conservative view of the counterculture, this song harks back to college days and focuses on the concerned viewpoint of the local inhabitants when confronted by the otherworldly denizens of Bard College. A flip for the benefit of the lyrics is that Barrytown, about a mile or so away from Annandale, is now the setting: 'In the beginning we recall that the word was hurled / Barrytown people got to be from another world.'

The strident intro gives way to an almost folky feel, and at times Fagen puts on his best Bob Dylan impression. The rising and falling cadence of the chorus is very engaging, it's a gentle song of low-level concern, the piano particularly effective in keeping things friendly. Baxter's steel guitar can also be heard adding warmth and a small-town feel in the background.

'Barrytown' is often noted as being directed at members of the Unification Church (the Moonies) who had a property in the town, but this isn't so as the church didn't locate their Unification Theological Seminary there until 1975, more than five years after the song was originally written.

'East St. Louis Toodle-oo' (Duke Ellington / James Miley) (2:45)

This is an anomaly; a fun romp through the Duke Ellington classic, the only time the band attempted anything like this on an album, and it's very successful. Taken at a faster pace than the original with guitar and voice effects replacing the slide trumpet melody.

Not only is this the only cover that the band ever put on an album, it is also the only instrumental. Walter Becker 'sang' the melody through a talk box to imitate 'Bubber' Miley's trumpet style and coupled it with wah-wah guitar (the first time Becker had played guitar on a Steely Dan recording). Baxter used pedal steel for the trombone part, the clarinet solo was covered by Fagen's piano, and he also played saxophone for the only time on a Steely Dan recording. With Jim Gordon on drums and Dean Parks' banjo, it's an eclectic line-up, Roger Nichols banging the gong at the end.

Overall, it's a quirky way to end a superbly rendered side one. Only played live a couple of times in 1974, it returned to the set in 1995 and 1996 but has only appeared a couple of times since, in 2011.

'Parker's Band' (Becker / Fagen) (2:36)

Another song resurrected from the early demos, this is a barnstorming opening to the second side, a blast of fun that underlines the jazz influences and shows where Becker and Fagen's hearts really lay.

After the tribute to Duke Ellington, we get a celebration of saxophone legend Charlie Parker, including a brief quote from his 'Bongo Bop'. The riffs are Parker influenced, and the lyric invites the listener to 'take a piece of Mr Parker's band'. There's a double drum showcase for Jim Gordon and the still teenage Jeff Porcaro, and Jeff Baxter integrates jazz phrasing into his playing. The lyrical change of direction in the middle is unexpected but adds to the variety, another sharp and to the point splash of enthusiastic creativity.

'Through with Buzz' (Becker / Fagen) (1:30)

Another strange piece, the shortest song the band ever recorded and regarded by many as their worst, although I like it a great deal. Yes, it feels incomplete, but with a lovely string intro, with subtle hints of 'Eleanor Rigby' to me, and a good chorus, it always feels that it finishes too soon. The B-side of the *Pretzel Logic* single, the words could be relating to an annoying acquaintance or a desire to clean up a drug habit – you takes your choice – but Fagen described it as being 'just about a more-or-less platonic relationship between two young people. There's nothing really sexual about it until one of the young people in the relationship realises he's being used and starts having paranoid fantasies and breaks off the relationship. There's no symbolism or anything. We never used puns. It's a very saccharine sounding track with a very cynical lyric.'

Or it could still be a talk with yourself about giving up the drugs. When asked about it, Becker responded, 'The less said, the better.'

Having got the strings thing out of their system here, they didn't use them again until 1978 and 'FM (No Static at All)'.

'Pretzel Logic' (Becker / Fagen) (4:32)

The second single from the album, the title track reached number 57, but that's not bad for what was always an odd single choice – a bluesy stomp about time travel.

With references to meeting Napolean and touring with a minstrel show, it's a capricious set-up. Fagen has confirmed that the 'platform' referred to was conceived as a teleportation device, and it seems that the full-bridge 'I stepped up on the platform / The man gave me the news / He said, "You must be joking son / Where did you get those shoes?"' suggests arriving at your destination in time and the locals making fun of your strange attire, as they no doubt would. Fagen also said that the 'I've never met Napoleon, but I plan to find the time' line means that he plans to find the time in which Napolean lived.

The 'travelling minstrel show' of the first verse could be a cynical jibe at the remorseless scheduling of the band's early tours, that saw them give up on the idea of going out on the road for almost 20 years. Another theory is of the band looking to the future and not sticking with their already successful formula: 'These things are gone forever, over a long time ago...'

Steely Dan frequently head into blues territory, but this one sounds the most authentic, probably based on Fagen's delivery in the verses. Other elements are brought in elsewhere, such as the jazzy chorus with close-harmony vocals, but the basic blues formula remains throughout. It appears that Becker played the guitar solo in one of his first appearances as lead guitarist.

'With a Gun' (Becker / Fagen) (2:15)

The scenario might be based on real incidents, but it's cryptic enough to keep you guessing, the murderous outcomes throughout the song are clear enough though. It's about cowards hiding behind guns, letting their weapons do the taking in the squaring of debts or grievances. No doubt a constant in their lives, both in New York and LA, Becker and Fagen were not fans of the gun culture so prevalent in the US. Commenting on the glamorising of it through westerns and cop shows and the worry that if someone feels crossed or hard done by, they'll 'hide in the bushes / Murder the man / With Luger in hand.'

The jaunty acoustic country of the intro, with interjections from Baxter, suggest a western, but a very good-natured one with much hoe-downing. It romps along with purpose, the key moment being the pause before the chorus. Becker's bass bounces along in toe-tapping style and the harmonies are as spot-on as ever. Perhaps strangely there are no keyboards to speak of in this one. It's fun, but again, the message is a dark one.

'Charlie Freak' (Becker / Fagen) (2:41)

Another re-recording of one of the early demos, it's one of my favourite pieces in the catalogue. The wonderful driving piano has a baroque edge, which is both at odds and perfectly in sync with the vocal line. It's just brilliant, I often listen to this breathtaking song multiple times on repeat and will never *ever* get bored of it. It's one of the most striking and unusual songs they did, and all the more precious for that.

It's like a tragic opera with a moral denouement, all delivered in a breathless two-and-a-half minutes, during which Becker and Fagen craft one of the finest songs you're ever likely to hear. It tells the story of a hungry and homeless junkie, Charlie Freak, told from the perspective of another who cynically buys his only possession ('Three weight ounce, pure golden ring, no precious stone') for peanuts. The whole lyric is an object lesson in delivering a story efficiently, with all the dramatic detail intact.

Charlie is in a poor way and needs to eat so 'in our plot of frozen space he told his tale', and the man takes advantage of him:

Poor man, he showed his hand
So righteous was his need
And me so wise I bought his prize
For chicken feed.

Unsurprisingly, Charlie uses his newly acquired cash for drugs and subsequently dies, the lines 'Poor kid, he overdid it / Embraced the spreading haze / And while he sighed his body died / In fifteen ways' are so beautifully descriptive and so desperately sad. The cynicism of the start turns to guilt when the man hears of Charlie's fate, and then human decency, but too late. He returns to find Charlie, ''round his arm the plastic tag read D.O.A.' and returns 'the ring I could not own' to the junkie's corpse.

All this in a little over 150 exquisitely chosen words.

The bass matches the piano with steady drum support. Guitars circle in the air above, like angels, vocal harmonies used sparingly to highlight detail. It builds slowly into the second verse, the guitar more apparent, then for the third verse sleigh bells appear, giving a feel of winter, which is appropriate as in my mind's eye the story is set in the bitter snows and harsh cold of the city. There's almost a hymnal feel, the final verse raising the stakes and expanding the instrumentation for a rousing conclusion that resolves in strident piano chords and then airy trills, as if for Charlie's departing soul.

It's a masterpiece, and if it isn't being used as a fine example in every songwriting course, there's something wrong.

'Monkey in Your Soul' (Becker / Fagen) (2:31)

A song about addiction, the 'monkey' in question, and the effects it can have on yourself and those around you, particularly poignant due to Walter's problems in that area, he clearly knew what he was talking about.

After all that has gone before in this wonderfully unorthodox album, this song almost feels like a letdown. The distorted bass is unexpected and Fagen, at his most manic, truly inhabits the largely impenetrable words. Walter sang this one on later tours. The brass and stabs of guitar bring the necessary funk, and there's a quirky little solo in the middle. It's fun, but again, not really when the words are considered. Well delivered but not exceptional, and it departs quite suddenly.

After all the other delights on this album, we could do with a rest. Just over half an hour and it sounds like 10 minutes, a rare work of extreme creativity.

Related Tracks:

'This all Too Mobile Home' [unreleased]

Played several times live before the band's retirement from the stage, it has only appeared once since the return to the stage, in 2011, and has never been officially recorded.

It's worth a search to find it. I'm not sure it would have made a good fit on *Pretzel Logic* – but Lord knows, there was enough room for it if they'd wanted to. It's big and bold with a lovely piano arrangement. There are a couple of bootleg live performances and a version recorded live at the Record Plant in March 1974 featuring the regular touring line-up, including Michael McDonald, Jeff Porcaro and Royce Jones.

It doesn't feel completely finished, although the harmonies are just right and the driving rhythm works well. McDonald certainly makes his presence felt in the harmonies. The introduction of a snippet of the theme from *A Summer Place* on guitar is typically odd. It seems to be about a road trip, possibly after a break-up, while living in your car.

Katy Lied (1975)

Personnel:
Donald Fagen: Vocals, Piano, Keyboards, Saxophone
Walter Becker: Bass, Guitar
Michael Omartian, David Paich: Pianos, Keyboards
Hugh McCracken, Denny Dias, Rick Derringer, Dean Parks, Elliott Randall, Larry Carlton: Guitars
Wilton Felder, Chuck Rainey: Bass Guitars
Jeff Porcaro, Hal Blaine: Drums
Victor Feldman: Vibraphone, Percussion
Phil Woods: Alto Saxophone
Jimmie Haskell: Horn & Horn Arrangement
Bill Perkins: Horn
Michael McDonald, Myrna Matthews, Sherlie Matthews, Carolyn Willis: Background Vocals
Producer: Gary Katz
Engineer: Roger Nichols
Record Labe: ABC Records
Recorded: ABC Recording Studios (Los Angeles), late 1974 to early 1975
Released: March 1975
Running Time: 35:25
Highest chart place: US 13, UK 13

Free from the need to tour – and the rest of the band – Becker and Fagen were in their songwriting element. 'We found ourselves back in Los Angeles with no band, no manager, no plans to tour, no money, some minor albeit possibly irreversible brain damage, and, thanks to Gary Katz, the keys to a certain unused office on the ground floor of the ABC Dunhill Records complex equipped with a leather couch, a piano, a lamp, and nothing else. It was there that we repaired on an autumn evening to lick our wounds and hopefully, begin work on a new suite of songs which would someday adorn the greatest Steely Dan album ever.'

The retreat into the studio added to the band's mystique; every year or two they would emerge blinking into the daylight with another piece of handsomely crafted vinyl to beguile the ever-expanding fanbase.

By now their fame was increasing, the privilege brought by the popularity and success of their songs were a particularly beneficial sideline, but the stardom was anathema, as Fagen said, 'Popularity has everything to do with business and nothing to do with music'. They always sought to avoid the limelight and never attended glitzy music industry gatherings. 'I got a thing that said: "Wear beautiful clothes"', Fagen said in response to a Grammy invitation. 'I don't have any beautiful clothes! Now I know what they wanted me to come like, they wanted me to come dressed like Cher!'

When it came to recording *Katy Lied*, Jeff Porcaro and Michael McDonald were retained from the last live band, the latter's first appearance on a Steely Dan album, Porcaro stepping up to play on all but one of the tracks. A diverse group of LA session players were also recruited, including saxophonist Phil Woods and guitarist extraordinaire Larry Carlton. It seems that Becker and Fagen intended to put a new band together at some point, but just never got around to it and the mix-and-match set-up of swapping musicians in and out as required ultimately suited their needs. Despite the different musical styles and the varying of player input, it all held together as a beautifully cohesive whole.

Session personnel were hired and often replaced on the spot if their performance didn't come up to scratch. Despite this, the sessions were challenging and fun for the musicians and being called in to participate was a real coup. Becker and Fagen were modest about their own playing and somewhat overawed by the technique of the hired guns, seldom playing with them and being respectful of their talents.

Fagen had grown more used to his voice and found ways to use it to the benefit of the songs, inhabiting characters and imbuing the words with individualistic traits which took advantage of the plaintive tones and inherent sinister edge, his performances going from strength to strength.

As with *Pretzel Logic*, the songs on *Katy Lied* are notable for their brevity, with only 'Your Gold Teeth II' running longer than four minutes. The album went gold on the strength of the 'Black Friday' and 'Bad Sneakers' single releases.

Fagen once described Steely Dan's music as 'pop songs with some sort of structure that's interesting and can be developed... the chords are usually more interesting than most rock 'n' roll, I think'. Becker called it 'Planned diversity'. They primarily wrote for themselves, the old cliché 'the music's all that matters' definitely coming into play, it was always all about getting the songs heard and presenting them in the best possible light, the fastidious perfectionism just part of that aim. The results were built for play on the thriving FM radio stations of the time – so long as the deejays didn't look too closely at the death, cynicism, and deviancy lurking within the lyrics.

However, once again there were problems during the recording process, this time with a faulty noise reduction system used in the mixing. The sound was recovered, but the consensus was that the final mix bore no resemblance to the original recording, Gary Katz calling it 'the best sounding thing I'd ever heard before it was mixed'. It was touch and go as to whether the album would be released at all – Becker and Fagen were so dissatisfied with the quality of the sound on *Katy Lied* that they felt it necessary to add a public apology to the reverse of the cover, refusing to listen to the completed album for many years.

The unusual cover image features a close-up of a katydid, an insect related to crickets and grasshoppers, once again put together by Dorothy White. The reverse featured six images; Becker, Fagen with Dias, Michael McDonald and Jeff Porcaro, plus Katz and Nichols.

The album itself was perceived, unfairly, as 'cool, cerebral and one-dimensional' jazz-rock. The *Rolling Stone* review acknowledged that while the music was 'immaculately tasteful and intelligent' it remained 'exemplarily well-crafted and uncommonly intelligent schlock', while others felt that it did not reach the heights of *Pretzel Logic*.

In 1989 Becker talked about the duo's writing process and the homogenous whole of their work: 'We were writing together for such a long time that we really adapted to one another. We had a tremendous rapport from the very beginning of our collaboration where we knew what we wanted to do and we weren't working at cross-purposes. That became more and more the case. We developed a way of working together that really combined our sensibilities. There were a lot of things that I never learned because Donald already knew how to do them. I could manipulate elements of his technique without having to master the same things myself. A lot of the themes that we developed, we developed together. Over the years, just bouncing things off of each other in ordinary conversations we'd be having, and I still find this when I talk to Donald.'

They worked separately, bringing in pieces and putting them together. 'Usually, we would get a melody first and then stretch it or do what we needed to do to accommodate words. Typically, we'd get a chorus together first with the lyrics. Ideally. Not having a chorus was a real pain in the ass. Once you had the chorus, then you could construct the music for the verse, and then the melody for the verse, and then actually write the verse.' Fagen: 'We try to make it "unboring", If it's boring that's the main indication that there's some failure.'

For all the problems in the recording, *Katy Lied* remains a beautiful collection of songs, maybe not scaling the heights of some of the other albums but awash with quality and containing some true classics.

The Songs:

'Black Friday' (Becker / Fagen) (3:40)
From the spooky fade-in electric piano, this is a thumping opener. There's no let up from start to finish, it bristles energy with some suitably blistering soloing from Walter. Donald is at his cynical and vindictive best relating the tale of a crooked speculator who makes a killing and ducks out at the last minute before the inevitable 'Black Friday' crash, watching 'the grey men when they dive from the fourteenth floor' and praying that when Black Friday falls, 'Don't let it fall on me'.

He intends to skip town with as much cash as possible and head to the distant rural hinterland of Australia as refuge from the inevitable fallout. The small town of Muswellbrook in New South Wales is chosen as the location, both to fit the metre and because it rhymed with 'book', but also because, as Fagen later explained, 'it was the place most far away from LA we could think of'. He's going to lie low in the outback, leading a comfortable life 'with nothing to do but feed all the kangaroos', seemingly faking his own death to live under an assumed name until everything blows over.

The momentum of the track comes from the combination of Michael Omartian's piano and David Paich's Hohner electric. The first single from the album, it charted at number 37.

'Bad Sneakers' (Becker / Fagen) (3:16)

A song of homesickness for New York, Don and Walt in conversation, thinking back to simpler, happier times in more comfortable (to them) East Coast environs, written from the soulless wastes of LA. The 'five names that I can hardly stand to hear, including yours and mine and one more chimp who isn't here' seems to refer to the original members of the band, so could the 'one more chimp' be a sixth name? If it is then that's got to be David Palmer.

West Magnolia Boulevard runs from Sherman Oaks to Burbank, where ABC Dunhill had their headquarters, and where Becker and Fagen had their writing studio at this time. The enigmatic nature of the song continues with the fellah in the white tuxedo 'tearin' up the streets'. A bit of a mystery, but could it be ABC's Jay Lasker, his quest for Steely Dan success likely to drive the band to its death and the 'ditch in the valley that they're digging just for me'? The final lines might reference Becker's understanding that his increasing use of drugs could prove to be terminal.

Soft and melancholic, with another great chorus, it was released as the second single from the album, but it did not chart, Gary Katz later regretting that the song was not released as the first single. What sounds like a return to the electric sitar opens this one, the piano part and vocals follow each other, with a rhythm guitar groove from Hugh McCracken and jaunty solo from Becker. This song marked Michael McDonald's first credit on a Dan album, his distinctive backing vocals adding a lot to Fagen's dynamic performance.

'Bad Sneakers' marked the first use of a common device in later Steely Dan songs, the referencing of alcoholic drinks (although 'poison wine' did appear in 'King of the World' on *Countdown to Ecstasy*, but I don't think that counts!). Beginning here with the weirdly out of context piña colada, *Katy Lied* also features the switched for lyrical continuity. This includes 'Coke and rum' (in 'Daddy Don't Live in that New York City No More'), the zombie appears on *The Royal Scam*, but it's *Aja* where things really take off – 'Black Cow', Scotch whisky and retsina all appearing, with grapefruit wine in the linked track, 'FM (No Static A All)'. *Gaucho* glugs down both kirschwasser and cherry wine, and Cuervo Gold, later albums keeping up the trend with Tanqueray, Cuban breeze and margaritas. Cheers!

'Rose Darling' (Becker / Fagen) (2:59)

This is a great song with a fantastic chorus built on the harmony vocals. The title comes from Vladimir Nabokov's novel *Lolita*, the song concerning an illicit affair with Rose, conducted while your partner sleeps, or possibly – just possibly – a song about late-night masturbation?

The lugubrious way Fagen sings 'I would guess she's in Detroit / With lots of money in the bank', with the elongated slide on 'moneyyy' is typical of Fagen's way with a lyric, the lewd and sneaky always coming through in his characterful voice.

Piano again drives this brief and uptempo little gem. In most cases, the musicians selected to play specific parts were given the space to improvise their solos, but for this song, Dean Parks was given a specific solo line to play, which he does with panache.

'Daddy Don't Live in that New York City No More' (Becker / Fagen) (3:12)

This strutting bluesy funk follows an alcoholic pimp, or another nefarious character (whose heavy drinking appears to be causing issues in the bedroom department), out and about in his Chevy Eldorado and up to no good. This is until – most likely, as 'Driving like a fool out to Hackensack / Drinking his dinner from a paper sack' isn't conducive to road safety – he crashes while under the influence and dies, therefore rendering himself no longer a resident of The Big Apple. It's probably the lowest point of *Katy Lied*, but it's still good stuff.

Becker and Fagen heard about Larry Carlton too late in the recording for him to play any major part, but he was invited to record some rhythm parts for this song, his sweet trills standing out, but he would really make his presence felt on the next album.

'Doctor Wu' (Becker / Fagen) (3:59)

From a lower point to one of the album's definitive peaks. This beautiful and painfully sad song is just wonderful in so many ways; the impassioned vocals from Fagen, the supreme confidence of the piano chords, the undulating chorus and Phil Woods' evocative first take alto sax solo. Michael McDonald remembers struggling with his part, Walter pushing him to do better: 'They were harsh taskmasters. Not harsh, but they set the bar high.'

The song focuses on a guy in need of his next fix, and his dealer (Doctor Wu) is not coming through for him, or possibly the flip side; a guy in rehab whose doctor is refusing to give him the medication he craves for his own good? In 2009 Becker said, 'It's about that uneasy relationship between the patient and doctor. People put faith in doctors, yet they abuse their power and become dangerous.' Fagen described it as a 'love-dope triangle', the third party in the relationship being heroin (personified as 'Doctor Wu'), which eventually leads to its ending; Katy tries to help him, but the hold of the drugs is too strong. So again, only they really know.

There are some beautiful words here, the ironic pain of 'All night long, we would sing that stupid song, and every word we sang I knew was true' not the least. The album's title comes from the line 'Katy lies, you could see it in her eyes', the paranoia coming out in the last verse as the addict convinces himself that his lover is lying to him and that the dealer (or the drug) is the only one telling the truth. 'I was halfway crucified / I was on the other side of no tomorrow. / You walked in and my life began again' – does that refer to Katy, the dealer or the drugs themselves? Or is the drug in fact Katy? It's a confusing business… but a wonderful song.

A great way to end side one and a fan-favourite, 'Doctor Wu' has perhaps surprisingly only been played live half a dozen times, between 2009 and 2011.

'Everyone's Gone to the Movies' (Becker / Fagen) (3:41)

Opening side two is a much more wholesome, family-friendly scene – but it so isn't, as we move from drugs to seedy sexual predator Mr LaPage, who loves nothing more than to entice teenage girls to his place to watch selections from his adult movie collection. Did ABC actually know what they were releasing?

It starts out with a cheeky and fun Latin rhythm, but the sinister edge soon creeps in – 'Bobbing for apples can wait…'. In typically ironic fashion, the chorus is pure pop with delicious female harmonies.

The line 'I know you're used to 16 or more, sorry we only have eight' refers to the film stock being viewed. Professional film would be shot on 16mm or 35mm, but home movies (and cheaply produced pornography) would be available on 8mm film.

This song had been around for ages and was originally recorded as a demo with Flo and Eddie (of The Turtles) in 1971, that version eventually released on the *Citizen Steely Dan* box set.

'Your Gold Teeth II' (Becker / Fagen) (4:12)

A second helping of chance, this one is not a sequel to the first 'Your Gold Teeth' (from *Countdown to Ecstasy*) and has less in the way of a definitive storyline, being more about the vagaries of luck in general. The opening verse is particularly worthy of note:

Who are these children
Who scheme and run wild?
Who speak with their wings
And the way that they smile?
What are the secrets
They trace in the sky
And why do you tremble
Each time they ride by?

It's positive in tone and lacking the regular dose of cynicism and irony, rolling the dice to see what will happen next ('If you're feeling lucky you best not refuse, It's your game the rules are your own, win or lose.'). One school of thought has it that the song references musical experimentation and discovery, the unexpected variations and new ideas brought in by the session players drafted in to work their magic in this new Dan era.

The laid-back swing of Michael Omartian's piano introduction, supported by vibes (from Victor Feldman) and Fagen's synth lines, moves on through strident chords into the verse, Fagen's tone warmer and more intimate than usual. Harmony vocals bulk out the chorus until Denny Dias' lovely percolating and jazzy solo, again supported by piano.

The musicians struggled to get the feel right, until Fagen referred Jeff Porcaro to some Charlie Mingus recordings and everything fell into place, Porcaro later describing 'Your Gold Teeth II' as 'pure bebop'.

It's a gorgeous hug of a song, a soft pick-me-up to dust yourself off and move on refreshed, and as a result, it's perhaps surprising that it does not appear to have been played live since 1974.

'Chain Lightning' (Becker / Fagen) (2:57)

Starting from electric piano, this is a sultry blues with the words sung in close harmony. You really wouldn't guess from the music what the subject matter might be referring to.

At the time, Fagen stated that the clue to the song was in the guitar break before the second verse, 'I was going to sing "40 years later", but we decided it wasn't a good musical idea', but in an interview in the early '80s he admitted that it was about two Nazis, possibly SS (the song title indicating their insignia) attending a rally in 1930s Germany. Hitler is on the rise, and swept up in the excitement of the ceremonial gatherings with no need to consider the darker meanings behind it all. Read the words and it all falls into place: 'Some turnout, a hundred grand / Get with it we'll shake his hand. / Don't bother to understand, / Don't question the little man. / Be part of the brotherhood. / Yes it's chain lightning / it feels so good.' Fast forward to decades later and the pair furtively return to the same spot: 'We're standing just where he stood...'

It seems odd for Fagen in particular, with his Jewish heritage, to write a song like this with not even a hint of revulsion. There is no comment on the immorality of the regime or its actions, just matter-of-fact acknowledgement that not only did people gladly go along with it all on a wave of hysteria, many of them continued to feel the same 40 years later, after all the horrible truths had emerged. Sobering stuff.

Rick Derringer was selected because of his gritty style to play the bluesy solo on this song, which featured as the B side of the 'Bad Sneakers' single.

'Any World (That I'm Welcome To)' (Becker / Fagen) (3:56)

Only attempted once live, in 2006, this song is notable for Michael McDonald's contribution and drummer Hal Blaine's only appearance on a Steely Dan recording. Blaine is considered one of the most recorded studio drummers ever with over 35,000 sessions to his name, and here he pitches his performance perfectly with a light touch, picking things up into the verse.

Another slow-burn start, a lonely man in a dead-end job in the city, yearns for a new life, a new start in a more welcoming community in a rural setting. It seems pretty clear-cut and straightforward, another song of hope for a better future ahead. It could be an older song written before the move to California ('A kingdom where the sky is burning'). The bridge changes the pace to fully upbeat before sliding into the final verse.

Thematically there could be some parallels with older demos, such as 'Sun Mountain', except this one is more distinctively drawn and realised with more flair. Ultimately, the positive outlook carries it through.

'Throw Back the Little Ones' (Becker / Fagen) (3:11)

A song discussing the Dan's awkwardness with the music industry, 'Hot licks and rhetoric / Don't count much for nothing' as the label bosses seek out the big hits and discard work deemed to be of lesser commercial stature. Alternatively, it could easily be about cruising for women, or suckers to scam (the 'fish'). Whatever, the opening line 'Lost in the Barrio I walk like an Injun / So Carlo won't suspect something's wrong here' are suitably engaging and enigmatic.

The soft downward movement of the opening chords shifts into a mid-tempo strut, Fagen in slightly sleazy character. The brass additions before the verses and in the chorus are set back but spot-on as waymarkers, and the guitar solo from Elliott Randall is boisterous without being too flashy. This gives way to the final verse where Donald is 'done like a matador', ready for the weekend and the 'little girls' throwing roses as a sign of their devotion, either to his manly charms or in adoration of his pop hits.

Always receptive to the ideas of the musicians, Becker and Fagen kept Michael Omartian's semi-classical - with hints of Gershwin - piano coda. It's at odds with the rest of the track but underlines everything beautifully, probably making the song work better as a whole and bringing the album to a warm and typically unorthodox end.

Related Tracks:

'Mister Sam' [unreleased]

A victim of the problems caused by the faulty noise reduction system, the hook-laden 'Mister Sam' is a great song that deserves more attention. Upbeat and easy to like, it could have made a great single, in completed form.

Michael Omartian's piano is the first feature, with Chuck Rainey and Jeff Porcaro, Hugh McCracken adding acoustic guitar. It is certainly unfinished, but it's a real toe-tapper. The words are sarcastic and subversive, yet funny. There's a theory that the story was inspired by Jerry Kosinski's book *Being There*, later made into a film with Peter Sellers as the simple gardener who is taken to be more than he actually is.

From the strutting opening, a steady snare rhythm leads into staccato verses that keep the momentum rolling. Again, the story is at odds with the music:

Mr Sam used to work as a gardener for the lady in the big house. Brilliantly described as a 'Cocker Spaniard', he is seduced by the lady, but things take an unexpected turn, and it appears that – whether intentional or not – she ends up dead, leaving Sam in anguish ('Mister Sam don`t look so good no more / I've never seen him cry out loud before'), and more than likely in prison.

The short bursts of words suggest songs like 'Green Earrings', from the next album, so they seemed to be in that mode around this time. Fagen is reaching a little for the highest notes, but I'm sure that would have been fixed in a finished version. It's fun and frisky, driven by the sparse piano and steady drums, guitar additions punctuating the gaps.

Upon listening to the song after the noise-reduction calamity, Denny Dias was heard to say: 'Mr. Sam don't sound so good no more...'

'Funky Driver' [unreleased]
Another unreleased and rather cool two-minute instrumental, piano front and centre with Jeff Porcaro's drums driving it along. It would no doubt have worked best as an upbeat break in the context of another, longer song, but unfortunately, it never found a place and languishes in the Dan outtake graveyard.

The Royal Scam (1976)

Personnel:
Donald Fagen: Keyboards, Lead & Background Vocals
Walter Becker: Bass, Guitar
Paul Griffin, Don Grolnick: Keyboards
Denny Dias, Larry Carlton, Dean Parks, Elliott Randall: Guitars
Mark Davis, Chuck Rainey: Bass
Jim Horn, Plas Johnson, John Klemmer: Saxophone
Chuck Findley, Bob Findley, Dick Hyde: Brass
Rick Marotta, Bernard Purdie: Drums
Gary Coleman: Percussion
Victor Feldman: Percussion, Keyboards
Timothy B. Schmit, Venetta Fields, Clydie King, Sherlie Matthews, Michael
McDonald: Background Vocals
Producer: Gary Katz
Engineer: Roger Nichols
Record Label: ABC Records
Recorded: ABC Studios (Los Angeles); A&R Studios (New York), Nov. 1975 to Mar.
1976
Released: 31st May 1976
Running Time: 41:11
Highest chart place: 15 US, 11 UK

The Royal Scam is Steely Dan's most guitar-centric release - perhaps oddly as
Jeff Baxter was no longer involved - due to the prominent positioning and
significant contributions from guitar whizz Larry Carlton, who first appeared
on a single track on *Katy Lied*. Also heavily featured are bassist Chuck Rainey,
his third Steely Dan album, and drummer Bernard 'Pretty' Purdie, appearing
for the first time and radically increasing the groove factor. R'n'B and funk man
Purdie is *the* groove drummer par excellence, a master of the technique, his
'Purdie Shuffle' a thing of wonder, looking simple but fiendishly complicated.
Groove had always been a vital component of the songs, but the pairing of
Purdie and Rainey ramped it up considerably.

It sold well in the US without support from a hit single, but 'Haitian Divorce'
became the band's first Top 20 hit in the UK. In typical style, the album is
littered with cryptic allusions to people and events, both real and fictional,
the cover showing a down at heel businessman sleeping on a radiator and
apparently dreaming of skyscraper-beast hybrids. This satire on the American
Dream, created from a painting by Zox and a Charlie Ganse photograph, was
originally meant for Van Morrison's unreleased 1975 album, *Mechanical Bliss*.
Fagen and Becker have claimed it to be 'the most hideous album cover of
the seventies, bar none (excepting perhaps *Can't Buy a Thrill*).' The reverse
showed a close-up of the hole in the man's shoe, while the inner bag had the
lyrics on one side and mirror-image photos of Becker and Fagen on the other.

At the start of the sessions, players were switched in and out, into almost every possible configuration, to see which worked best, songs being dropped after innumerable takes if Becker and Fagen decided that the recording would not measure up to the perfection they heard in their heads. The time this all took saw the recording budget, which had been growing album by album, skyrocket to $100,000, but that was nothing compared to the next two releases.

This was storytelling in song, with only 'The Fez' and 'Green Earrings' featuring abstract words. There's world-weary cynicism swathed in a cloak of sophistication, the album moving through numerous styles towards the strange title track, epic in feel if not stature, dark but with an odd humour in the words. The counterculture of the late '60s was in decline, in the wake of Vietnam and Watergate, the resulting album having spikier edges than some of the other releases.

The blend of pop, jazz, R'n'B and doo-wop influences with quirky, cryptic and often sarcastic lyrics is underpinned by the sophistication of the studio techniques, benefitting from the crisp and bright sound delivered by Roger Nichols, and now we're in overdrive. The detail captured in these recordings is remarkable, in a warm 'sound' with little echo and reverb. The mid and late '70s albums are still hallowed by audiophiles for their pristine sound and attention to even the most minute detail. It's clean and there's space for all the instrumentation to be heard, Fagen likening the sound to the jazz albums released on the Prestige label in the late 1950s.

Now is a good time to talk about the lyrics. Throughout the Dan songbook, the stories and the words used to portray them are vital, turning these from great songs into works of depth that you can truly immerse yourself in. The songs themselves cover a lot of ground, often featuring fictional (or fictionalised) places and characters, usually of the low-life variety, and dealing with illicit passions. They eschew the love songs and wholesomeness of traditional popular music in favour of obsession, disturbing twists and irony, with subject matter taking in drugs, alcohol, prostitution, sexual desire, pornography and the like. There is nefarious crime, murder and extra-marital relationships in a world that appears at odds with the sophistication of the music, oozing NYC smarts and delivered with such poetic expression that you can't help but be drawn into the seedy beauty of it all, while the music suggests West Coast jazz inflexions or Floridian Tropicana. Things are seldom as clear cut as they may at first appear.

The cryptic and open-ended nature of the songs derived from extracting the key parts of the story, making many of them subtle and hard to decipher, open to the listener's interpretation, which is the way Donald and Walter liked it. They didn't give much away about the meanings or their inspirations. Imagery is often used out of context, for effect or the sound of the words, with plenty of slang terms and references, many of which, just to confuse the issue, are made up. It's a game, anyone keen on getting clear meanings and understanding will, in most cases, be disappointed. Interpretations of the often inscrutable and expressionistic lyrics are hard to pin down, with alternatives available for listeners to find different meanings.

Becker: 'All our lyrics are calculated and literary, they are not personal documents. We use autobiographical material, but the autobiography is not what the lyrics are about. I don't expect anyone to understand me the way I understand myself. Whatever people get out of these songs, it's fine ... songs can't be too funny, they can't be too obscene, they can't be too nasty, they can't be too pretentious, we have to sort of try and juggle the different elements that we're using in the songs, and I think we've learned how to do that over the years so that the songs will sort of work on a bunch of different levels at once. You can listen to them one way and hear one thing, and you can listen to them one way and hear something different.'

To me, song after song, the lyrics are a joy, stylistically fascinating, ironic and sardonic in equal measure, seeking out the dark underbelly of society and ribbing it mercilessly while integrating often obscure references and themes from jazz, movies and literary works. This is what keeps me coming back for more – the words are probably without peer in the rock'n'roll pantheon and are worthy of a book in themselves.

The overall partnership was an equal split, all the songs carrying the 'Becker / Fagen' writing credit, however, a few were predominantly put together by one or the other. Fagen could start songs but needed Becker to finish them, and for Becker it was the other way around. From looking at the history of their relationship, particularly in the first ten years, the sense of symbiosis and a real closeness come through – the two come as an individual package – but towards the end of this period Fagen said, 'we're friends, but we're not the closest friends in the world ... we understand each other's working habits and needs and limitations. But we aren't hanging out together that much.'

The Songs:

'Kid Charlemagne' (Becker / Fagen) (4:38)
From the start, this is a massive funky kick in the pants of what has gone before, probably the archetypal Steely Dan track. The rhythm section of Purdie and Rainey is imperious, but as soon as Larry Carlton steps up to the plate, the whole thing lifts skyward with one of the most ridiculously melodic guitar solos you'll ever hear.

Purdie excels, creating a pocket so capacious that Rainey can't help but slip right into it. As Becker said in 1989: 'I'm kind of a drum freak myself, so I would always have a pretty good vision of what I wanted. We would describe what we wanted to a drummer, listen to what he did and then take it from there. But in the case of Bernard Purdie, there was no point in having any ideas because he was going to do something that you couldn't really imagine. And he was the kind of guy who could look at a chart and see a record in his mind's eye. He would put it together and make it orderly, make the transitions work.

If he found something he liked, he would use that over and over and give it structure in that way. Basically, he just did what only he could do.'

The single release only made number 82 in the *Billboard* charts, but that doesn't detract from it being one of the mightiest tracks in the catalogue. The song was inspired by notorious San Francisco drug chef Owsley Stanley, and his ultimate downfall. The purity of Stanley's product was legendary, supplying LSD to Ken Kesey and the Merry Pranksters, with whom he travelled in a 'Technicolor motor home' known as 'Further'.

For all its funk, R&B and jazz influences and techniques, 'Kid Charlemagne' remains a rock track, the flavourings of the other genres adding a tasty spice. From Don Grolnick's Fender Rhodes intro, we're already cooking, Fagen's vocal, possibly inspired by the quality all around him, sharp and on point, conveying the seat-of-the-pants lifestyle of the always on the lookout social pariah ('Careful what you carry / 'Cause the man is wise / You are still an outlaw in their eyes'), the female backing singers imploring 'Get along Kid Charlemagne'. The call and response falsetto ending the line 'Is there gas in the car? / Yes there's gas in the caaaar' is unexpectedly wonderful, and right through to the outro, Carlton is The Man.

'The Caves of Altamira' (Becker / Fagen) (3:34)
Inspired by Hans Baumann's book *The Caves of the Great Hunters*, and also Plato's Cave Allegory and Keats' 'Ode to a Grecian Urn', the song takes its name from the renowned prehistoric site in Spain. Another re-recording of one of the early demos, a child discovers a 'hall of rock and sand', filled with wonderful ancient paintings; 'A woolly man without a face / And a beast without a name'. The song contrasts art as it was originally intended – for its own sake – with the for-profit business it has become, cynically noted in the line 'When there wasn't even any Hollywood'.

The swelling brass intro leads into electric piano and bass, Fagen in intimate form as the child alone discovering a lost world. The chorus is catchy, brass again working with the rhythm to lead into the following verse. John Klemmer gets the tenor sax solo, and the extended outro on a repeated brassy groove almost suggests the unchanging world inside the cave.

Originally a final verse saw the child return to the caves to find that others have discovered what was once his own secret world, leading to a loss of innocence, but this was omitted in the final version, allowing the song to retain its otherworldly sense of mystery.

'Don't Take Me Alive' (Becker / Fagen) (4:16)
Another song that the duo did not play on, highlighting their contention that 'If we ever received an award, we'd like to receive it for songwriting. At least we'd rather be recognised for that than our musicianship.'

It's a siege situation, possibly based in part on the Sterling Hall bombing in 1970, a response to the Vietnam War and the shootings at Kent State University, from the perspective of one of the perpetrators. There's also a hint of *Dog Day Afternoon* in there, and Becker and Fagen's unease with the level of LA street violence, particularly a series of armed sieges at the time, is palpable: 'Agents of the law / Luckless pedestrian / I know you're out there / With rage in your eyes and your megaphones.'

From the opening lines, it's a frantic scene, the holed-up and cornered fugitive waiting for the next move in a tense game of chess. But the song itself is uplifting, a compelling exploration of the criminal's inner mind, moving from the bravado of 'don't take me alive' to the breathtaking realisation of what he has become in the final verse:

Can you hear the evil crowd
The lies and the laughter
I hear my inside
The mechanized hum of another world
Where no sun is shining
No red light flashing
Here in this darkness
I know what I've done
I know all at once who I am.

The ragged sliding guitar intro and following solo from Carlton are fantastic, and he features throughout with some wonderful playing right through to the outro, supported by superb bass from Chuck Rainey and drums from Rick Marotta.

'Sign in Stranger' (Becker / Fagen) (4:23)
An unexpected deviation into sci-fi shot through with corruption in a brutal society. Fixers are on hand to change identities and airbrush the past – 'You zombie / Be born again my friend / Won't you sign in stranger' – allowing fugitives to escape justice to the lawless planet Mizar Five, the lack of any significant policing attracting criminals of all kinds to make it big in shady ways; 'And who are you? / Just another scurvy brother'.

It's almost a Western, but the reggae groove tells you differently. Rainey is again on thumping form and you can't keep the funk down. Paul Griffin brings the jazz with some gorgeous chords and a deliciously improvised solo, Elliott Randall returning to add his own unique spin in an unusual ending guitar section. A session demo without horns and vocals is also in circulation.

'The Fez' (Becker / Fagen / Paul Griffin) (4:01)
The descending piano line gives way to a full-on disco parody, an ode to condom use, and how you should never do it without one, 'Fez' being a '70s slang term for a condom, making it much more humorous with images of Tommy Cooper never far away!

Uniquely, keyboardist Paul Griffin was given a co-writer credit – the only person to ever get such acknowledgement on a Steely Dan song – for writing the main theme, as acknowledged by Fagen, although Becker played that down: 'I wouldn't call it the main theme, he wrote a melody that is featured.' They couldn't resist adding plenty of chord changes, Fagen saying 'you can dance to parts of it, you just have to stop in the middle once in a while.' Rainey is the man here, keeping things bouncing, with Becker adding the expressive guitar solos.

It's lyrically the simplest song the band ever released, a one-point message with repeated phrases and many 'oh no's, but it is also one of the catchiest, although even this change to a possibly more populist style wasn't overly successful, the second single from *The Royal Scam*, it only managed number 59 in the US.

'Green Earrings' (Becker / Fagen) (4:05)
A song of lust, sparkling jewellery enticing a would-be thief – or is it a scene of rape? The significance of the earrings 'of rare design' suggests a theft, in some theories possibly from a girlfriend to fund a junkie's habit, but the earrings might just be a glittering and peripheral part of the complete package. The abstract and minimal lyric leaves much to the imagination, and the song can be taken in many ways.

The music is as stop/start as the words, Dias taking a short solo, with bursts of snare and hi-hat from Purdie, a second solo coming again from Elliott Randall, getting more deranged as it progresses to the fade. The funky groove drives the song along, Purdie and Rainey locking in, to wonderful effect. In fact, the interplay between the rhythm section and the lead instruments is a fascinating listen in its own right. There's also a seven-minute instrumental version from the sessions, without horns and vocals, nothing but the amazing groove.

'Haitian Divorce' (Becker / Fagen) (5:53)
A clever little nugget with a lilting Caribbean swing, it's a lovely listen with a cheeky story. Babs and Clean Willy are very much in love and get married, but soon constant fighting sees them heading for the rocks. A popular option with US citizens for many years, when divorces were more difficult to get, was Haiti where you could get a divorce by the appearance of just one of the parties, who does not have to be resident, the consent of the spouse not being required, so Babs heads for the sun, seemingly funded by her father. Once there, presumably having signed the requisite paperwork, she's in the mood to celebrate and takes a taxi to the Grotto, where 'In the greasy chair / Sits the Charlie with the lotion and the kinky hair'. They dance the Merengue and one thing leads to another…

Upon returning home Babs and Willy make up and get back together. Babs is pregnant, to the family's delight, until the offspring appears – 'Who's this kinky so-and-so?' Once more Papa has to fund a trip…

The idea for the song came from advice engineer Elliot Scheiner received from his lawyer about quickie divorces in Haiti – the gender switched to incorporate the 'surprise' ending.

A soft reggae with plenty of jazz chords, the song is noteworthy for the 'talkbox' effect, Becker altering Dean Parks' guitar through a voice box, the call and response with electric piano in the last part a lovely thing and the backing vocals set low in the mix behind the chorus add to the warm and sunny vibe. It wasn't released as a single in the US but was the band's first and biggest UK hit, reaching number seventeen.

'Everything You Did' (Becker / Fagen) (3:55)
'Where did the bastard run?' A guy comes home to discover that his girlfriend has been cheating. He wants to find the guilty party, but the thought of the infidelity also turns him on and he's keen to hear the gory details, and then experience them for himself...

The lyric relates the guy's side of the conversation, anger at the evidence 'everywhere in our happy home' turning to disgust at the end of 'I jumped out of my easy chair – it was not my own!', suggesting that there are noticeable 'traces' of the earlier sexual shenanigans.

The ensuing argument brings us to one of the best lines – 'turn up the Eagles, the neighbors are listening.' Glenn Frey of the Eagles said, 'Apparently Walter Becker's girlfriend loved the Eagles, and she played them all the time. I think it drove him nuts. So, the story goes that they were having a fight one day and that was the genesis of the line.' The Eagles stated their admiration for Steely Dan, so this was more than likely a friendly bit of fun rather than a feud, and later the same year they returned the compliment by adding the line 'They stab it with their steely knives' to 'Hotel California'.

The pace is easy, Rick Marotta's style markedly different to Bernard Purdie, and this is a less funky outing than much of the album. Larry Carlton adds sustained notes in the background, almost like despairing howls of anguish, and a woozy solo that is highly effective, rising to the heights before sliding back into the chorus.

I'm not sure of the significance of her being a rollerskater, and what exactly she was gonna show him later, but I'm pretty certain it's not her skates...

'The Royal Scam' (Becker / Fagen) (6:28)
How dreams shatter in the dog-eat-dog real world, relating specifically to the experiences of Puerto Rican immigrants to New York City as part of the 'great migration' of the '50s and '60s in search of better lives. Visions of the island, its capital San Juan ('the city of Saint John'), the colours of the coat of arms, the sunshine, traded for a harsh winter in an unforgiving city, the immigrants descend into a murky world in the enclaves of Spanish Harlem. They work hard for low pay ('the royal scam'?), suffering oppression and racism from other groups with some falling into addiction, while sending positive letters home to comfort loved ones, in turn encouraging more people to make the trip.

It's bleak but beautifully poetic. Once when asked what it was about, Becker replied 'About four and a half minutes.' Becker was irritated by the notion that 'in order to enjoy a song you have to know exactly what it means.' Fagen remained fond of the lyric, with its biblical undertones.

Easily the album's longest track, the tone is stately, a mini-epic of gravitas and dignity. Carlton's additions are again deployed with pin-point accuracy amid mournful muted trumpet wails, the backing singers imploring us to 'See the glory of the royal scam.' A notable element is the use of trombone, Dick 'Slyde' Hyde pushing this element to its lowest extremes.

Related Tracks:

'Here at the Western World' (Becker / Fagen) (4:00)

This is a beautiful song. About a brothel.

Michael Omartian's piano is key to the homely nature and relaxed atmosphere of the establishment, which is also a drug den, frequented by the mayor and his friends (the 'rap with your cane' line suggesting that the place is high class) but everyone is treated the same. Covering hedonistic lifestyles in general, it is full of drug slang; you lay down your 'Jackson' (a $20 bill features seventh president Andrew Jackson), take the hit and experience the effects in the security of the Western World, the languid tone having an appealing elegance.

Recorded during the sessions for *The Royal Scam* but not used, it was considered for *Aja* but was passed over again as there were already enough songs in the same tempo, finally appearing on the 1978 *Greatest Hits (1972-1978)* album. It has subsequently turned up on the *Gold – Expanded Edition* compilation in 1991, the first time on CD, and then the *Citizen Steely Dan* box set.

Aja (1977)

Personnel:
Donald Fagen: Lead & Backing Vocals, Synthesizers, Police Whistle
Walter Becker: Bass, Guitar
Victor Feldman: Piano, Electric Piano, Vibraphone, Percussion
Joe Sample, Paul Griffin, Michael Omartian, Don Grolnick: Keyboards
Larry Carlton, Lee Ritenour, Denny Dias, Dean Parks, Steve Khan, Jay Graydon:
Guitars
Chuck Rainey: Bass
Paul Humphrey, Steve Gadd, Bernard Purdie, Rick Marotta, Ed Greene: Drums
Jim Keltner: Drums & Percussion
Gary Coleman: Percussion
Tom Scott: Tenor Saxophone, Lyricon, Horn Arrangements
Wayne Shorter, Pete Christlieb: Tenor Saxophone
Jim Horn, Bill Perkins, Plas Johnson, Jackie Kelso: Saxophones, Flutes
Chuck Findley, Lou McCreary, Slyde Hyde: Brass
Michael McDonald, Timothy B. Schmit, Clydie King, Sherlie Matthews, Venetta
Fields, Rebecca Louis, Paul Griffin: Backing Vocals
Producer: Gary Katz
Engineers: Roger Nichols, Elliot Scheiner, Al Schmitt, Bill Schnee
Record Label: ABC Records
Recorded: Village Recorders; Producer's Workshop; Warner Bros.; ABC Recording
Studios; Sound Labs (all Los Angeles); A&R Studios (New York), Jan. to July 1977
Released: 23 Sept 1977
Running Time: 39:51
Highest chart place: US 3, UK 5

With a more direct jazz influence, *Aja* is a classic. Released in September 1977, it's the band's best-selling album, top five in both the US and UK charts. One of the first albums to be certified 'platinum' for sales of over 1 million copies, it has since topped 5 million sales. It won Roger Nichols an engineering Grammy in 1978 and was inducted into the Grammy Hall of Fame in 2003 and the Library of Congress National Recording Registry in 2010, based on its artistic significance. The album's history was also documented on TV in an episode of *Classic Albums*.

Aja is often cited as one of the best test recordings for audiophiles, due to its high production standards, and as Gary Katz said, 'Roger Nichols made those records sound like they did. He was extraordinary in his willingness and desire to make records sound better. The records we did could not have been done without Roger. He was just maniacal about making the sound of the records be what we liked ... He always thought there was a better way to do it, and he would find a way to do what we needed to in ways that other people hadn't done yet.'

Around the time of *Aja* Becker said, 'It's not more jazz or less pop. It's just rock. We write rock songs because when we were starting, rock was the most exciting field. It was actually more interesting melodically than jazz in the post-Coltrane period'.

Aja solidified Becker and Fagen's reputations as songwriters and studio perfectionists. The first album to credit the musicians who played on each individual track, it features such jazz and fusion luminaries as guitarists Larry Carlton and Lee Ritenour, bassist Chuck Rainey, saxophonists Wayne Shorter, Pete Christlieb and Tom Scott, drummers Steve Gadd, Rick Marotta and Bernard Purdie, pianists Joe Sample and Michael Omartian, plus the ubiquitous Victor Feldman.

In a 1989 interview with *Q Magazine*, Becker was asked about the duo's reputation for being studio tyrants and telling musicians exactly what to play: 'Not at all. We would go in with a piano chart that showed Donald's chord voicings and Donald would usually go through the keyboard chart with the keyboard player. Because if you just write chord symbols, everyone will play them differently. The keyboard parts, in most cases, were so integral to what we were doing that a lot of the ingredients had to be there in that way. But then the keyboard player was free to articulate and add things to that, so there was a lot of just blowing. And that's basically what was written, no bass parts were written. Usually, Chuck Rainey would listen to our demo in which I played bass and take the things off that that he thought were appropriate and just come up with the rest. The guitar players had nothing written for them and they would come up with their own parts. We would listen and suggest things, but there certainly wasn't any score.'

Fagen has said that *Aja* was named for a Korean woman who married the brother of a high-school friend ('We thought that was a good name, just a very romantic sort of image, the sort of tranquillity that can come of a quiet relationship with a very beautiful woman'). The cover photo by Hideki Fujii features Japanese model and actress Sayoko Yamaguchi, the rear of the sleeve is plain black with only the track titles printed, the inner gatefold photos of Becker and Fagen were taken by Dorothy White and Walter.

Rolling Stone's review at the time felt that 'the conceptual framework of their music has shifted from the pretext of rock & roll toward a smoother, awesomely clean and calculated mutation of various rock, pop and jazz idioms'. The album had lyrics that 'remain as pleasantly obtuse and cynical as ever' it went on to call Becker and Fagen 'the perfect musical antiheroes for the Seventies.'

Stereogum considered that it 'redrew the parameters for sophistication in the midst of pop music's weirdest year', the antithesis of punk, but Ian Dury was a fan: '*Aja*'s got a sound that lifts your heart up, and it's the most consistent up-full, heart-warming, even though it is a classic LA kinda sound. You wouldn't think it was recorded anywhere else in the world. It's got California through its blood ... It's a record that sends my spirits up, and really when I listen to music, really that's what I want.'

Each record had increased in sales, but the *Aja* sessions were ramping studio costs to a whole new level, and ABC were getting nervous, pushing for more press and a tour to break the band further internationally. Becker and Fagen did plan to tour in support of the album, getting to the point of rehearsing a live band. However plans were scrapped when arguments over pay started among the musicians, and the duo became fed up with trying to sort out the logistics of getting the show out on the road.

William S. Burroughs finally heard Steely Dan for himself around this time in, deeming them to be 'too fancy', to which Becker retorted, '*Naked Lunch* is a fairly difficult work. William Burroughs at one point claims that he didn't remember writing it. I don't see why I should remember having read parts of it.'

During this period Becker and Fagen decided to sign to Warner Bros., apparently fuelled to some degree by their enthusiasm for Bugs Bunny and Daffy Duck cartoons, but their deal with ABC required another album after *Aja*, and by the time that one was completed Steely Dan would effectively be no more.

The Songs:

'Black Cow' (Becker / Fagen) (5:10)
A Black Cow is a root beer or Coke float, or more likely in this context an alcoholic drink including Kahlúa, a popular drink for party girls. The characters appear to be in a relationship, he is stable and conscientious, she is reckless and irresponsible, getting wasted on a regular basis, often in Rudy's (which is still going in NYC's Hell's Kitchen), and possibly turning tricks under an assumed name down on Greene Street in Lower Manhattan. The song describes his internal monologue; he is in love with her, but each time she comes home in a mess he has to try to 'make everything right', and he's sick of it, to the point where he needs to tell her to 'Drink your big Black Cow and get out of here.' It's a heartfelt but bitterly sarcastic song about a relationship that is doomed to fail, no love lost, just get out and move on.

Crusaders keyboardist Joe Sample plays chunky clavinet on this catchy disco-funk number with jazz-crossover harmonies. The horns add a subtle wooziness while the beat is infectious, Victor Feldman's thoughtful electric piano solo followed by Tom Scott's earthy tenor sax.

'Aja' (Becker / Fagen) (7:57)
From the album notes by 'Michael Phalen' (Don and Walt in disguise): 'a rather ambitious work in which a Latin-tinged pop song is inexplicably expanded into some sort of sonata or suite.' Humorously, the liner for the remaster contained the duo's rebuttal to Phalen's original words!

By 1977 Becker and Fagen decided that the time was right to expand their songwriting, 'Aja' combining several other songs they were working on, including 'Stand by the Seawall' which they had recorded as a demo. The result is a mysterious and compelling jazz-based eight minutes, the longest song the band recorded in the '70s, with a captivating solo from the legendary Wayne Shorter before the final verse and an explosive Steve Gadd drum solo – the only one on a Steely Dan album – that fits the piece perfectly. It's tonally sophisticated and structurally complex, and probably the most ambitious song that they ever produced. Denny Dias gets to solo, but it's his last appearance with Steely Dan, and the final performance by any of the other founding members.

Despite the complexity of the arrangement, it took less time to record than most other tracks on the album. Becker played guitar, alongside Dias and the returning Larry Carlton, parts of performances by all three being edited together in the final mix as it was extremely difficult to play, Dias citing 'clusters where the notes are so close together that you can't stretch your fingers far enough to get all the notes out at the same time ... open voicings that are so wide apart that you can't reach the notes.' Becker adds blues phrases over the main theme.

Fagen sang the lead with Timothy B. Schmit backing him. Fagen also played the synth parts, plus a police whistle during the instrumental break. Michael Omartian played piano, with Joe Sample adding its electric variant. Chuck Rainey played bass, and Victor Feldman added vibraphone. Gadd discussed the piece with Becker and Fagen, then recorded his part, including the solo, in just two takes, the final mix containing edits from both. 'He just knew what to do,' said Becker.

As part of a conscious effort to expand the range of musicians, Becker and Fagen hoped to get Wayne Shorter from Weather Report involved. A member of Miles Davis' late-1960s fusion band, he had played on *In A Silent Way* and *Bitches Brew*. A confirmed jazzer, Shorter was sceptical, so he declined Katz's invitation. They then asked Dick LaPalm from the Village Recorder, who knew Shorter, to contact him on their behalf. He vouched for them, and Shorter agreed, this performance introducing the jazz legend to millions who had not previously heard him.

Shorter listened to the parts before and after where his solo was to be and then just played, said Becker: 'He was very thoughtful and probing about the musical possibilities ... He was influenced by the contour of sections other than the part he played over', Gadd's playing inspiring him in a similar way to that of Tony Williams in Miles Davis' band.

With only three short verses, all beginning with the same line, and with the same chorus, the piece is largely instrumental. It's another internal monologue, but more enigmatic, a man yearning for his lover, 'Aja', to escape the regimented emptiness and stresses of his working life 'up on the hill.' Fagen described the song as 'a journey in time and space' to where 'Aja' is. Eastern themes feature frequently, with imagery of the 'angular banjos' familiar in Chinese music, soothing sounds among the banyan trees when 'Aja' is near. The vision of hills, trees, sky and the sea are the antithesis of life 'dime-dancin'' in the city rat-race, but I've no idea what the enigmatic 'double helix in the sky' might refer to.

Opening with Omartian's lilting piano, Gadd and Sample come in before Fagen's mellow vocals, the tempo building towards the chorus. Vibraphone and guitar additions expand the sound, harmonically it's like a warm breeze, expansive and all-encompassing. The space within it is what makes it work, there's room for the instruments to breathe, while still having lots going on. There are numerous tempo and key changes, and it's fascinating from start to finish – in many respects so far removed from their early work that it could easily be someone else, while retaining a recognisable Dan quality. They are not shy of their jazz influences, the love of bebop shining through, and that's before we get to Shorter's solo, which is beautifully presented.

It has a shifting feeling and throughout you're never sure where it's going to go next, and ultimately that's the song's major triumph – airy, beautiful and unpredictable, all presented in pristine condition. AllMusic are right in describing the piece as 'an absolute masterpiece, not only one of Steely Dan's finest songs but also a pinnacle of '70s studio rock.'

'Deacon Blues' (Becker / Fagen) (7:33)

With the fragility of Fagen's delivery and the sophisticated words and arrangement, 'Deacon Blues' could be a textbook for songwriters. I can't envisage it being done any better. The smoothness of the setting brings through the coolness of the jazz heroes and the yearning to become one of them, set against the sometimes grimy world of an ultimate loser, sacrificing himself in a live fast, die young quest for a worthy legend.

The descending opening chords from Feldman's electric piano lead into the rhythm from Bernard Purdie, with Becker's lyrical bass. Delicate picked guitar from Carlton and the swelling brass of Tom Scott's arrangements give breadth, the clarity keeping everything in place in the space created by the perfect separation. The female backing vocals in the chorus take it to another level, the beat pin-sharp as always. Given the number of tracks used to record these songs, the sound never becomes 'everything and the kitchen sink' dense.

Set immediately after thumping opener 'Black Cow' and the jaw-dropping otherness of 'Aja', it is at 'Deacon Blues' that the realisation of what a special album *Aja* is, dawns. The heart-rending sax solo by Pete Christlieb, with brass support, exemplifies the Deacon character, 'learning to work the saxophone' as he dreams of scaling artistic heights, putting his all into his music: 'I cried when I wrote this song, sue me if I play too long.' There may be parallels with Charlie Parker here, his star burning out sooner than it should have, fuelled by the lifestyle of his art.

Christlieb came to be involved as Becker and Fagen admired his playing in the band on Johnny Carson's *Tonight Show*. They told him to play what he felt, he recorded two takes and the second was used – 'I was gone in half an hour', he later said, 'the next thing I know I'm hearing myself in every airport bathroom in the world.'

The 'Crimson Tide' line relates to other nicknames that aim to build an aura around the recipient, making them appear more grandiose than they would otherwise be, this one belonging to the University of Alabama football team. Autobiographical in the sense that both Fagen and Becker dreamt about becoming jazz musicians in their early days, the 'Deacon' epithet came from football player Deacon Jones, who was big at the time; they liked how the name sounded.

It plays until it's done, and is nearly the length of 'Aja', Becker and Fagen confidently extending themselves. The second single from the album, it reached number 19 on the *Billboard* charts, Becker clearly feeling something for what they had recorded: 'I remember the night that we mixed that one thinking that it was really good and wanting to hear it over and over, which is never the case.'

'Peg' (Becker / Fagen) (3:58)

The last song to be recorded and the shortest track on *Aja*, it reached number eleven on *Billboard* as the first single.

A sassy and upbeat song about pornography, and lust for one of its unattainable stars? Quite possibly, but it could also be about actress Peg Entwistle, who jumped to her death from the Hollywood Sign in 1932, before her first film was released.

The guitar solo was attempted by several top sessioners – including Robben Ford and Larry Carlton – before Jay Graydon successfully laid down the final version. Drummer Rick Marotta said of his work with Chuck Rainey on 'Peg', 'You could have hung your coat up on the groove' and regards it as one of the greatest tracks he ever played on. Tom Scott plays the riff on Lyricon, an electronic woodwind instrument, and it's probably the most played live Dan track, with over 600 set appearances since 1993.

'Home at Last' (Becker / Fagen) (5:34)

The B-side of the 'Deacon Blues' single, it was inspired by Homer's *Odyssey* and a weary traveller making his way back home, maybe as Becker and Fagen were homesick for NYC. The line 'Still I remain tied to the mast' refers to Odysseus, wanting to hear the Sirens' song, which rendered all who heard it incapable of rational thought. He put wax in his men's ears so that they could not hear, and had them secure him to the ship's mast so that he could not jump into the sea.

Victor Feldman's piano intro moves into a lilting reggae shuffle with horn blasts, the guitar accents standing out as anchoring points. It's laid-back but with a funky groove from Rainey's bass. The chorus features lovely harmony vocals, and there is space for a synth solo and some tasty guitar from Walter, piano stabs and swelling brass driving things along.

Bernard Purdie again excels, adding an odd, loping rhythm, finger-snapping and making you want to move while being languid and easy at the same

Above: Donald Jay Fagen in 1999, taken from the *Classic Albums* documentary for *Aja*. (*Eagle Rock*)

Below: Walter Carl Becker in 1999, again from the *Aja Classic Albums* documentary. (*Eagle Rock*)

Left: The scattershot cover for the *Can't Buy a Thrill* debut by Robert Lockart, probably dissuaded more potential listeners than it drew in. *(Universal)*

Left: The finished cover for *Countdown to Ecstasy* by Dorothy White having being adapted at the insistence of ABC Records' Jay Lasker. *(Universal)*

Right: The cover for *Pretzel Logic* from 1974, photographed by Raeanne Rubenstein at the Miners' Gate entrance to Central Park in New York. *(Universal)*

Right: The original ABC release of *Katy Lied* (1975), again by Dorothy White, features a 'katydid'. *(Universal)*

Left: Jeff 'Skunk' Baxter and Walter Becker performing 'Reeling in the Years' live in 1973 on The *Midnight Special* TV show. (*NBC*)

Right: David Palmer live with the band in 1973 during his brief tenure as lead singer. From The *Midnight Special* performance. (*NBC*)

Left: David Palmer and Donald Fagen from the 1973 *Midnight Special* performance. (*NBC*)

Right: Denny Dias in 1973, the longest-serving member of the original band, after Becker and Fagen. (*NBC*)

Left: Palmer, Dias and Becker (l to r) on *Midnight Special* in 1973. (*NBC*)

Right: Burt Sugarman's *Midnight Special* ran on NBC from 1972 to 1981 and featured bands playing live to a studio audience. (*NBC*)

Left: *The Royal Scam* from 1976: 'the most hideous album cover of the seventies, bar none (excepting perhaps *Can't Buy a Thrill*).' *(Universal)*

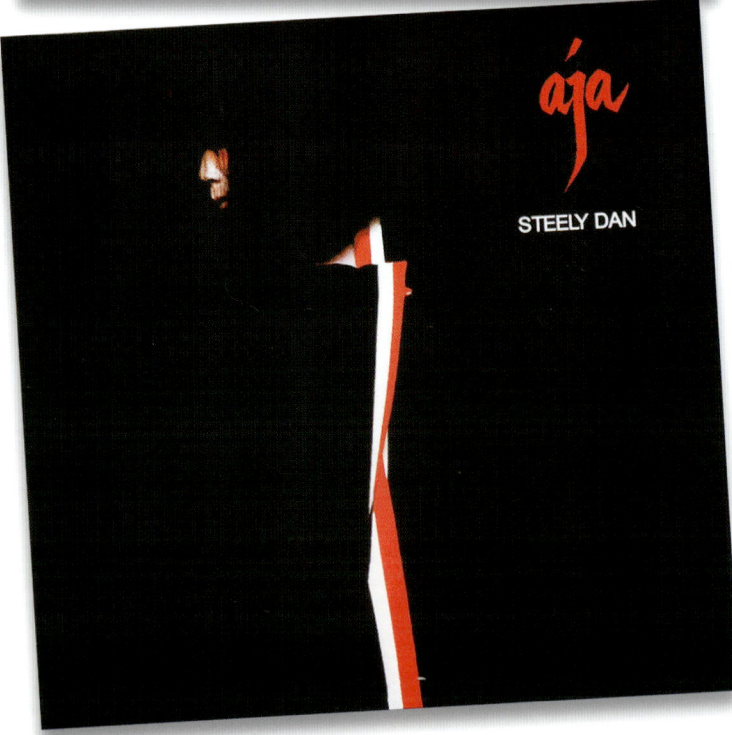

Left: The cool sophistication of the *Aja* album cover from 1977 beautifully complemented the sounds found within. *(Universal)*

Right: Gaucho from 1980. An enigmatic album with cover art based on a wall plaque in Buenos Aires created by Israel Hoffmann. *(Universal)*

Right: The band's comeback live album *Alive in America* from 1995, featuring an image from the 1940 film *The Mummy's Hand*. *(WEA)*

Left: Rick Marotta added his drums to *The Royal Scam*, *Aja* and *Gaucho*. (*Eagle Rock*)

Right: Toto drummer Jeff Porcaro played on *Pretzel Logic*, *Katy Lied*, *Gaucho* and Fagen's *The Nightfly*. He sadly died in 1992.

Left: Legendary soul drummer and shuffle specialist Bernard Purdie added his magic to *The Royal Scam*, *Aja and Gaucho*. (*Eagle Rock*)

Right: Soul and funk bass master Chuck Rainey played on every Dan release from *Pretzel Logic* to *Gaucho*. *(Eagle Rock)*

Left: Denny Dias from the *Aja Classic Albums* documentary in 1999. *(Eagle Rock)*

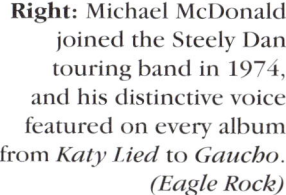

Right: Michael McDonald joined the Steely Dan touring band in 1974, and his distinctive voice featured on every album from *Katy Lied* to *Gaucho*. *(Eagle Rock)*

Left: Jazz guitarist Larry Carlton's stunning solos were a vital contribution to *Katy Lied, The Royal Scam, Aja* and *Gaucho.* *(Eagle Rock)*

Right: Sheet music for *Aja*, arranged by Larry Carlton. *(Eagle Rock)*

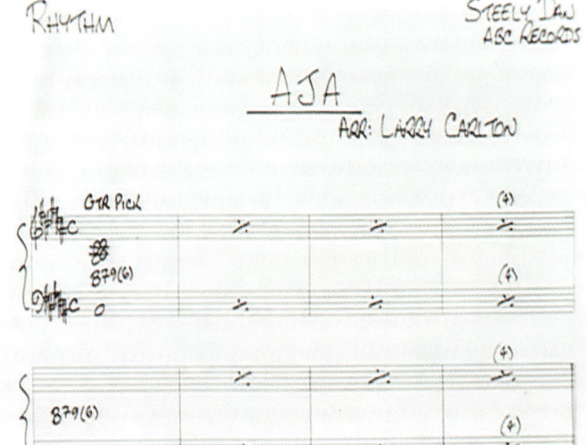

Left: A regular '70s contributor, guitarist Dean Parks also played on *Two Against Nature, The Nightfly* and both Becker's solo albums. *(Eagle Rock)*

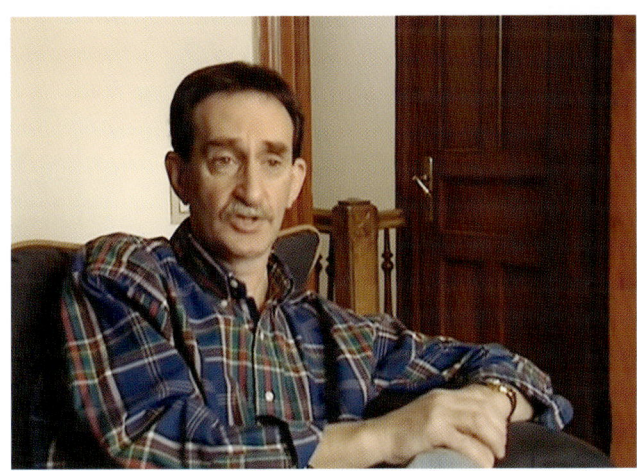

Right: Fagen and Becker at the mixing desk during the *Classic Albums* documentary for *Aja* in 1999. *(Eagle Rock)*

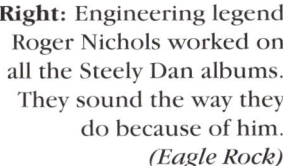

Left: Producer Gary Katz, an intrinsic part of Steely Dan's 1970s success. *(Eagle Rock)*

Right: Engineering legend Roger Nichols worked on all the Steely Dan albums. They sound the way they do because of him. *(Eagle Rock)*

Left: *Two Against Nature* from 2000, the first Steely Dan studio album in twenty years. *(Revolution)*

Left: The final album to carry the Steely Dan name, *Everything Must Go* from 2003. *(WEA)*

Right: Released shortly after *Two Against Nature* in 2000, the *Plush TV Jazz-Rock Party* DVD sees the band playing live in the studio. *(Image Entertainment)*

Below: Donald Fagen in 2000, taken from *Plush TV Jazz-Rock Party.* *(Image Entertainment)*

two against nature

STEELY DAN'S

PLUSH TV **Jazz-Rock** PARTY IN SENSUOUS SURROUND SOUND

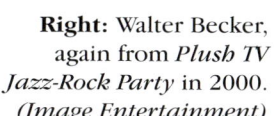

Right: Walter Becker, again from *Plush TV Jazz-Rock Party* in 2000. *(Image Entertainment)*

Left: Fagen's first solo album, *The Nightfly*, released in 1982 shortly after the break up of Steely Dan. *(Reprise)*

Right: The cover of Fagen's 1993 solo album, *Kamakiriad*. *(Reprise)*

Left: Donald Fagen looking suitably uncomfortable for the cover shoot of his 2006 *Morph the Cat* solo release. *(Reprise)*

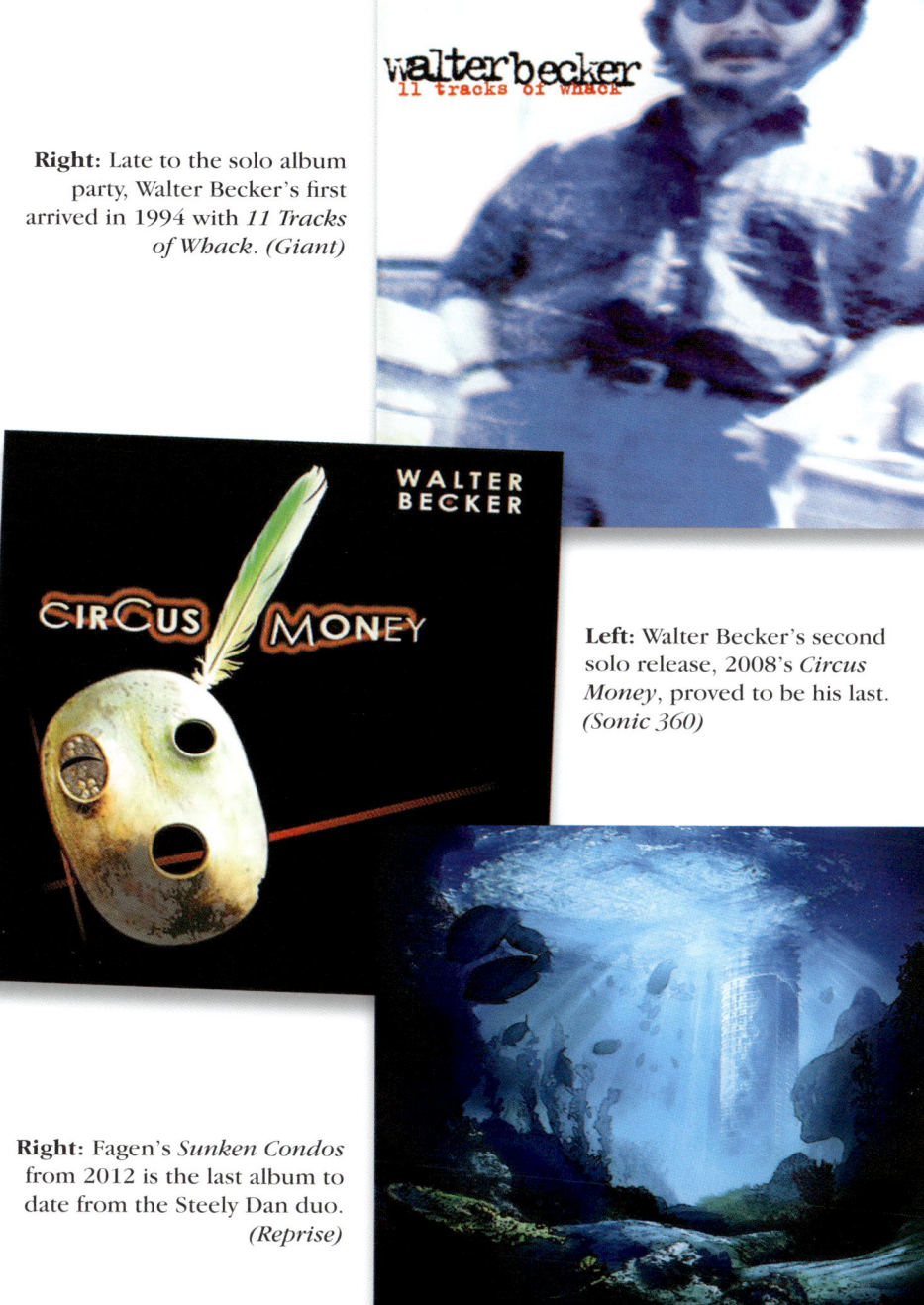

Right: Late to the solo album party, Walter Becker's first arrived in 1994 with *11 Tracks of Whack*. *(Giant)*

Left: Walter Becker's second solo release, 2008's *Circus Money*, proved to be his last. *(Sonic 360)*

Right: Fagen's *Sunken Condos* from 2012 is the last album to date from the Steely Dan duo. *(Reprise)*

Left: The first *Greatest Hits* collection from Steely Dan, a double album released in 1978 covering all the albums to *Aja*. *(Universal)*

Below: The 1991 expanded version of the *Gold* compilation from 1982 included a couple of Fagen solo songs from film soundtracks. *(MCA)*

Left: The *Citizen Steely Dan* boxset from 1993 collected all the '70s albums with a few additional tracks. *(MCA)*

time. His bass drum has a wonderful thump to it, and there's real meat in the playing. The rhythm section rules this piece, the embellishments to the groove perfectly placed to accentuate the dynamics. As with a lot of Steely Dan numbers, you could just listen to the rhythm track on its own and be enthralled. Purdey had the temerity to request a co-writing credit for 'Home at Last', and you can see why, his drum sound is integral to the song. However, no dice.

This is a piece that hides its light somewhat; in the esteemed company it is a slow-burn but get stuck into its layers, and it's an exemplary piece of work, an uplifting hymn praising the security of the familiar. It always seemed to me to be one of the lesser tracks on *Aja*: it isn't, lingering long once properly heard, slinking off into the night on a wave of uplifting horns.

'I Got the News' (Becker / Fagen) (5:06)

A diversion into almost funk disco, with another beefy shuffle, Rainey this time paired with the drums of Ed Greene, whose bass drum properly punches you in the chest. Feldman's piano stabs around the staccato words in a suggestive lyric that dwells on the wonders of oral sex. Michael McDonald comes to the fore again with his unmistakable soulful tone during the 'Broadway Duchess' section, and Walter adds a solo that seems at odds with the rest but works. Fagen only sang on this one.

Like 'Home at Last', it's the rhythm that makes this one work and Greene shows off a great deal of technique, that he most likely learned from Bernard Purdie, Rainey hitting sparse and short notes.

'Josie' (Becker / Fagen) (4:33)

Local party girl and ringleader comes home, to the wild approval of the local lads. Is she back from college, or maybe prison? She could have made it out of the neighbourhood to make it big in the wider world. Whatever the detail, the original liner notes speak of a song 'rich with images of random violence, copulation, drug abuse, loitering with intent and other misdemeanors.'

From a simple guitar line, the song moves into the drum track, this time from Jim Keltner, that is at the root of everything, even utilising garbage can lids. There's less jazz and funk in this one, an LA rocker with brass and a distinct groove, synths adding a sheen. Becker's distinctive solo has a hint of blues, supported by disco-like keys, and the brass section is used to good effect, as and when required.

There's a classic bit of Becker and Fagen made up nonsense in the lyric – 'Walter and I enjoy making up our own slang', said Fagen, 'a street gang uses a weapon called a "battle apple". I don't know what that is, but it sounded better than anything else we could come up with.'

After the strutting verses, the chorus is smoother and hooky, and as the third single from the album 'Josie' reached number 26 on the *Billboard* chart, falling short of cracking the top 20, as the two previous singles from the album had done.

Related Tracks:

'The Bear' [unreleased]

The sessions for *Aja* produced several outtakes, including this one, never officially released, but occasionally played live on some of the later tours.

A woozy electric piano intro adds cymbals, then Clavichord and bass. From the simple beginning, it becomes a powerful sub-funk, with chords as big as a bear, Fagen in fine voice. It's a very odd listen to start with, but the more familiar you get, the more natural it seems. 'Sir, I parked my juggernaut at your gate / Fifteen-thousand miles, and I'm feeling great' suggests an enhanced state, and the song is about drug smuggling, with a warning to not try the product as it might become unclear 'If you got the bear or the bear got you'.

This bear is only too happy to take over, it 'wants your ass' and you have to be careful. In a possible link to 'Kid Charlemagne', 'Bear' was Owsley Stanley's nickname. As a well-known supplier of pharmaceuticals to the open-minded and sometime soundman for the Grateful Dead, the beatnik vibe may confirm this.

Things go askew again in an off-kilter piano solo, but it's so good they repeat it, and the second verse suggests that the advice to avoid testing the goods has not been heeded: 'Drive the coach and six for the county line / Point me towards the tube, and I'll be just fine.'

It's a great shame that this excellent song, along with many others that most people would die to have written, has been relegated to the 'also-ran' bin of obscurity. It would be wonderful to see them rehabilitated, but the desire is clearly not there, even to include them as bonus tracks on expanded reissues. For now, at least, we must content ourselves with low-res versions online, but they are so worth checking out.

'Stand by the Seawall' [unreleased]

A funky instrumental with Steve Gadd, the middle part was incorporated into the mid-section of 'Aja'. The breakdowns could be Chick Corea, it has that Latin jazz vibe, and it's around five minutes of escapism with some great changes. A shame that it never saw the light of day in its own right.

'FM (No Static at All)' (Becker / Fagen) (4:52)

After the success of *Aja*, Becker and Fagen were asked to write the title track for the movie *FM*. The film was a box-office disaster, but the song was a hit, earning Roger Nichols another Grammy. Fagen felt the song could have been bigger if the movie had been more successful. 'I think we should have seen the movie before we committed ourselves', he said in 2007, claiming that neither he nor Becker had seen it. That appears to have changed by 2014 where he described it as 'a rotten movie.'

The film revolves around an FM radio station, of the kind burgeoning across the US at that time, but the song takes the 'no static' selling point of FM radio and equates it to a situation where the mood is right and the girls are more likely to put out. No static = no problem, 'Give her some funked up Muzac, she treats you nice / Feed her some hungry reggae, she'll love you twice … The girls don't seem to care what's on / As long as they play till dawn.' Lyrically, it's quite light with a minimal chorus and the second verse being repeated as the third. However,the words that are used are just right, at odds with the film's premise of celebrating the FM format, a cynical edge creeping in with the plea for more choice on the stations: 'Nothin' but blues and Elvis and somebody else's favorite song.'

Their first soundtrack music since 1971's *You've Got to Walk It Like You Talk It or You'll Lose That Beat*, it also features a string section, arranged and conducted by Johnny Mandel, which they had not used since 'Through with Buzz' on *Pretzel Logic*. Fagen: 'We wrote a song that would sound good with a big production, and an overdub of strings that would sound good coming out of movie-theater speakers.'

'FM' was released as a single in 1978, between the *Aja* singles 'Deacon Blues' and 'Josie', confusing some listeners into thinking that it must be on the album. It reached number 22 in the US and there were four official versions of the song: the full length from the film soundtrack, a 12" which features Becker's guitar solo outro, a 7" radio edit with shortened solo, and the B-side 'FM (reprise)' instrumental which extended Pete Christlieb's sax solo and dropped the guitar solo. There is also a hybrid version, that appeared on the *Citizen Steely Dan* box set and some other compilations, which replaced the guitar outro from original with the sax solo from the instrumental. An additional unauthorised version was created by AM radio stations that played the single as part of their Top 40 format. AM had been steadily losing listeners to FM stations, due to the latter broadcasting in stereo with minimal interference. Not wishing to promote their competitors, AM stations spliced in the harmonically compatible 'A' from the chorus of 'Aja' to make the chorus say 'AM' instead!

A good fit with the rest of the band's work at that time, it's jazz-rock driven by bass, guitar and piano with the duo handling most of the instrumentation themselves, the only time this happened. The arpeggiated keyboard intro adds bass and guitar stabs, then we're into the verse, bass and drums (from Porcaro) with two-note piano punches. The strings sweep in for the end of the verses, keeping things smooth, backing vocals from Don Henley, Glenn Frey and Timothy B. Schmit of the Eagles expanding the chorus. Becker's guitar additions are perfect and Christlieb's sax slinky and lush, Victor Feldman adding marimba and other percussion.

MCA released the film soundtrack and 'FM' was the first release by Steely Dan on the label, predating MCA's acquisition of ABC Records by a year.

Gaucho (1980)

Personnel:
Donald Fagen: Lead & Backing Vocals, Keyboards
Walter Becker: Bass, Guitar
Rob Mounsey: Keyboards, Horn Arrangements
Don Grolnick, Pat Rebillot, Joe Sample: Keyboards
Steve Khan, Mark Knopfler, Larry Carlton, Hugh McCracken, Hiram Bullock, Rick Derringer: Guitars
Chuck Rainey, Anthony Jackson: Bass
Bernard Purdie, Rick Marotta, Steve Gadd, Jeff Porcaro: Drums
Errol 'Crusher' Bennett, Victor Feldman, Ralph MacDonald, Nicholas Marrero: Percussion
George Marge, Walter Kane: Clarinet
Tom Scott: Clarinet, Alto & Tenor Saxophone, Lyricon, Horn Arrangements
David Sanborn: Alto Saxophone
Michael Brecker, Dave Tofani: Tenor Saxophone
Ronnie Cuber: Baritone Saxophone
Randy Brecker: Trumpet, Flugelhorn
Wayne Andre: Trombone
Michael McDonald, Patti Austin, Valerie Simpson, Frank Floyd, Diva Gray, Gordon Grody, Lani Groves, Lesley Miller, Zachary Sanders, Toni Wine: Backing Vocals
Producer: Gary Katz
Executive Engineer: Roger Nichols
Record Label: MCA Records
Recorded: Soundworks; A&R Studios; Sigma Sound; Automated Sound (all New York); The Village Recorder; Producer's Workshop (both Los Angeles), 1979 to 1980
Released: 21 Nov 1980
Running Time: 37:58
Highest chart place: US 9, UK 27

Donald and Walter took time out from writing and recording in 1978, both moving back to the East Coast. Big band leader Woody Herman was introduced to their music and recorded the 'Chick, Donald, Walter and Woodrow' album as a tribute to them and Chick Corea, featuring covers of 'Green Earrings', 'Kid Charlemagne', 'I Got the News', 'Aja' and 'FM', with 'Deacon Blues' also appearing on a later reissue, the tracks selected by Donald and Walter who attended the recording session, Becker recalling the experience as 'the happiest two days of my life'.

Denny Dias, whose contributions were shrinking year by year, finally severed the last remaining ties after *Aja*, going on to tour with Toto and record with Wayne Shorter. He continued to play with various low-key bands while working as a computer programmer in Los Angeles.

Steely Dan took on a new manager in Irving Azoff, later president of MCA

Records, having been managerless since the previous incumbent, Joel Cohen, was dismissed in 1974.

The quest for studio perfection was ratcheted up for *Gaucho*, as the need to replicate the success of *Aja* added extra pressure. Once work began, things did not go smoothly. Early on, an assistant engineer managed to accidentally erase most of the tape of 'The Second Arrangement', a favourite track of Katz and Nichols. Despite fevered attempts to re-record the missing section, it was never recovered, the abandoned recordings being a tantalising insight into what might have been.

In March 1979, ABC was bought by MCA Records who claimed ownership of the new Steely Dan album as they now owned their contract, delaying the release and preventing any move to Warners. Becker's personal life also became an issue. His drug habit began affecting his reliability, Fagen noting that 'music wasn't his first love at that point.' Things got worse in January 1980 when Becker's girlfriend, Karen Stanley, died from a drug overdose in their New York apartment. Her family sued Becker for $17 million for introducing her to the substances that ultimately led to her death. However, Becker had been encouraging her to seek help for her addiction and the court eventually awarded in his favour. The unwanted press attention and accusations were a source of anxiety for him, but things went further downhill that February when he was hit by a taxi while crossing the street, shattering his right leg in several places. He suffered infections and took six months to recover. While in the hospital he and Fagen continued to discuss the recording process by telephone, but when Walter was finally back on his feet the need to use crutches affected his mobility, the pain limiting the time he could spend working in the studio.

Fagen said of his perfectionism, 'I have a critical nature, in the sense that when I look at something I often look for the flaws', and drummers struggled to achieve the strict tempos required, leading to Roger Nichols developing the first professional drum machine, which he christened 'Wendel', to provide millisecond perfect timings.

Gaucho was finally released in November 1980 on MCA, but more trouble lay ahead. Much to their chagrin, MCA priced the album at $9.98, a dollar higher than the standard price point for the time, costing them sales and attracting unwarranted accusations of greed. Then, in 1981, jazz pianist and composer Keith Jarrett heard the title track and promptly sued them, claiming a striking resemblance to one of his pieces.

In 1993, Fagen opined that on *Gaucho* 'the writing was hard, the recording was hard, everything about it was like pulling teeth', also calling the resulting album 'a document of despair', but despite the tortured process, *Gaucho* was another major success, Roger Nichols winning a third engineering Grammy award. The recording had taken over a year and featured 41 different musicians. The costs were always going to be high, but this one really pushed the envelope. The results were worth the pain, though, and this is undoubtedly up there with my favourite Steely Dan releases.

With cover art based on 'Guardia Vieja – Tango' by Argentine artist Israel Hoffmann (the reverse showing a gaucho's stirrup – no band portraits were included), *Gaucho* has a different vibe to the other albums, remarkably louche and laid-back, given the pain and suffering of its gestation. Originally intended to be a return towards short, punchy numbers, the songs naturally evolved into longer pieces. There was a move to electric piano and synths, away from the acoustic piano of *Aja*, the jazzier elements of that album reduced with more of an emphasis on space and atmosphere, but the killer grooves remain, although less obviously. It is musically complex, but the talent ascribed to it makes it sound almost effortless. Despite mostly positive reviews, there were some for whom it just didn't click, Robert Christgau referring to it as 'Countdown to Lethargy'. That does it a disservice, despite the squeaky-clean presentation there is heart and emotion, and it's a remarkable achievement that under the trying circumstances it manages to escape from the gravitational tug of *Aja*, which could easily have swamped it.

In *Musician* magazine in 1981, the duo discussed their songs and their approach to working. 'I feel we've progressed a lot since our first records', said Fagen. 'They are plain embarrassing, if you listen to them... I don't listen to our old records, but if I happen to hear one on the radio, my general feeling is humiliation. I don't really understand some of our earlier stuff.' Becker agreed: 'I don't listen to them either. I mean there were a lot of things that were very shoddily done, and a lot of things that were just bad, but probably different things for me than for Donald. We were doing the best we could, but fuck it, it wasn't very good.' He confirmed that they compose for themselves: 'We try to always make the lyrics not grab your attention. We want them to SOUND good with the music, even if you're not an English-speaking person, that's definitely a problem. We have to be clever, but not funny ... Every time someone's in the next room when we're writing a song they'd say, "Don't tell me you're fucking writing songs in there, you're not working, 'cause you're fucking screaming and laughing in there. You're not writing, you're making up Pope jokes!"', Fagen adding 'We have a problem, trying not to cross the comedy threshold.'

With regard to structure, Fagen said, 'It's not a short story, it's not a novel. Yeah, a miniature and sometimes you can't fill in the details. So, you hope that you give the proper signals, so that people will get a sense of what you're talking about ... The lyrics must be subordinate to the music and you can only give as many clues as you have time for', Becker adding, 'Some of the smaller, pettier details in a story are the best ones. The little things that you retain in your sense more than in your mind; they may not make sense but they color something... If something is open-ended, or means more than one thing, or is elliptical or whatever, someone listening to it carefully enough will in fact become creative and fill in the spaces with their own intelligence.'

With their relationship deteriorating, on 17 June 1981, the *New York Times* announced that Becker and Fagen had dissolved their partnership. Becker moved into production while Fagen had already composed an instrumental piece for the film *Heavy Metal*, released in 1981, and then started work on his debut solo album, *The Nightfly*.

Gaucho was the last Steely Dan album to be produced by Gary Katz, although he did work with Fagen on *The Nightfly*. He went on to produce many other artists and had a joint venture with Interscope called Jake Records before moving to Warner Brothers as a producer and A&R man, where he signed Prince, Dire Straits, Christopher Cross and Rickie Lee Jones.

The Songs:

'Babylon Sisters' (Becker / Fagen) (5:49)
There's an immediate sparseness to *Gaucho*, the album's opening track starting with four descending drumbeats before Don Grolnick's lyrical electric piano, space-filling out the arrangement. Chuck Rainey's bass and horn stabs come in with Bernard Purdie's slow shuffle, moving into a reggae vibe with subtle guitar from Steve Khan. The opening verse sets the scene of a Californian evening in the sun, but with a sense of pathos, a first encounter with the album's underlying theme of ageing and not being the hedonistic hipster that you once were, 'That I'm not what I used to be / And that love's not a game for three':

Drive west on Sunset
To the sea
Turn that jungle music down
Just until we're out of town
This is no one night stand
It's a real occasion
Close your eyes and you'll be there
It's everything they say
The end of a perfect day
Distant lights from across the bay.

The title is a biblical reference to fallen women and degenerate lifestyles, the ageing singer realising he is too old for the shallow sex, drugs and partying of old. Fagen's voice has a yearning quality in the verse before the 'Babylon Sisters' give the chorus a seductiveness that is very appealing, responding to Fagen's 'So fine so young' with a smouldering 'Tell me I'm the only one' and making the song. The repeated 'You gotta shake it baby' outro is sassy and compelling, but it took more than 50 attempts to complete a satisfactory mix of it.

Muted brass adds to the sultry atmosphere, and Randy Brecker's flugelhorn works with Purdie in a fascinating slow dance. Rob Mounsey's horn arrangements are the icing on a particularly delicious cake while elsewhere, the use of bass clarinet is pithily described in the reissue liner as 'a cross between a clarinet with glandular problems and Palladin's spittoon.'

Unusually, 'Babylon Sisters' was recorded on the second take. Becker and Fagen don't play on it, as Fagen said, 'We've got it all except the fingers. Both of us have terrific feel. I think we get a lot of points for style, but technique and execution are weak. There tend to be a lot of mistakes and inconsistencies. If we can't find a musician who's comfortable with a particular feel, then we'll haul out our instruments', Becker adding, 'The B band is me and Donald. The A band is anyone else – professionals.'

It's a beautifully crafted and mature work that you can indulge in, bury yourself in the richness of the arrangement and the sadness of the message, and it's one of the many reasons why I love *Gaucho* so much: 'Son you're playing with fire / The kid will live and learn / As he watches his bridges burn / From the point of no return...'

The third single, backed with 'Gaucho', it was released only weeks before Becker and Fagen announced their split and failed to chart.

'Hey Nineteen' (Becker / Fagen) (5:06)

Funky and more upbeat than 'Babylon Sisters' – but still very sparse – it's a continuation of the theme, an older guy trying to pick up a girl so young that she doesn't know who Aretha Franklin is, making him realise that they really have nothing in common ('No we can't dance together / No we can't talk at all').

The first verse sees Fagen at his lecherous best, continuing with the 'Nice, Sure looks good, Mmm-mmm-mmm, Skate a little lower now...' section. The song closes with the repeated lines 'The Cuervo Gold, the fine Colombian, make tonight a wonderful thing', ambiguous as we are left to wonder whether the guy is enjoying an evening of tequila and drugs with his young lover, or whether he is, in fact, alone. When discussing this song and the perspective of the post-30-something male, Becker made the observation, 'At one time I felt I would be morally obliged to blow my brains out at this age, but I no longer feel that.'

From the abrupt start, the kick drum does exactly that, Roger Nichols' pioneering work in digital drum replacement with the Wendel sampler being used to fine effect alongside Rick Marotta's analogue skills. Walter's bass bulks out the basic but effective rhythm, without the shuffle element that Purdie might have brought in, and it's all about the drums, electric piano accents, including two note slides which add to the slinkiness, and Hugh McCracken's sophisticated guitar touches adding new cadences. McCracken gets a solo, but again, it's sparse, the close harmony backing in the chorus giving a doo-wop feel. A synth solo from Fagen leads into the outro fade with electric piano.

The album's first single, 'Hey Nineteen' was backed with a 1974 live version of 'Bodhisattva', reaching number ten in the *Billboard* charts in early 1981.

'Glamour Profession' (Becker / Fagen) (7:29)

This one pumps away from the start, the bobbing Wendel bass drum giving it a disco edge, augmenting Steve Gadd's playing.

It's fun and devilishly naughty, the 'Illegal fun under the sun' always bringing a smile to the face, Fagen confirming that it's about the power a drug dealer holds over his clients, which he would otherwise be unable to achieve. In this case, the client is top basketball star 'Hoops McCann' ('Brut and charisma poured from the shadow where he stood'). Hoops is at the top of his game, 'Crashing the backboard, he's Jungle Jim again', possibly facilitated by the specialist substances provided by the dealer, who is only too happy to be associated with him for his own prestige – 'Who inspires your fabled fools? That's my claim to fame.'

Next stop, the geography no doubt taken for the sound rather than the ease of access from LA, it's off to Barbados aboard the 'Carib Cannibal' with some wealthy clients, 'just for the ride' to service their requirements, then back to LA just in time to meet with Columbian supplier Jive Miguel. In typical Dan manner, the successful deal is celebrated with Szechuan dumplings at Mr Chow, a Chinese restaurant in Beverly Hills.

The piano additions, from Rob Mounsey, are beautiful, including a salacious solo, adding a sophistication at odds with the basic and unchanging rhythm. Anthony Jackson's bass brings the funk, horns adding a slightly sleazy aura. Steve Khan's guitar is back, similarly spacious to 'Babylon Sisters', an extended solo taking the song to the close. Becker doesn't play on this one. The chorus comes from a song written in college, the words changed to fit, and Fagen admitted that the bridge was taken from Kurt Weill's 'Speak Low'.

At seven-and-a-half minutes, it's long, plenty of space to add detail to the elements of the story, adding to the humour and intrinsic 'otherness' of the Dan's words.

'Gaucho' (Becker / Fagen / Keith Jarrett) (5:32)
There's a change of pace for this one with languid sax from Tom Scott, electric piano and a steady rhythm from Becker and Porcaro. Other instruments were tried over many months before the sax solo was deemed to be the best fit.

The laid-back nature belies the scenario, which could be an argument between a gay couple, but I prefer the idea of it being an agent and his high-flying film star charge, the words being the agent's side only. The star is 'golden', at the top of his game, famous and in demand, but he is secretly gay and, in the climate of the time, this is not good for business. He has turned up at an important meeting with a handsome and flamboyant Latin American ('You say this guy is so cool / Snapping his fingers like a fool'). The star doesn't seem to get the problem, and the effect it could have on the agent's livelihood, hence the argument. The agent is losing it: 'Can't you see they're laughing at me? / Get rid of him. / I don't care what you do at home / Would you care to explain!?', the chorus a wonderfully humorous summation of the situation:

Who is the gaucho, amigo?
Why is he standing

In your spangled leather poncho
And your elevator shoes?
Bodacious cowboys
Such as your friend
Will never be welcome here
High in the Custerdome

The 'Custerdome' being another Becker and Fagen invention, a huge office building, the kind in which important meetings are held.

Seemingly shocked by the realisation, the star looks for a way out, the agent ruling out the suggestion that the cowboy stays with him ('No, he can't sleep on the floor, what do you think I'm yelling for?!') and offers to drop him off near the freeway, but it appears that the gaucho has nowhere to go. Describing the star as a 'nasty schoolboy' the agent attempts to re-book the meeting for the next day – without the gaucho.

Becker adds a lovely guitar solo before the second verse, his only one on the album, and Mounsey's piano is again central. According to an article in *Modern Drummer* magazine, Jeff Porcaro recalls the drum track being assembled from 46 different takes: 'From noon till six we'd play the tune over and over and over again, nailing each part. We'd go to dinner and come back and start recording. They made everybody play like their life depended on it. But they weren't gonna keep anything anyone else played that night, no matter how tight it was. All they were going for was the drum track.'

I love this song, probably my favourite on the album. it's witty, well-observed and deliciously scripted, all supported by playing of the highest quality, but there was a slight problem. After release, jazz pianist Keith Jarrett sued Becker and Fagen for copyright infringement, claiming the song plagiarised 'Long as You Know You're Living Yours' from his 1974 album *Belonging*. Jarrett won the case and has since been credited as a co-author, Fagen admitting that he loved the Jarrett track and had been strongly influenced by it.

'Time Out of Mind' (Becker / Fagen) (4:13)

Another song with a four-beat drum intro, moving straight into a strutting rhythm, twangy double-tracked guitar supporting before Fagen steps in, using a range of his vocal mannerisms, sliding up into phrases and adding brief pauses in the middle of words ('Perfec-tion and Grace') in a bravura performance brimming with confidence, with expansive backing singer support. The horns season both chorus and verses beautifully amid Rick Marotta's metronomic pulse.

The instrumental break half-way through is great; the full power of the horns coming through. It's as sharp as a tack, a fabulous piece of late-period efficiency that slowly fades on horns and guitar. The music has a crunching upbeat confidence; there is power to be had, perfection and grace that certainly puts a smile on my face.

There are no veiled references here, this is a song about heroin and its beguiling effects – without the downside, possibly strange given Walter's problems with addiction. But more likely, it's an honest appraisal of how that addiction came to pass in the first place, from someone who knows and has the scars to prove it: 'Tonight when I chase the dragon / The water may change to cherry wine / And the silver will turn to gold / Time out of mind.'

Upon hearing Dire Straits' 'Sultans of Swing', Mark Knopfler was hired to play guitar. From several hours of recording, his contributions as heard on the record are limited to a matter of seconds in the intro, elsewhere overshadowed by Rick Mounsey's horn parts. In a 1993 interview, Becker said that Knopfler seemed a little intimidated during the session as he wasn't a music reader and communication was difficult as they couldn't describe things to him in jazz terms.

Fagen played electric and acoustic piano and synth for most of the track, Mounsey playing the same in the instrumental sections, but to simplify things Mounsey was credited with piano, Fagen the electric instruments.

The second single release, it bizarrely featured the same 'Bodhisattva' live B-side as 'Hey Nineteen', but that didn't stop it reaching number 22 on the *Billboard* charts in April 1981.

'My Rival' (Becker / Fagen) (4:34)

The furtive keys and bass intro adds Steve Khan's elusive guitar. It's atmospheric, and the words are fun, but what's it about? It appears to be a mash-up of a detective noir where a two-timed man seeks the identity of his love rival ('I struck a match against the door / Of Anthony's Bar and Grill'), and a new father whose nose is out of joint at the arrival of his first child, a boy who he feels replaces him in the affections of his other half ('The milk truck eased into my space / Somebody screamed somewhere'). Alternatively, does it allude to a father's angst at his daughter's first relationship? I think I edge towards the new baby explanation, 'I still recall when I first held / Your tiny hand in mine / I loved you more than I can tell', however, the jealousy has got the better of him and 'now it's stomping time.'

There's a lovely synth solo after the first verse from Fagen, but Becker again doesn't play here. Rick Derringer recorded a solo, but Steve Khan's got onto the record. 'My Rival' featured in John Huston's 1980 film *Phobia*, but it has been played live less than a dozen times since first appearing in the set in 2009.

'Third World Man' (Becker / Fagen) (5:15)

Again, there's no Becker contribution, and Fagen only sings. Originally demoed during the *Aja* sessions, with different words as 'Were You Blind That Day', upon the demise of the intended final track, 'The Second Arrangement', it was brought off the subs bench to complete the album. As a result, Joe Sample and Larry Carlton appear on *Gaucho* despite not playing the sessions, Carlton later relaying his surprise when he heard, via *Billboard* magazine.

The words are again open to interpretation but suggest a victim of post-traumatic stress disorder, a veteran, most likely of Vietnam, struggling to deal with life back in suburbia ('He's been mobilized since dawn / Now he's crouching on the lawn'). The lines 'I saw the fireworks / I believed that I was dreaming / 'Til the neighbors came out screaming' is probably a flashback to some traumatic event in the combat zone, but there's hope that 'Soon you'll throw down your disguise / We'll see behind those bright eyes / By and by / When the sidewalks are safe / For the little guy', the final verse seemingly coming from a loved one, 'When he's crying out / I just sing that Ghana Rondo', to soothe his pain.

But why the line in Italian? Spanish would be a better fit with the 'Gaucho' theme. The phrases in both languages are very similar, but 'e l'era del terzo mondo' is Italian for 'and he was from the third world' and was used as a better fit.

With a very similar arrangement and the same solo from Carlton, the lyric for the demo version of 'Were You Blind That Day' covers similar ground to the finished song, but if anything, is bleaker still.

It's a subdued end to the album, I like it a great deal – and Carlton's solo is superb – but I can only feel that 'The Second Arrangement' would have rounded things off more successfully, and as was originally intended.

Related Tracks:

'The Second Arrangement' [unreleased]
The Steely Dan Holy Grail, a massive exclamation mark in the 'Big Book of Maybes'. There are several versions in circulation, most not great quality, ranging from instrumental to basic piano, voice and bass, to a fuller arrangement.

After weeks of recording, by late December 1979, the song was 75% complete. Katz had asked a junior engineer to ready the track for playback, but most of it was accidentally erased in the process. Nichols broke the news to the band, Fagen just stood up and walked out of the studio without a word.

They attempted to re-record the song, but none of the takes were deemed satisfactory in comparison with the lost original, and the song was abandoned. Of the fragments, demos and re-recordings that have appeared. None are perfect, but the best of them give an idea of what the final result might have sounded like, and it's a compelling listen that really gets under your skin. Hearing this for the first time is like unearthing a box filled with gold bars, it would no doubt have been a Dan classic. It's such a sad loss, I wish they'd stuck with it.

It's almost disco, but with the layers of sophistication that you'd expect. Hiram Bullock's majestic guitar features in a song of loneliness, adultery and sexual jealousy. Funky and slinky, it would most likely have been the album's centrepiece, a compelling listen that has you craving more. If it were to inhabit the album-closing slot, where its replacement 'Third World Man' appeared, then *Gaucho* would have ended in a much more exuberant fashion.

It's a fun lyric, opening with 'Pour out the wine, little girl / I've got just two friends in this whole wide world / Here's to reckless lovers / We all need somebody.' It goes on to become a study of abandonment – 'Stashed in the yellow Jag / I've got my life and laundry in a Gladstone bag' – but it's his own fault: 'Old friends abandon me / It's just the routine politics of jealousy.' The payoff line is the sincere request for 'Something I can dance to', more specifically 'A song with tears in it.' What a great line, delivered with real pathos.

It was unexpectedly played live on 17 September 2011, at a rarities show on the 'Shuffle Diplomacy' tour.

'Bodhisattva' (live in Santa Monica, 1974)
The B-side of both the 'Hey Nineteen' and 'Time Out of Mind' singles, the track also appeared on the *Gold – Expanded Edition* compilation in 1991, and the *Citizen Steely Dan* box set in 1993, where it was tucked away at the end of *Pretzel Logic*.

The only officially released record of the '70s live performances, shows what a rocking band the early line-up turned into. Recorded at the last but one show by the band, in Santa Monica in July 1974, it features Becker and Fagen with Jeff Porcaro, Jim Hodder, Denny Dias, Jeff Baxter, Michael McDonald and Royce Jones.

During the 1974 US tour, Steely Dan had hired a truck driver named Jerome Aniton, a character quite unlike his employers with an unquenchable thirst for alcohol and a devil-may-care attitude that, perversely, Becker and Fagan admired no end. As the comedian of the party, they started to let him introduce the band on stage. Jerome's fondness for alcohol meant that he crashed the equipment truck on more than one occasion, but it did wonders for his introductions.

He approached his role with exaggerated exuberance as if as master of ceremonies at a soul review, becoming a favourite with the fans. The band enjoyed the introductions so much they often played the opening song better as a result, as evidenced in this sparkling and pacey rendition of 'Bodhisattva'. Fagen referred to him in a 1974 *Rolling Stone* interview: 'We dig him, nobody does better build-ups than he does. "Mr Whatever"! Once he introduced us as "Stevie Dan"!' The more he drank, the more hilarious his introductions became, so it goes without saying that he was encouraged mercilessly in that area. As evidenced in this track, his rambling speeches might go on for more than two minutes, the obvious laughter from the band seeping into the recording, but it sets up a scintillating performance perfectly with just the right degree of quirkiness.

'Kulee Baba' [unreleased]
From the count in and swirling cymbal rhythm from Rick Marotta, again giving almost a disco feel, there's energy a-plenty and it would have been a great

addition to the album in finished form. There are two versions in circulation, a basic demo and a cleaner full band version, complete with studio chat from Fagen, the 'bash' in the final verse changing its location from New Orleans to Cameroon between them. The vocal on the more finished demo is excellent, again showing what a naturally gifted and idiosyncratic singer Fagen is.

Kulee Baba could be a sham mystic, fleecing his followers via TV appearances, but more likely it's the name of a TV show which broadcasts live rituals and events from the furthest reaches of the world, live to the masses every Sunday night.

The Fender Rhodes, presumably from Fagen is rich, the chords chosen to perfection to lay out the path for the song, sporadic guitar accents adding depth.

'Kind Spirit' [unreleased]
Almost certainly an unfinished lyric, based on the amount of 'na na na'-ing going on, but this is a quality melody with fine strident piano. It starts strongly, funky bass giving it groove. The verse is very nice, rueing the loss of a positive spark – 'Kind Spirit don't go / Tell me why / The time has come to fly on by.' The whole lyric is repeated twice, including the 'na na na's, so it was probably nowhere near ready for the album.

'Ladies Night' [unreleased]
A very rough instrumental demo recorded in 1980, it's nearly 5-minutes of electric piano, bass and drums, slowly building with, surprisingly, a lush backing of strings. An electric guitar motif is to the fore, double-tracked as the piece progresses. There's room for a piano solo and the whole is a nice laid-back listen with moody intent. It cuts out abruptly but could certainly have become the basis of a smouldering finished song.

'Talkin' About My Home' [unreleased]
A very rough piano and bass demo, but the chording is great and the whole thing quite uplifting. This could have turned out as a classic.

'I Can't Write Home About You' [unreleased]
It sounds a bit sentimental and probably wouldn't have made a good fit on *Gaucho*, but you can't deny it has charm in its basic piano and bass arrangement.

The Nightfly (1982) (Donald Fagen Solo)

Personnel:
Donald Fagen: Lead Vocals, Organ, Synthesizers, Synth Blues Harp, Electric Piano, Piano, Background Vocals, Horn Arrangements
Dave Bargeron: Trombone, Euphonium
Michael Brecker: Tenor Saxophone
David Tofani: Alto Saxophone
Randy Brecker: Trumpet, Flugelhorn
Larry Carlton: Lead & Rhythm Guitar
Ronnie Cuber: Baritone Saxophone
Rick Derringer, Dean Parks: Guitar
Hugh McCracken: Guitar, Harmonica
Steve Khan: Acoustic Guitar
James Gadson, Ed Greene, Jeff Porcaro: Drums
Anthony Jackson, Abraham Laboriel, Will Lee, Marcus Miller, Chuck Rainey: Bass
Greg Phillinganes: Synthesizer, Piano, Electric Piano, Clavinet, Synth Bass
Rob Mounsey: Synthesizers, Horn Arrangements
Michael Omartian: Piano, Electric Piano
Frank Floyd, Gordon Grody, Steve Jordan, Lesley Miller, Zachary Sanders, Valerie Simpson, Roger Nichols, Daniel Lazerus: Background Vocals
Starz Vanderlocket: Percussion, Background Vocals
Producer: Gary Katz
Engineer: Roger Nichols
Recorded: Soundworks Digital Audio/Video Recording Studios; Automated Sound (both New York); Village Recorders (Los Angeles), 1981 to 1982
Released: 30 Oct 1982
Running Time: 38:53
Highest chart place: US 25, UK 44

The first instance in the catalogue of a truly autobiographical release, focusing on Fagen's '50s suburban childhood, his discovery of jazz culture and another world via the late-night radio DJs. These ultimately led him to the life he followed, as the liner notes make clear: 'The songs on this album represent certain fantasies that might have been entertained by a young man growing up in the remote suburbs of a northeastern city during the late Fifties and early Sixties, i.e. one of my general height, weight and build.' The autobiographical element, of the future viewed from naïve adolescence, was surprising for someone as reserved and guarded as Donald, and he later feared that he had revealed too much of himself on the record.

Originally due to be called 'Talk Radio', in a break with Steely Dan tradition, Fagen appeared on the front cover as the 'Nightfly' character, replete with Chesterfield Kings cigarettes, as name-checked in the title song, and a copy of one of his favourite jazz albums, Sonny Rollins' *The Contemporary Leaders*.

Many of the sound elements of the album are similar to Steely Dan but the feel is somewhat different, Fagen himself noting that 'in all the albums I did with Walter, we never said, "We're going to write about a certain period or a certain motif", and I think that accounts for a lot of the difference right there.'

Fagen agreed to press and radio interviews but turned down all requests for TV appearances due to his shyness. Despite considering the possibility, Fagen did not tour the album. He found writing more difficult without Becker to bounce ideas around with, underlining the team dynamic behind Steely Dan, and the album was followed by a period of writer's block for Fagen. Musically he knew what he wanted to do with *The Nightfly*; lyrically he said that he was 'striving for a lack of irony'. Walter later noted that Fagen's album sounded like Steely Dan with lighter lyrical content, 'Donald was trying to move away, from the dark, ironic tone of the Steely Dan albums. And I think he was very successful in doing that.'

Roger Nichols developed a more advanced Wendel drum synthesizer for *The Nightfly*, appearing prominently on several tracks. At an early stage, the decision was taken to record digitally, originally as a back-up, but Nichols soon became an advocate for its use and advantages over analogue recording, allowing the album to be built up in layers.

The Songs:

'I.G.Y.' (Fagen) (6:03)
With its gorgeous electric piano chords and synth start moving into an easy groove, bouncing along on Anthony Jackson's bass and the instantly recognisable horn motif, 'I.G.Y.' is a positive and uplifting introduction to *The Nightfly*. Except that it really isn't.

The first single from the album, it performed well, reaching number 26 on the *Billboard Hot 100*, but its light and breezy positivity belies the ironic message that by 1982 things hadn't turned out as expected. A reminiscence of the 'International Geophysical Year' (I.G.Y) collaborative scientific project that ran around the world from July 1957 to December 1958 and the wonderful advances that technology was expected to bring in the subsequent 20 years – superfast transatlantic rail links, space station tourism, solar-powered cities and, of course, 'spandex jackets, one for everyone'. The post-war optimism and naiveté of the time stand in stark contrast to the realities of life in the early '80s.

The lines 'You'll be a witness to that game of chance in the sky – You know we've got to win' reference the early days of the Space Race, America vowing to launch satellites into Earth orbit, the USSR ultimately getting there first, leading to enhanced efforts from the US and the creation of NASA in 1958. The words fly in the face of previous Steely Dan lyrics and offer the idealistic thoughts of a suburban pre-teen in the late 1950s. There was a belief that science could provide all the answers and make those pesky important choices – 'Just machines to make big decisions / Programmed by fellows with compassion and vision'. As Fagen's most autobiographical work, it might be prudent to look at this song, and much of the album, through the eyes of a much younger and less cynical Donald Fagen: 'a child's view of the future'.

The lilting reggae chorus, 'What a beautiful world this will be / What a glorious time to be free', Fagen's optimistic enthusiasm and the brilliant arrangement make this song a complete winner, a joy to hear every time. Greg Phillinganes' electric piano is key, Fagen adding a quite lovely synth-harmonica solo with the horn section, featuring the Brecker Brothers, excellent throughout. Wendel features, and the song was nominated for a 'Song of the Year' Grammy.

'Green Flower Street' (Fagen) (3:42)
Another song that features an Asian woman, a couple getting together amid a scene of gang violence and rioting – 'Where once we danced our sweet routine / It reeks of wine and kerosene.' An unorthodox love song to be sure, sinister electric piano leading into Rainey's pulsing bass, locked in with Porcaro's propulsive rhythm.

'Where the nights are bright / And joy is complete / Keep my squeeze on Green Flower Street' – but there's a problem, conflict with her brother, Lu Chang: 'I'd like to know what's on his mind / He says "hey buddy, you're not my kind"', so there's possibly a hint of racial tension.

A key component of this song is Dean Parks' stuttering fast guitar picking. It's not in the forefront but vividly colours the music, meshing with Greg Phillinganes' sliding electric piano chords. Larry Carlton is also on hand to contribute a brief but suitably tasty solo, the song kicking along nicely.

'Ruby Baby' (Jerry Leiber / Mike Stoller, arr. Fagen) (5:38)
This is a very nice job on a fun Leiber and Stoller song, originally recorded by The Drifters in 1956. Leiber and Stoller liked Fagen's version so much they chose it as a selection on a UK radio show of their favourite songs, much to Fagen's delight.

It's about unrequited love: 'I got a girl and Ruby is her name `/ She don't love me but I love her just the same ... Ruby Baby how I want you / Like a ghost I'm gonna haunt you'. There is a theory, borne out in the lyrics, that Ruby, is in fact, a prostitute, the object of a young man's desire upon whom he wants to spend his 'lovin' money' and 'steal [her] away from all those guys.'

Fagen's vision was for separation in the right and left-hand keyboard parts, Michael Omartian struggled with this to the point of almost giving up, but eventually, the result was to Fagen's satisfaction with Omartian playing the left hand and Phillinganes the right while seated together at the piano.

The one-note bass pulse moves into a strange keys and brass intro, jazzy and with a hint of madness, opening out into Fagen singing the verse. The backing vocals have that close harmony '50s feel, and Phillinganes' spidery piano addition is sublime, opening out into a jazzy solo. There are parts with just the bass and drums and it's beautifully arranged, always coming back to the luscious vocal sections. The party noises towards the end were recorded in the studio, everyone getting drunk as a release from the tension of the recording process, the partying set over a walking bassline from Anthony Jackson. It's a Wendel song, but Jeff Porcaro also played drums with James Gadson adding tom-tom fills. It was not successful as the third single from *The Nightfly*.

'Maxine' (Fagen) (3:50)

There's a romantic thread of young love here, starting from Michael Omartian's rhapsodic intro. The couple plan a fantastic future for themselves, full of fun and happiness, and, sometime in the near future, a trip to Mexico – but first they have to graduate.

'Maxine' was written around a drum track by Ed Greene for a different song that wasn't working, Fagen coming back with a new song to accommodate it. The close harmony doo-wop, which carries most of the vocal, continues the '50s vibe in an idealised song of teenage romance. Fagen sings the 'Mexico City' part alone, and he's at his most dreamy, the beautifully languid rhythm smoothing out all the problems that might befall the pair.

Jeff Porcaro and James Gadson reversed their roles from 'Ruby Ruby' with Gadson playing the bulk of this song. There's a delicious sax solo, and the song ends in a beautifully arranged brass and piano coda.

'New Frontier' (Fagen) (6:23)

The second single from the album, again not a hit, it's another unorthodox love song as teens party in an underground fallout shelter, giving that Cold War vibe – something positive in the face of possible nuclear annihilation, 'In case the reds decide to push the button down'. Where 'I.G.Y.' carries an ironically positive edge, this song has more uncertainty, the world making rapid progress into the future – but where will that ultimately lead. The futility of domestic fallout shelters underlines a naïve and optimistic trust in science.

The protagonist is keen to get together with the blonde with 'a touch of Tuesday Weld / She's wearing Ambush and a French twist / She's got us wild and she can tell', and there's a suggestiveness in the line 'She loves to limbo, that much is clear' – he thinks he's on to a good thing. The song has a summery party feel, like a blowout before the return to the reality of high school, but the guy dreams of a bright future: 'I can't wait 'til I move to the city / 'til I finally make up my mind / To learn design and study overseas.'

Back at the party, the couple discuss their mutual liking for Dave Brubeck, and he can't help turning on the charm – 'I like your eyes'. At the end of the night, 'We'll open up the doors and climb into the dawn / Confess your passion your secret fear / Prepare to meet the challenge of the new frontier.'

The bass leads straight in, keyboard pulses adding to the drive of the melody line from Omartian, and there's even some blues from the harmonica of Hugh McCracken, complemented by Larry Carlton's guitar additions. Fagen's vocal is full of youthful enthusiasm and the four-note piano riff cuts calmly through the frenetic rhythm.

The song's title is taken from a term used by John F. Kennedy in his presidential acceptance speech in 1960 – but in the context of this song, it could also be taken as a reference to the wonderful new world of sex and experimentation opening up to teenagers.

The video for the song – an early MTV classic – combined animation and live-action and was included as a bonus feature on the DVD-Audio reissue of the album. Fagen wasn't a fan of the medium; 'It's more interesting to me to hear pure music. I don't need any visual imagery to go with it', and he only appears in a poster for *The Nightfly* seen on the wall of the bunker.

'The Nightfly' (Fagen) (5:47)

A funky swing takes us into the world of the late-night radio DJ, playing jazz and talking into the wee small hours of the darkness of Baton Rouge. He fields calls from cranks and lunatics, advising them to turn down their radios, in order to avoid on-air feedback loops, and to respect the seven-second delay, so that any unsavoury references can be cut off, while advertising whatever wonder product the station's backers are pushing this week – 'If you want your honey / To look super swell / You must spring for that little blue jar / Patton's Kiss And Tell'.

For a night-time song, it sounds sunny, but he's down on his luck and there are hints of the blues, which Fagen describes as 'music I associate with a time of innocence'. How did it come to this? Once he was happy, in a relationship, now all he has is loneliness, nights alone fuelled by 'plenty of java and Chesterfield Kings', as he reminisces about his lost love:

I sometimes wonder
What happened to that flame?
The answer's still the same
It was you you it was you
Tonight you're still on my mind.

Acoustic and electric pianos colour a simple rhythm, backing singers providing the station ident and jingles. There are a couple of brief guitar solos, with Larry Carlton involved again, and the song ends on a rising synthesizer note.

'The Goodbye Look' (Fagen) (4:50)

Sun, sea and sand – and political intrigue and potential death. The warmth of the synthetic Caribbean percussion and rhythms pervade, but the story isn't as relaxed, taking place at the time of a military coup on a small island. Fagen has always denied that the Bay of Pigs debacle in 1962 was an influence, but the developments of casinos along the beach, the reference to ordering a Cuban breeze and the Colonel 'with the stupid face, the glasses and the gun' could well refer to Cuba and Castro. There also seems to be a suggestion of Graeme

Greene's *The Comedians*, set in Haiti under 'Papa Doc' Duvalier, his Tonton Macoute ruthlessly silencing all opposition.

The music is relaxed but 'The rules are changed / It's not the same / It's all new players in a whole new ball game' and the narrator knows that he's in danger and must leave. To that end, he hires a motor launch from 'a skinny man with two-tone shoes' to avoid the 'small reception just for me / Behind the big casino by the sea.'

It sounds immaculately throwaway, but it isn't, and this is a song of hidden depths. Marcus Miller nails down the bass and Larry Carlton is effortlessly brilliant, but it's the keys and synths that are in charge here, soloing merrily to the fade-in steel drum style.

'Walk Between Raindrops' (Fagen) (2:38)

Based on a Jewish folk tale where a mystical rabbi could indeed walk between raindrops, here it's given an upbeat swing in what is, on face value, an optimistic way to close the album.

However…

Two lovers have a tiff during a downpour and seem to make up, but there's a profound sadness in the last few lines:

> In my dreams I can hear the sound of thunder
> I can see the causeway by the big hotels
> That happy day we'll find each other on that Florida shore
> You'll open your umbrella
> And we walk between the raindrops back to your door.

It feels like some terrible calamity has occurred and he is now alone, nostalgic for that perfect afternoon in Miami.

It's brief but fun, musically at least, with Wendel taking some of the rhythmic strain, keyboard bass from Greg Phillinganes doubled by Will Lee on bass guitar. The 'Oh, Miami!' interjection was an afterthought by engineer Dan Lazerus, and features him, Fagen and Katz.

Related Tracks:

From *The Nightfly Trilogy MVI* Boxed Set

In November 2007, Rhino Records released all three of Fagen's solo releases to that date, the so-called *Nightfly Trilogy*, in a box set with bonus tracks. This came as something of a surprise as the Steely Dan albums had all been reissued in their original format with no additional tracks, a shame as there were plenty of possible extras to include, as we have seen, but revisiting his past recordings is not something that Donald enjoys: 'I actually don't like that kind of stuff. But fans like it, so I've been looking to see if there's anything to put on there.' And this is what he came up with for *The Nightfly*. He admitted to not listening to his albums once they're completed, 'unless I hear them on the radio or had to remaster them, but that has to do with various subtle, psychological events that go on in my mind.'

'True Companion' (Fagen) (5:09)
Taken from the soundtrack to the 1981 animated film *Heavy Metal*, the music is anything but. The words are limited, but the music is rich, full of electric piano over jazzy rhythms, synthetic additions and restrained guitar – until Steve Kahn blasts off into a solo. It becomes lyrical in the middle before the vocals finally arrive three-and-a-half minutes in, sung in chorus throughout but with Donald's voice clearly in the mix. It's a strange track, smooth jazz with an edge of guitar rock, and an interesting diversion.

'Green Flower Street (Live)' (Fagen) (4:24)
This version was performed in the New York Rock and Soul Revue shows and appears on the *Live at the Beacon* album. Starting with Melodica, the rest of the band come in until we hit the main rhythm, and it's a jumping version to be sure, taken at quite a clip with Fagen in good voice. Drew Zingg's guitar is great, and the horns work beautifully. This is quite distinct from the studio recording and stands up well in its own right.

'Century's End' (Fagen/ Timothy Meher) (5:31)
This sounds like it could have come from *Kamakiriad*, synth rhythms and horns in abundance, and it's a cracking song, typically Fagen in melding two distinctive worlds – synth and jazz – into a rewarding and melodic listen that is easy to repeat play. It's taken from the end credits of the 1988 film *Bright Lights, Big City*, co-written with lyricist Timothy Meher as a picture of urban life at the time. The vocals are great, with excellent arrangements of both the backing singers and the horns. It's sharply written and striking, and it's a great shame that it has been somewhat lost down the cracks, with some great snappy lines like:

We cut to this blonde
Dancing on a mirror
There's no disbelief to suspend
It's the dance, it's the dress
She's a concept more or less

A remixed version appeared on the *Gold – Expanded Edition* compilation in 1991.

Interregnum (1982-1993)

During the 1980s, the duo remained largely inactive, the introduction of the compact disc and the continuing sales of the albums as fans replaced their vinyl copies meaning that new material wasn't essential, Fagen quipping that if the CD hadn't been invented, he'd probably be playing in a lounge bar somewhere.

Fagen contributed songs and performances to a number of projects, including Rickie Lee Jones' *Pirates*, Eye to Eye's debut (produced by Gary Katz), the soundtrack of the *The King of Comedy* movie, Diana Ross' 'Love Will Make It Right' and, with Steve Khan, 'Reflections' for a tribute album to Thelonious Monk. He also produced a gospel album, *The Gospel at Colonus*, but work on his second solo work was aborted in the mid-'80s.

Walter did production work for Michael Franks, Norwegian synthpop band Fra Lippo Lippi, Rickie Lee Jones' *Flying Cowboys* and China Crisis' *Flaunt the Imperfection*, on which he also played, briefly being listed as a member of the band (who were strongly influenced by Steely Dan). He'd moved to Hawaii and got married, producing China Crisis' *Diary of a Hollow Horse* album there so he did not have to leave his young family. Other recording was limited to only very occasional sessions.

Becker and Fagen spoke regularly on the phone and, reunited in 1986 to work on the so-far-only album from model turned singer Rosie Vela, *Zazu*. Gary Katz was to produce, Fagen coming aboard to provide keyboards, a real buzz for Vela who was a huge fan. Becker stopped by the studio to see his old friends and liked what he heard, staying for a few days to add some guitar and synthesizer. With the pair playing together again, the reunion rumour mill started up in earnest – and prematurely. Ultimately, Fagen played on seven of the nine songs, Becker on three. Their contributions are important, but they have no writing credits, and the publicity around their presence was largely inflated.

It's a nice album, Vela's voice is warm and sultry, the songs hooky and bear repetition, with an unusual quirkiness that she delivers confidently. It has that somewhat typical '80s sound, but the songs work well. Donald and Walter's contributions are more obvious on the UK Top 30 single 'Magic Smile', with its slightly bluesy edge and there are definite touches of Dan influence in evidence. The sessions rekindled Donald and Walter's relationship, and they began writing songs again soon afterwards, though these were quickly shelved: the time was not yet right.

In 1987, Fagen took a contributor role on *Premiere* magazine, his first article discussing his battle with writer's block, continuing to provide irregular articles until 1991. He co-wrote the score for the film *Bright Lights, Big City* with Rob Mounsey and provided music for some short art animations in the late 1980s, also donating the track 'Shades' to the Yellowjackets. In 1990, Fagen contributed to William S. Burroughs' *Dead City Radio* album, playing on 'A New Standard by Which to Measure Infamy'.

With encouragement from his partner Libby Titus, in 1989 Fagen played a low-key show with Dr John and Carly Simon in New York, his first stage work in 15 years. He enjoyed the experience and followed this up with a couple of shows of '60s soul standards, but he did not sing. The shows were about sharing his love of soul, and when Steely Dan was brought up in interviews, his response was an irritated 'Nobody should expect us to do a reunion concert. It would be ridiculous.' Fagen did sing at follow-up shows in November, after the quip 'I'd like to hear what I sound like!'

In 1990, the newly christened New York Rock and Soul Revue also included Michael McDonald. Fagen opened the shows with 'Black Friday' and 'I.G.Y.', ending the performance with 'Pretzel Logic', but he wasn't interested in putting on a nostalgia show for Dan fans. He began sitting in with the ten-piece Little Big Band at the Hades Club near his apartment, and eventually, Becker also turned up as a one-off, jamming on guitar while Fagen sang and played keys on some soul standards.

The New York Rock and Soul Review recorded the *Live at the Beacon* album in March 1991 with a line-up of more than twenty players but no Becker. The set included standards, solo track 'Green Flower Street' (noted previously as a bonus track in *The Nightfly Trilogy* box set), and Dan classics 'Chain Lightning' and 'Pretzel Logic'. Not included on the album release but part of the show was Fagen singing 'Home at Last' and 'Black Friday'. As an album, it's fun but inessential and, as is common with such things, the live experience on the night would no doubt be significantly more enjoyable.

Further shows with the Little Big Band introduced 'Josie', 'Green Earrings' and 'Deacon Blues' into the set, and in October 1991 Becker joined Fagen and the band to solo on 'Josie', 'Chain Lightning' and 'Black Friday'. On 25 October 1991, Becker attended a New York Rock and Soul Revue show and spontaneously performed with the group, subsequently being part of a 12-date tour in August 1992. Fagen was still reluctant to sing the Dan songs, but as so many in the audience wanted them, he felt he had to compromise, ultimately enjoying the experience.

Kamakiriad (1993) (Donald Fagen Solo)

Personnel:
Donald Fagen: Keyboards, Vocals, Horn & Rhythm Arrangements, Tenor
Saxophone Sample (as 'Illinois Elohainu')
Walter Becker: Bass, Lead Guitar
Georg Wadenius – Guitar
Leroy Clouden: Drums & Percussion
Dennis McDermott, Christopher Parker: Drums
Bashiri Johnson: Percussion
Randy Brecker, Alan Rubin: Trumpet, Flugelhorn
Cornelius Bumpus, Tim Ries: Tenor Saxophone
Ronnie Cuber, Roger Rosenberg: Baritone Saxophone
Lawrence Feldman, David Tofani: Flute, Tenor Saxophone
Birch Johnson, Jim Pugh: Trombone
Lou Marini: Clarinet, Flute, Alto Saxophone
Paul Griffin: Hammond Organ
Amy Helm, Angela Clemmons-Patrick, Frank Floyd, Diane Garisto, Mindy Jostyn,
Brenda King, Curtis King, Jenni Muldaur, Catherine Russell, Dian Sorel, Fonzi
Thornton: Background Vocals
Producer: Walter Becker
Recorded: New York & Maui, 1990 to 1993
Released: 5 June 1993
Running Time: 50:31
Highest chart place: US 10, UK 3

Finally overcoming the writing block, Fagen had been working on his second
solo album since 1990. He was originally going to produce himself but got
cold feet, and Becker was brought in, also co-writing one song and providing
all the bass and lead guitar, upfront playing some lovely funky stuff, Fagen
crediting the revitalising of their partnership as the kick he needed to complete
the album. By 1993 it was finished, the first Steely Dan related recording with
no involvement from Gary Katz. *Kamakiriad* was conceived as a sequel to *The
Nightfly*, the hero now older and more experienced, but no less idealistic.

The Japanese word for 'Praying Mantis', the Kamakiri is a futuristic steam-
powered car, complete with hydroponic farm to provide the driver with fresh
fruit and vegetables during long journeys. The opening track describes the
delivery of the vehicle and the *Kamakiriad* setting off on the road, the next six
describe the journey through an idealised America, and the adventures along
the way, with the final track considering the arrival at his destination, where he
must decide whether to continue on into the unknown.

The story takes place 'a few years in the future, near the millennium', but it
comes across like it could be a 1950s American suburban utopia. There are sci-
fi elements in order to advance the story, but it isn't a work of science fiction in
itself, that element used to futurise the allegory of Fagen's life through the '80s,

suffering his block and the end of a relationship.

He admitted that his songs were still basically inspired by 'music I listened to as a kid', dance music of the late '50s and '60s, commenting that, in general, the songs are quite theatrical, but to keep them punchy bits were left out of the narrative. With a 12-year gap between albums, Fagen discussed the delay in a 1993 interview for Dutch radio. He said that the '70s Steely Dan songs and *The Nightfly* were fuelled by the 'energy of youth', you then need to live a bit more before you can produce new material.

Fagen's obsessional fastidiousness remained undimmed, weeks spent making micro-adjustment to drum tracks in a quest for perfection, but his belief in drum machines had waned, and he much preferred live drummers, despite the need to continue to massage the results for minute changes. This was the first album where Fagen wrote the horn arrangements himself. Whereas Steely Dan songs to date were generally within the three to four-minute range, although *Aja* and *Gaucho* had stretched the format with a few of the tracks, *Kamakiriad* extended the songs to an average of six minutes.

Three singles were released but failed to chart, however, the album ultimately outsold *The Nightfly*, probably due to the Steely Dan tour in the summer immediately after the album's release, Becker and Fagen assembling a 14-piece band, including themselves, Fagen introducing himself at shows as 'Rick Strauss' and Becker as 'Frank Poulenc'.

The cover image features the dashboard of the Kamakiri with Fagen's face on an integral screen, the reverse showing him stood in a dilapidated doorway with goggles around his neck as the *Kamakiriad*. There are technical drawings, maps and other images in the CD artwork to depict parts of the storyline. The album is dedicated to Dorothy White, Donald's former girlfriend and designer of Steely Dan artwork in the early days, who had since died, Libby Titus noted as 'inspiration'.

The Songs:

'Trans-Island Skyway' (Fagen) (6:30)

It's a low-key start on a repeating guitar figure with bass drum and cymbals until finger-snapping leads into a funky little rhythm with electric piano additions as the driver describes his newly collected Kamakiri: 'The frame is out of Glasgow / The tech is Balinese.' The car is not fast, but it is ethical, a steam-powered biosphere with everything the driver needs for the trip, including 'Good, fresh things / Every day of the year' from the hydroponic vegetable garden and a Tripstar sat nav system, very futuristic at the time.

Not long after setting off, he encounters a car crash. His response is less ethical than his car – with the suggestion that the kid who was driving is dead, he picks up the 'beautiful survivor with dancer's legs and laughing eyes' (although why her eyes would be laughing after a fatal car smash is anyone's guess), reassuring her with 'C'mon snakehips, it's all over now'! He tries to get her to relax, 'put some sounds on / I'll brew up some decaf / C'mon kick off those heels ma'am / Now breathe in and sigh out.' This sounds like it could relate to Donald, the 'crash' as a relationship ends – or he hits the wall of writer's block – having to take stock and reset before starting out again ('Let's talk about the good times').

They reach the 'sprangle' where he was brought up, and he visualises his father mowing the lawn of their old home. It's a suburban idyll of 'motels and drive-thrus'.

The production is state of the art, but there's a slight retro feel to the sound, the chorus harmonies again having a doo-wop feel. It's bright and snappy, an engaging groove to kick things off, horns well placed for accent, all ending abruptly. A sparse bass drum and vocal mix of the song appeared on the b-side of the 'Snowbound' single release.

'Countermoon' (Fagen) (5:05)
As Fagen noted, the title refers to 'a moon that makes people fall out of love.' It's an anti-love song, telling of 'How the women get restless / And the men grow cold' in the blue rays of the Countermoon – 'Spitewaves are threatening' and 'There's a heartquake on the way'. The second verse ends with the realisation that 'Last night you loved her / Tonight you wonder why'.

It continues in the same style as 'Trans-Island Skyway' initially but then builds into a more strident strut, with horns to start and scratchy guitar adding to the rhythm track. Again, the chorus harmony is very strong. The sax solos, credited to Illinois Elohainu, are Fagen in disguise, his only solos on the album, played on a sampling keyboard.

'Springtime' (Fagen) (5:06)
Arriving at Laughing Pines, an amusement park on the Funway, the Kamakiriad stops to have his brain scanned and old romances replayed. An easy tambourine rhythm with smooth horns that pick up the jazziness when he encounters old flames Connie Lee ('We're cruisin' at about a thousand miles an hour / But the car is standin' still') and Mad Mona (baking 'gospel candy'), with John Coltrane getting a namecheck as the soundtrack. The chorus is as groovesome as it should be:

Swing out to Lake Nostalgia
Route 5 to Laughing Pines
Get off at Funway West
Drive into Springtime.

Becker's twangy guitar additions stand out, and he gets to solo in typically laid-back Walter style. The horns are on fine form with a soulful '60s tone.

'Snowbound' (Becker / Fagen) (7:08)
The weather turns bad, with thunder effects, the icy road conditions leaving the driver stranded in a city with nothing to do except party and enjoy some

decadent and carefree living until the weather clears, thermasuits protecting them from the intense cold while they turn the town 'Into a city of lights'. At the Metroplex, the driver has his eye on a dancer who he'll wait for at the stage door. Meanwhile, Club Hi Ho has a new art piece by Charlie Tokyo – 'It's a kind of pyramid / With a human heart / Beating in an iron grid.' Later, they sail 'icecats' on the frozen river; someone sets off a flare and 'For seven seconds it's like Christmas day / And then it's dark again.'

Originally written in 1985, during an attempt to revive Donald and Walter's writing partnership, it fitted the concept, so made the cut here. It's an easy slide of a song, 'let's sleep in today' suiting the mood; take it easy during the day, party all night. It gives itself plenty of time, and the bass sound is spectacularly wonderful.

The third single release from the album, it also included a sparse bass, drum and vocal version on the b-side. The video, by Michel Gondry, mixed stop motion and live-action in a futuristic city where Donald is the tower-dwelling overlord of robotic worker drones, ultimately pushing them to retaliation.

'Tomorrow's Girls' (Fagen) (6:17)

A space opera, referencing Philip K. Dick's short story *Second Variety*. It's just another day in suburbia, people blissfully going about their business, 'Then the milkman screamed / And pointed up at the sky'. They're here, aliens from another world, disguised, in full-on '50s/'60s schlock style, as beautiful women who lull men into relationships, and then turn into a mass of whirling blades and cut them to pieces:

We fall asleep with the TV on
 Dream about a laughing angel
Then the laugh becomes a furious whine
Look out fellas
It's shredding time

The inference being that in relationships it sometimes feels like you're with an alien.

As with much of Fagen's best work, it's dark and funny, shrouded in the smooth jazziness of the music. The intro from electric and acoustic pianos moves into a thumping little number, Fagen's voice lower and with more edge on this one. The chorus is jazzy, as are Walter's guitar additions. The bridge is wonderful, a soft and engaging section introduced by a horn fanfare, the blend of Donald with the backing singers reminding me, surprisingly, of vocal trio the Roches, moving back into horns and guitar to carry the song forward, playing out on a long vocal 'improv'.

A video was produced, featuring Rick Moranis, underlining the idealised 1950s suburbia, Fagen, in sunglasses, lip-syncing some of it; but Fagen still felt that videos detracted from songs, making listeners passive, unlike radio where they had to actively listen and use their imaginations to come up with their own imagery.

'Florida Room' (Fagen / Libby Titus) (6:02)

After the cold of 'Snowbound', it's some Floridian sun and the back room of a house where his love sits and dreams, but 'does she dream of me?' The calm and languid air gives him the relaxation he needs, 'But in her Florida room / There's a hurricane'. He's wondering, 'Can she bring me back to life once more?'

It's an airier, sunny sound, with Cornelius Bumpus' warm tenor sax prominent. Chris Parker's propulsive groove is lovely, and the whole thing is an easy toe-tapper, with great work from the backing vocalists in the chorus. At over six minutes, there's plenty of room for the band to stretch out. Libby Titus, who married Donald shortly before the album's release, got a co-write on this one for helping him with the words.

'On the Dunes' (Fagen) (8:07)

This song was written as far back as 1983 but fitted the eventual project so found its place. The longest track on the album, it's languid and easy-going, stately horns and piano leading into a low-key vocal, the Kamakiriad heading along the coast 'To a misty beach / That's where my life became a joke'. His love ends their relationship, and the warm romanticism of the words is shot through with despair: 'As you spoke you must have known / It was a kind of homicide / I stood and watched my happiness / Drift outwards with the tide.' The beaches attract fun-seekers and lovers, but 'For me it's just a joyless place / Where this loneliness began.'

Guitar adds mournful accents, and Cornelius Bumpus' tenor sax again features largely. After the lyric ends, piano leads into an extended instrumental play out – that takes in the whole of the second half – built on Chris Parker's unplanned drum break, he was into the tune and just kept playing, Bumpus returning to solo with a bluesier edge. It's downbeat but uplifting at the same time.

'Teahouse on the Tracks' (Fagen) (6:09)

After the despair of 'On the Dunes', the Kamakiriad arrives at the end of his journey – depressing Flytown. While walking down Bleak Street he hears 'a wailin' combo' that gets him finger-popping. He seeks out the sound and is told 'If you've got eyes / To rhythmatize / Bring your flat hat and your axe / 'Cause tonight at ten / We'll be workin' again / At the Teahouse on the Tracks.' The music is hot, 'The crowd was bouncin' in sync with the pulse / You get a case of party feet ... Some frozen stuff begins to crack', and his despair starts to lift, resurrection through music and dancing. The next day he's revitalised and back at the wheel, ready to continue the journey, a reference to the end of the block that had hampered Donald's writing for a number of years.

It's upbeat, in similar vein to 'Trans-Island Skyway', piano, horns and synth strings featuring along with an extended trombone contribution from Birch Johnson, a fun way to finish the album.

Related Tracks:

Bonus tracks from *The Nightfly Trilogy MVI* boxed set:

'Big Noise, New York' (Fagen) (5:21)

The B-side of the 'Trans-Island Skyway' single, alongside a live version of 'Home at Last' from the New York Rock and Soul Review shows. Fagen supplies synth-harmonica via the Melodica in a city-smarts post-breakup lament; 'Without your love, this town's no fun at all'. It was written around the same time as 'Century's End' (from the *Bright Lights, Big City* film soundtrack), and parts of the melody line surprisingly reappeared in the title track of the final Steely Dan album, *Everything Must Go*. It's a decent song, with a bold if not overly catchy chorus, but it wouldn't have fitted the album.

'Confide in Me' (Fagen) (4:15)

The B-side of 'Tomorrow's Girls', bluesy piano leads into Drew Zingg's strident guitar with Mindy Jostyn's harmonica. Donald's vocal is full to the brim with confidence and brings in some big band swing to the chorus. With Lincoln Schliefer on bass and Denny McDermott's drums, it's a full-steam-ahead bluesy rocker that has a real live feel, moving into a gospel vibe towards the end. Well worth hearing.

'Blue Lou' (Fagen) (7:01)

Recorded for the *Glengarry Glen Ross* film soundtrack, a lugubrious sax adds its lonely footprint to start, eventually joined by piano and string bass. The downbeat slow jazz is blue indeed, and more authentic than most of Donald's other excursions into this territory, the horn section bulking it out here and there, in a subtle arrangement that builds to full-on big band towards the end, then back to basics and the saxophone again. Quite beautiful.

'Shanghai Confidential' (Fagen) (4:54)

With an obvious oriental sound, this is a lovely instrumental, a synthetic rhythm and an engaging melody line. The funky slapped bass, and guitar additions sit nicely amid the boxed rhythms and synth washes, and it's a smooth toe-tapper. There's quite a Dan feel to some of it, so it could well have turned up as part of another piece, but that was not to be.

11 Tracks of Whack (1994) (Walter Becker Solo)

Personnel:
Walter Becker: Bass, Guitar, Ukulele, Vocals
Dean Parks: Acoustic & Electric Guitars
Adam Rogers: Electric Guitar
John Beasley, Donald Fagen: Keyboards
Fima Ephron: Bass
Ben Perowsky: Drums
Paulinho Da Costa: Percussion
Bob Sheppard: Saxophone, Woodwinds
Bruce Paulson: Trombone
Jon Papenbrook: Horns & Brass
Catherine Russell, Brenda White-King: Background Vocals
Producers: Donald Fagen, Walter Becker
Engineers: Tom Hardisty, Earl Martin, John Neff, Roger Nichols, David Russell
Recorded: 1993-1994
Record Label: Giant Records
Recorded: Hyperbolic Sound (Hawaii), 1993 to 1994
Released: 27 Sept. 1994
Running Time: 56:46
Highest chart place: US 11, UK –

Walter Becker's solo recordings were considerably less frequent than Fagen's, who took the plunge straight after the demise of Steely Dan in 1981. Walter had his demons to conquer first. He moved to Hawaii in 1982, cleaned himself up, met someone, settled down and had a child, enjoying a 'groovy little lifestyle' on the idyllic island in preference to the fast-paced dog-eat-dog world of the wider recording industry, becoming, in his own words, an 'avocado rancher and self-styled critic of the contemporary scene.'

In 1989, Walter was asked by *Q* magazine whether he would ever do a solo album: 'If Walter Becker could sing a little better, there probably would have been one already. I'm beginning to realise that I don't have the luxury of sitting around wishing I was a better singer than I am ... I'd like there to be a Walter Becker record now which I never really thought about before.'

Fagen returned the favour to Walter for working on *Kamakiriad* by co-producing, arranging and playing keyboards on *11 Tracks of Whack* in 1994. Roger Nichols was also involved in the engineering and mixing.

As the voice of Steely Dan, Fagen's albums have received far more attention than Becker's, but that's a shame as Walter was a vital element of the Steely Dan formula. His albums are more laconic, carried along by his easy drawl and with less of the funk and jazz that inhabit Donald's work, seeming comfortable away from the more fastidious perfectionism and unremitting precision of Steely Dan and Fagen's solo work. He was keen to get a more organic sound and make it a fun experience.

It is the solo albums of both men that show more detail regarding the contributions they made to the greater Dan. Whereas Fagen's are whip-smart groove-a-thons oozing clever wordplay, situations and characters, they downplay the sardonic edge of Steely Dan, and that's where Walter comes in. Fagen has admitted that a lot of the Steely Dan attitude came from Walter.

Becker sang lead vocals on record for the first time since a few verses on the debut Steely Dan album. He had originally considered an instrumental album, then he thought about hiring a singer before finally deciding to sing himself. It turns out he was more than up to the task.

The songs have an autobiographical feel, with a flavour of his now seemingly idyllic life in Hawaii, but he still manages to bring in the characters and lowlifes that you would expect. Having gathered a collection of around two dozen songs, Walter admitted to tying himself in knots trying to decide on which to record for the final album, Donald helping hone it down upon his arrival and putting the project back on track.

In typical Walter fashion, *11 Tracks of Whack* features twelve tracks, which he put down to being 'a clerical error', although the reality is that there are eleven tracks of 'whack', and one song of love, for his son. The sleeve is helpful in explaining two appropriate meanings, playing down Walter's skills in typically dismissive mood: 'Whack. 1. A blow, intermediate in intensity between a wallop and a smack. 2. A first stab or crude attempt,'

With a blurred image of Walter on the front cover, the album is laconic but still biting, the cynical edge clearly visible, while the jazz and Fagen's more neurotic tendencies are toned down. It's an easy and witty listen, Dean Parks saying of the beautifully crafted songs, 'If you listen close, you can hear Walter's contributions [to Steely Dan] – his sense of humour and odd choice of subject matter.' Walter's albums have a different tone and feel to the Dan albums, unlike Fagen's, and they're well worth investigating.

The Songs:

'Down in the Bottom' (Becker) (4:16)
Immediately, Becker unveils the darkness of his soul; it's a bleak vista, inhabited by demons of his past, a life he clearly knows.

Becker loved the line 'if you got the bear or the bear got you' from 'The Bear' outtake from the *Aja* sessions, a song about the confused life of the junkie, so reanimated it for use here. Are you in control, or are the drugs taking over?

There's a weariness and longing in this song, despite some upbeat flashes, as the singer remembers a lost friend, a victim of the habit to which the singer introduced him. There's guilt, blame and regret, probably built on personal sorrow after the death of Walter's girlfriend in 1980, where he found himself 'down in the bottom of the wine dark sea.'

A drum-machine gives quite an '80s feel, supported by bass. The instrumentation is sparse, only touches of guitar, until the solo, by Walter, bass and bell-like keys making themselves known here and there. It's a great start, the relentless rhythm set against Walter's rich and warm voice and poetic delivery. He might not have the range of others, but he has a lovely tone.

'Junkie Girl' (Becker) (4:07)

There's already a theme developing with this album and 'Junkie Girl' states it pretty openly. It could again refer to Walter's guilt around the loss of Karen Stanley, but most likely it's a more general observation on junkie culture.

The references revolve around the lifestyle: 'through to the white side of her China curtain' appears to refer to the spectre of death, while after getting money for her drug of choice she sends it 'bubbling down the thin blue line', the vein through which she administers. Later she appears to be overdosing: 'Now I can hardly hear you anymore / Your eyes are empty, and your voice is hollow / I see you waving from a distant shore…' Becker seems to be saying that at one time he wishes he had died with her, but he has managed to get his own life back together and move on.

There's a warmth in the music, you believe everything that Walter says, the 'F' Bomb dropped with passion. The pace is easy, driven by guitar and a rhythm track with snare upfront. The tone of the guitar is great, smooth but with enough of an edge, the unorthodox solo not quite cutting through, but its waywardness is almost certainly the point.

Stanyan Street probably refers to the avenue that cuts across the Haight Ashbury district of San Francisco, where junkie girls are more than likely to be found.

'Surf and/or Die' (Becker) (6:15)

There's a spikey edge to this one, shards of guitar against a strong rhythm from Ben Perowsky's drums. The lyric sweeps in and out of the instrumentation, the vocal line carrying the song along. Already, it's obvious that Walter's songs are often wordier than the more concise efforts with Steely Dan. This one is almost stream of consciousness, directed to the young victim of an accident. His thoughts on the sad waste of life clearly gave him plenty to say. After an angular guitar solo, probably from Dean Parks, the piece ends with Buddhist chanting.

Becker said that it was 'about an incident that happened with some friends of ours in Hawaii where a young guy was killed in an accident, and it was very shocking, for a young, healthy person that you know well, and that you loved the family, and everything, to suddenly not be there one day. And I remember they had a little sort of a memorial service for him, and one of the Tibetan lamas from the Dharma Center in Paea, the town I live in, in Hawaii, came and said a little piece there. And it was very moving, and I could see how his perspective on the continuum of life and death and the whole Tibetan Buddhist thing kind of made the whole thing a little less meaningless and senseless seeming.'

The cynical edge to the title is typical, but the message within the song is heartfelt and the guitar gives it an original sound.

'Book of Liars' (Becker) (4:09)

Performed on Steely Dan's reunion tour in 1993 and included on the *Alive in America* live document (which was not released until after *11 Tracks of Whack*), Walter calls out a compulsive liar with whom he thought he was secure, and he tries to remember what it was that they had. The relationship is clearly dead, Walter musing that 'if my bad luck ever blows me back this way / I'll just look in the book of liars for your name.'

The electric piano is warm, it's a quiet start, Walter's voice quite plaintive. The drums click and guitars bubble, a perfect support for the poetic words. The arrangements on most of these songs are subtle and basic, the words and Walter's delivery of them being the stars of the show, but there's space for a lilting and jazzy sax solo from Bob Sheppard followed by a quirky little keyboard solo before the final verse.

Walter obviously had a love for this one, as it featured regularly in later tours, the version on *Alive in America* probably the better given the expanded instrumentation of the bigger band.

'Lucky Henry' (Becker) (4:39)

This one kicks straight off into a swirling, swinging rhythm, off-kilter rhythms throwing you sideways. Initially upbeat, Dean Parks' guitar follows the vocal line before taking a hard-edged solo. The pace slows for a lyrical mid-section, the energy returning with a twin guitar attack that is very well done, followed by a solo from Adam Rogers. The drums have a jazzy pulse, and the guitars get more chaotic towards the fade.

It's an inscrutable song with some lovely lines, like 'On the bus across from us seen once in silhouette / The old man's face you couldn't place that now you can't forget', Walter delivering the song well, handling the twists and jumps with ease, his easy drawl used to good effect. It's tricksy and interesting, a testament to his skill in arranging.

'Hard Up Case' (Becker) (4:56)

A brooding opening of drums, bass and keys moves into a Latin-edged groove with added percussion. Brass is almost unexpected for the chorus, a lilting phrase before the words, adding piquancy. The sporadic backing vocals work well, including a sole voice echoing some of the lines. Words like 'I know you gave your little heart to me / I guess I threw the thing away' suggest another failed relationship.

Becker adds a couple of brief solos which point towards the sound of the final two Steely Dan albums, and it's a neat little number that adds some different elements to the album's sound.

'Cringemaker' (Becker / Dean Parks) (5:11)

Another failed relationship, but where it seems to have been Walter's fault in the last song, here it's 'What ever happened to my college belle / When did she turn into the wife from hell?' It's a stalking, bluesy number with some country to spice it, upbeat with lovely female backing vocals. Walter's solo is sparse but effective, and it rocks out gently in the choruses on a lovely guitar riff.

Again, Walter delivers the words well, a growling edge giving a distinctive character to his world-weary vocal, and there's cheekiness in there too, 'Nobody told us when we started out / Just what this life is really all about / Sometimes I wonder and you do too / If I could do it all over would I / Still do it all over you?' Co-written with Dean Parks, it's certainly one of the album's winners.

'Girlfriend' (Becker) (5:43)

Another great opening couplet, possibly with hints of Becker's life immediately after the Dan break-up in 1981: 'Alone in my cave / It's corn flakes and Camels / And the long restless shadows of my life.'

Bright and breezy, keys take the lead with a soft rhythm and guitar accents. The chorus is a delight, you could see this one in a Dan song, although Donald's delivery would be very different. While festering in his apartment, Walter needs someone 'to tell my story to', but he's not making an appealing picture, wasting time watching re-runs rather than getting out and about.

There's a world-weariness in 'The time that remains / What good can it do me / Now that I know that too much is not enough.' A clarinet appears and goes a little crazy, and then Bugs Bunny arrives, 'With a fluffy white tail and long grey floppy ears / Who looks up at me and says, "Doc don't you worry / All you got to do is, hide in here"', in the rabbit hole, away from the world until he's able to fully face it again. Altogether this is a lovely song, witty, strange and fun.

'My Waterloo' (Becker) (4:02)

Another shift, into a tight reggae, starting with keyboards but driven by the bass. It builds into a sharp number, Walter soloing briefly amid a variety of keyboard textures, the synthetic edge giving it an otherworldly quality.

The words hint at disaster after disaster, 'It's still no easy thing to hold your head up high / When every time you turn around / Somebody kicks your statue down', Walter realising that this time he's really met his match and he's not going to get up. This is a relatively simple but engaging song that gets the foot tapping.

'This Moody Bastard' (Becker) (5:18)

Walter is the 'moody bastard' in a song of self-pity, synth lines giving it a low-key opening that remains for the whole piece. It considers an old friendship that has seen difficult times, seeming to refer back to the early days when he met Donald, happily reminiscing about the good times. But 'These days it's like a tomb / Amid in the stacks of gloom'.

Instrumentally it's very sparse, hints of guitar, basic drum rhythm and a lugubrious clarinet appearing briefly to change the texture, with subtle backing voices in the chorus. An odd little song, but it works well in the context of the album.

'Hat Too Flat' (Becker) (5:26)

Probably the strangest song on the album, clanking percussion and odd synth tones preface a spidery guitar. It's a tale of alienation set in a sci-fi scenario, but the underlying principle of outsiders not finding it easy to be accepted remains clear. The immigrant has arrived from Arcturus and tries to assimilate ('My English she is much better now') and works hard at his job, but the locals can't see past his hat which, in true Arcturan style, is flat – far too flat for the indigenous population.

The chorus is fun, with female backing, and there's another weird little keyboard solo – it kind of makes me think of the 'cantina' band in the original *Star Wars* films – the song playing out with a brief off-kilter guitar. The quirkiness continues a path that takes the album in unexpected directions.

'Little Kawai' (Becker) (2:44)

With all the 'Whack' out of the way, here comes the unadulterated and complete love in a brief ode to Walter's son, Kawai. In a cheerful, country-tinged acoustic song that smacks of sunshine and island life, Walter can see beyond the lapses in behaviour: ('Here's a note from one Miss Turnbull / Certain homework was not done / Tiny holes in brand new windows / From an unknown bb gun'), the annoyances ('That new squirt gun Eric got you / Don't you aim it over here / That's a mean song Eldon taught you / I no longer wish to hear') and the misinformation ('And where he says babies come from / This is not completely true…') to declare 'But they don't love you / Little Kawai / Not the way that I do.' It's A heart-warming way to end a relaxed but idiosyncratic solo debut.

Related tracks:

'Medical Science' (Becker) (4:31)

The bonus track for the Japanese market features a similar template to much of the rest of the album, being sparse with a subtle groove, synthetic elements and bits of guitar. It's a worthy addition, strange but beguiling with synth horns supporting the warm drawling vocal, cool and impervious, punctuated by recreated ambulance sirens.

The song considers the wonders of medical science, but also its limitations ('Does it hurt when I do this? / Can you laugh when I go like this? … Just look for big pieces when we sweep up tonight boys') and Walter is more than aware that 'You know medical science is helpless / Helpless in a case like this' when it comes to drug use – 'And all the jive-asses and the true believers / The bullshit givers and receivers / Here today tomorrow gone / To the triage tent in the great beyond / Wherein the angel tangos with the infidel.' It's a hard-hitting addition, worthy of the main album rather than a slightly throwaway bonus.

Alive in America (1995)

Personnel:
Walter Becker: Guitar, Lead Vocals (on 'Book of Liars')
Donald Fagen: Lead Vocals, Melodica, Electric Piano
Warren Bernhardt: Piano
Georg Wadenius, Drew Zingg: Guitars
Tom Barney: Bass Guitar
Cornelius Bumpus: Tenor Saxophone
Chris Potter: Alto & Tenor Saxophone
Bob Sheppard: Soprano & Tenor Saxophone
Dennis Chambers, Peter Erskine: Drums
Catherine Russell: Percussion, Background Vocals, Human Whistle
Bill Ware: Percussion, Vibraphone
Diane Garisto, Brenda White-King: Background Vocals
Producer: Donald Fagen
Record Label: Giant Records
Recorded: Irvine, CA; St. Petersburg, FL; Charlotte, NC; Detroit, MI; Chicago, IL;
Phoenix, AZ, 19 Aug. 1993 to 19 Sep. 1994
Released: 17 Oct. 1995
Running Time: 66:36
Highest chart place: US 40, UK 62

In 1993, Donald and Walter finally embraced the idea of taking a show out on the road to play Steely Dan music. Fagen was initially uneasy about using the SD brand name but was finally convinced that the increased revenue that would undoubtedly be made would alleviate many of the issues that had soured the touring process for them in the '70s, and he warmed to the idea.

The initial line-up included drummer Peter Erskine, pianist Warren Bernhardt, bassist Tom Barney, guitarist Drew Zingg. Michael McDonald declined as he was promoting an album of his own. Pat Metheny was also invited but believed that three guitar players would be too many.

They were looking to reinterpret Dan songs, and if they didn't enjoy playing them, they'd be dropped. Fagen did not relish 'Do It Again' ('I despise that song') or 'Rikki Don't Lose that Number' so they were omitted, but 'Reelin' In the Years' appeared, albeit extensively rearranged. Becker admitted to going and buying CDs of the old albums so that they could relearn the chord changes.

The tour began in August 1993 at Auburn Hills, Michigan and after six weeks and 32 gigs ended in Cleveland. It was a great success, also including some solo material, but a lot of this was dropped as the tour progressed. Denny Dias guested for a couple of songs at the Los Angeles show.

Alive in America appeared in 1995, compiled from recordings of the 1993 and 1994 concerts, promoting the recently released *Citizen Steely Dan* box set. Roger Nichols recorded all the shows, and he and Fagen ploughed through the tapes for the choice performances to produce the band's first-ever live album.

The result was a somewhat sterile record of the tour. It felt like Becker and Fagen were going through the motions, a one-hour souvenir of a two-and-a-half-hour show not doing it justice. The double live album has been a standard since the '70s, but Steely Dan's one and only official live album is a relatively flimsy affair – and with almost 1,000 shows played to date (around 150 in the '70s and more than 800 since the return to the stage), that's probably unique for a major band. The insecurity that comes with live performance clearly remains an issue, despite the quality of the sidemen and the serene confidence displayed during the shows. Nevertheless, it's nice to have a live record of some of the songs, and the band is pure quality.

The sleeve features a still from the 1940 film *The Mummy's Hand* (probably a reference to the corpse of Steely Dan being reanimated) with a series of live shots in black and white and a photo of an open-air venue.

Most of the tracks are played pretty straight, the band in very good form, the earliest recording being of Becker's 'Book of Liars', a good year before it was released and probably better than the studio version, benefitting from the larger band. The other 1993 recordings are 'Green Earrings' (with extra solos), 'Aja' and 'Third World Man', the latter being slowed down into a laid-back and pretty emotion-free jazz version. The bulk of the set is from shows in 1994, with 'Babylon Sisters', 'Bodhisattva', 'Peg', 'Kid Charlemagne, 'Sign in Stranger', 'Reelin' In the Years' and 'Josie'. Most of the tracks chosen fit easily within the big band format.

It's interesting to compare 'Bodhisattva' with the 1974 version; that was a rock band, this is most certainly a jazz orchestra. 'Josie' is a straight-ahead version with embellishments and a short drum solo, though not as funky as the original. 'Sign in Stranger' has been jazzified, but not as much as 'Reelin' In the Years' which is resplendent in its new jazzed-up arrangement, the Rhodes piano intro throwing the audience off, it only becoming obvious what the song is over a minute in, when the words start. Saxophones replace the guitar of the original and it's completely reworked. It's still fun, different but entertaining in a new way, a mature work that loses some of the bravado of the original.

Two Against Nature (2000)

Personnel:
Donald Fagen: Lead Vocals, Keyboards, Horn Arrangements
Walter Becker: Bass, Lead & Rhythm Guitar, Horn Arrangements
Ted Baker: Piano & Fender Rhodes
Jon Herington: Rhythm & Acoustic Guitar
Paul Jackson Jr., Hugh McCracken, Dean Parks: Guitars
Tom Barney: Bass
Keith Carlock, Leroy Clouden, Vinnie Colaiuta, Sonny Emory, Ricky Lawson, Michael White: Drums
Gordon Gottlieb, Will Lee, Daniel Sadownick: Percussion
Dave Shank, Steve Shapiro: Vibraphone
Amy Helm: Whistle
Lawrence Feldman: Clarinet, Tenor & Alto Saxophone
Roy Hitchcock: Clarinet
Lou Marini, Chris Potter, David Torfani: Alto & Tenor Saxophone
Roger Rosenberg: Bass Clarinet, Baritone Saxophone
Michael Leonhart: Trumpet, Wurlitzer, Horn Arrangements
Jim Pugh: Trombone
Cynthia Calhoun, Carolyn Leonhart, Michael Harvey: Background Vocals
Producers: Walter Becker, Donald Fagen
Executive Engineer: Roger Nichols
Record Label: Giant Records
Recorded: River Sound; Clinton Sound; Electric Lady (all New York); Hyperbolic Sound (Hawaii), Nov. 1997 to 1999
Released: 29 Feb. 2000
Running Time: 51:25
Highest chart place: US 6, UK 11

Hints that a new Steely Dan album might be forthcoming started appearing in 1995, and after the 1996 'Art Crimes' tour, which included dates in the US, Japan, and their first European shows in 22 years, they began work.

Finally released in early 2000, the sound was more mature, as would befit two now middle-aged dudes, but *Two Against Nature* delighted many eager fans with a collection of songs that grooved mercilessly while staying true to the heritage of the band and the wickedly unexpected nature of the duo's songs. Produced by Donald and Walter with Roger Nichols in an executive engineer capacity, it's as pristine as you would imagine, maintaining the band's quest for the immaculate.

The album is not often held aloft with the likes of *Aja*, *The Royal Scam* or *Pretzel Logic*, but it is a fine collection, which was rewarded with four Grammy Awards, including Album of the Year. On the back of this success and their return as a fully functioning studio and live band, Steely Dan were inducted into the Rock and Roll Hall of Fame in March 2001, an experience that brought out the devils in them. The induction speech by a clearly suspicious Moby set the tone as he pondered on why he had been chosen for the role: 'Either they like me, or for some reason they really hate me, and this is some sort of monstrous practical joke.' Donald seemed willing to play the game to some degree, but Walter is quietly acerbic, entertainingly throwing the floor open to questions rather than making a speech, then ending with, 'Thank you very much, we're persuaded it's a great honour to be here tonight.' Class! They followed it up with a sweet rendering of 'Black Friday' with Paul Shaffer and the house band from David Letterman's *Late Show*, Walter on fine form, and despite his understated view of the honour, he was quietly proud.

There's a seam of sexual degeneracy through *Two Against Nature*, typical of much of their work, but possibly a little more prevalent, the horny old goats. After the LA years, which thematically continued on into *Gaucho*, this album is far more centred around the environs of NYC, with references to the likes of Gramercy Park, Lower Broadway, the Strand book shop and Dean & DeLuca's food store. Some of the original ideas for the songs dated back to the mid-'80s when occasional writing sessions had briefly recommenced, but most came together in the '90s when the band was back on the road, and the partnership was fully rekindled.

The songs are often less cryptic than before, consisting of beautifully scripted stories, Fagen later commenting 'I think we've become better at writing more lucid, narrative things than we used to do.'

The title suggests our heroes standing up to the ageing process. Fagen: 'it's kind of an axiom that when you get to be our age, you can't have a rock 'n' roll band anymore. So we're fighting nature in that sense. There's also the idea of art vs. nature.' The oblique cover depicts the shadows of Don and Walt (shadows of their former selves?) amid nature, although clearly not too far out into the wilds, probably at Walter's home in Hawaii, with the reverse of the CD inlay featuring, obviously, incongruous garden ornamentation, including fake flamingos.

The sound is possibly less widescreen than the classic late-'70s releases, a trait continued into the final studio album, *Everything Must Go*, but there is plenty going on, stellar performances and finger-snappin' rhythms. It's an album I go back to regularly and like most of the Dan's work it makes me groove, and it makes me smile. It's probably less gritty and a touch smoother than before, but it's just so listenable, and it's good to hear Walter out front and centre playing the lines as only he could. As Fagen said, 'Self-reflective like our earlier work, but more sophisticated.' He again countered the accusations of overt perfectionism due to their ongoing insecurities: 'We don't think of ourselves as being perfectionists. To us, it's more like desperately trying to have it sound more or less OK.'

The Songs:

'Gaslighting Abbie' (Becker / Fagen) (5:53)
What better way to commence your return album than with a delicious psychological shocker, set to bouncy upbeat and struttin' rhythms of course,

whereby a man and the woman he's having an affair with ('boppin'' all summer) devise a plan to remove the man's wife, Abbie, from the picture by driving her to madness? 'It's a luscious invention for three / One summer by the sea', the period from 4 July to slowly push Abbie over the edge, finally doing her in over the Labor Day weekend at the start of September.

The track takes its name from the film *Gaslight*, of which two versions were made in the 1940s (one starring Ingrid Bergman and Charles Boyer). The term 'gaslighting' coming to mean a manipulation of the target's mind in an attempt to sow subconscious doubt, making them question their own memory and perception with the aim of driving them to insanity, deriving from Boyer's character changing the settings on the gaslights each night to try to make his wife think she's delusional.

It took 26 straight 8-hour days of studio fastidiousness to nail the song. Walter's guitar is all over it, stabs of delight displaying his wonderful vibrato, mixed with Tom Barney's growling bass, even getting a briefly skeletal solo that fits the moment beautifully. Ricky Lawson's drum sound is so crisp and razor-sharp that you could cut cheese with it and the ubiquitous horn section continues the record of wonderful brass additions to Dan albums, seeming more prevalent here, Chris Potter taking the tenor sax solo to the end.

The scene-setting detail is marvellous, planning how to pull off the deed, Fagen describing it as 'the aural equivalent of an Alfred Hitchcock movie'. All the while the man salivating over his mistress wearing clothes stolen from Abbie ('That black mini looks just like the one she's been missin' / Feels good on you'), and could there be a better name for a reality-altering drug than Deludin? Also, as we're talking made-up stuff, whatever a 'spitelock' is, it sounds nasty.

The references to solitaire come from the 1962 film *The Manchurian Candidate*, a man brainwashed to become an assassin whenever someone suggests 'a nice relaxing hand of solitaire'. This reference may also throw a different spin on the situation: Is the perpetrator just one person, with a split Norman Bates-like personality who also enjoys dressing in his soon to be deceased wife's clothes? It's darkly deranged enough to be a Steely Dan song!

'What a Shame About Me' (Becker / Fagen) (5:17)

A laid-back slide carried on some wonderfully sparse soloing from Becker. The deft piano touches are a delight, but, like 'Gaslighting Abbie', this one is all about the beautifully realised story, delivered to perfection by Fagen.

Fagen's character is down on his luck in a dead-end job, still working on the novel that he'll probably never finish, while all his friends from college appear to have done well for themselves. He bumps into Franny, an old flame ('the goddess on the fire escape'), now successful in Hollywood.

It's a conversation, verses sung from different perspectives, first Donald, then Franny asking about other members of their college crowd. Donald responds with what he knows of them (including Bobby Dakine, 'Da kine' being Hawaiian slang for 'whatshisname'), finishing with 'And somebody told me in the early '80s / You were gonna be the Next Big Thing', to which Franny responds 'Well now that was just a rumor / But I guess I'm doin' fine / Three weeks out of the rehab / Living one day at a time.' Ultimately, they're both in a depressing place, culminating in the line 'it's a shame about me' repeated twice, inferring that it's a shame about both of them.

They chat for a while, but 'the connection seemed to go dead', their lives have diverged so much that they have little in common anymore. As they're about to part, Franny suggests they go to her hotel to rekindle some youthful passion, but Don demurs.Maybe this is due to the self-pity he's feeling, but most likely it's because he needs to move forward, not back, eliciting the wonderful lines, 'Babe you look delicious / And you're standing very close / But like this is Lower Broadway /And I'm talking to a ghost.'

The song is reminiscent of 'Springtime' from *Kamakiriad*, Becker playing so well that they never got around to hiring a session guitarist or bassist. The easy pace is delicious, but the sadness seeps through in the horn sections.

'Two Against Nature' (Becker / Fagen) (6:17)

Becker said of the album's title track, 'It's about the songwriters' invocation of their own powers to overcome the natural and supernatural forces arrayed against them. They're offering to help their audience prevail in the face of all sorts of mysterious and frightening beings', the voodoo imagery conjuring up the mystical skill of the master songsmith. The 'Two Against Nature' are Walter and Donald, in a world of younger artists, still trying to come up with the goods in middle age – 'Two against nature tan and lean / Puttin' big heat on skanky things unseen'. Fagen: 'We made it the title because we thought it was descriptive of our condition at the present time. Because when you start to get older, you really are fighting nature all the time. And musically you're fighting nature, trying to organise the atoms of sound. You're trying to manipulate or overcome obstacles in nature.'

In the second verse, Erzulie is the goddess of love, the black hat a symbol of Baron Samedi, the spirit of death and debauchery, the song being full of Creole phrases and pronunciation, conjuring up the supernatural elements of Caribbean religion. There's a one-night stand, encouraged by Erzulie, the suggestion being that the night of passion is a mid-life crisis, but the next day, realisation dawns that it was a futile attempt to resurrect youth, and possibly, thanks to Samedi's way with such things, the woman you thought you'd slept with was actually a man!

The chorus of 'Two against nature don't you know / Who's gonna grok the shape of things to go / Two against nature make them groan / Who's gonna break the shape of things unknown' suggests that Donald and Walter understand (grok) where music is going and are here to save us from banal mass-media entertainment – 'Two against nature they got that stuff / Good things happening when you see about us.'

I love this song, it's unlike anything else in the catalogue, totally unique to my ears and I doubt anyone else could have pulled it off. It's wild and freaky, packed with weird energy and full of spectacular performances, particularly Fagen's vocal. From the rhythmic percussion and random sax squalls, we are off riding a wave of a groove, spiced with sunshine and magic. Keith Carlock's indefatigable rhythm is wonderful and the percussion adds to the atmosphere as it clips along, horns and guitar having their say. The band is on fire, frantic and spicy from start to finish. The songs from the last two albums recorded by the band have fared poorly in terms of the number of live outings, but this one has been played regularly over the last 20-odd years.

'Janie Runaway' (Becker / Fagen) (4:09)

The album's fourth single is a breezy number, like a summer day in the sun, strutting in on Leroy Clouden's hi-hat. Soundtracking the seduction of teenage Janie from Tampa, now 'the wonderwaif of Gramercy Park', by a seedy older guy with considerable available wealth, it's light and very dark all at the same time.

Fagen is furtively creepy, noting how lucky he is that 'Your dad went on that spree / Before the crew could put out the fires / You hopped a bus for NYC'. He good-naturedly mocks her naïveté and youthful outlook – 'Who makes the morning fabulous', 'Who says today's a fun day' and 'Who makes the traffic interesting', the words spoken in a juvenile tone, her energy reviving and energising him. They go to Dean & Deluca and buy 'a hearty gulping wine', probably to reduce her inhibitions while he cajoles her into acting out one of his fantasies; he's Frank Sinatra, and she's a showgirl he seduces in 1959 – 'Come to old blue eyes, tell me – who do you love?'

He suggests that they drive to his friend Binky's 'sugar shack' in Pennsylvania, considering whether taking Janie across state lines for immoral purposes would make it a federal case, hinting that she may be underage. He wants more and encourages her to bring along her friend Melanie, 'who's not afraid to try new things', the inference clear. The final chorus suggests that if she goes along with his sordid wishes, he might take her to Spain for her birthday.

It is always surprising how the depravity inherent in many of these songs sounds so innocent when set to such smooth and sophisticated music. The horn additions are perfectly placed and delivered, with slinky solos from Chris Potter, the purity of Carolyn Leonhart's backing vocals underlining Janie's innocence.

'Almost Gothic' (Becker / Fagen) (4:09)

This could be a love song to a younger woman with severe mood swings, which paradoxically makes her even more alluring. She's a Goth with blue-black eye make-up, hence the 'Sloe-eyed creature' description, her look severe, exciting and fascinating to him. He's in 'a dark place', emotionally bereft, she is his cure – 'She's pure science with a splash of black cat ... almost gothic in a natural way'.

He tries to convince himself that this is not simply lust and his 'house of desire is built foursquare' – but is she actually a hooker, 'the cleanest kitten in the city'? 'It's kind of like the opposite of an aerial view...' suggests that she's a dominatrix and he is tied up, looking at the ceiling, but possibly too tightly, 'so cut me some slack'. He's 'sizzling like an isotope', a great way to describe his excitement, in 'amen corner now' where the church's most fervent vocal exclamations can be heard, suggesting that she's giving him exactly what he wants. Finally, he notes his desire as 'L-U-V', rather than love, acknowledging that the attraction is predominantly physical.

Ted Baker's Fender Rhodes wafts us in, there's an insecurity, Fagen's voice fragile with spot-on support from Carolyn Leonhart and Michael Harvey. The snare rhythm picks up, like a raised heartbeat, and there's a Gothic quality to the horns, the muted trumpet solo from Michael Leonhart one of his finest, full of emotion, lugubrious clarinets adding depth.

'Jack of Speed' (Becker / Fagen) (6:17)

This finished version is transformed in tempo and key from the live debut on the 1996 tour, the first fruits of new labours, where it was sung by Walter. Here the intro is low-key with bass, guitar and electric piano before a strident horn riff kicks things off, repeated throughout the song.

The pace is easy in a discussion concerning a friend whose drug of choice boosts his confidence to become the centre of social situations, but ultimately he's 'skatin' backwards at the speed of light', his personality changing, subtly at first but then more noticeably, 'in a thousand different ways'. His use of right-wing rhetoric at a party offends the other guests, and with 'his new best friend at the throttle' he won't be the one to decide when the ride is over, 'moving on metal' like a runaway freight train, a 'one-way rider' with no return ticket.

The final verse is a poignant warning to his partner to get out before it's too late:

He can't hear you honey – that's alright
Pack some things and head up into the light
Don't stop – he'll be callin' out your name
But don't stop when you hear him plead,
You better move now little darlin' or you'll be
Trading fours with the Jack of Speed'

'Trading fours' being musical slang for an improvised duel between two soloists, four measures each, attempting to get one up on each other, and in the tone of this song, the partner will always lose.

Becker's guitar additions cut through nicely, a bluesy counterpoint to the jazziness of the horns, with plenty of space for an extended laid-back solo.

'Cousin Dupree' (Becker / Fagen) (5:28)

The breakthrough single from the album concerns a wannabe familial love affair. Another strange little tale, the detail makes it work, with a massive slap 'round the chops at the end. Could it be the only incest-light song to ever receive a Grammy?

Touring musician Dupree is back at his aunt's house, sleeping on the couch, where he notices that his cousin has grown into a highly attractive woman: 'She turned my life into a living hell / In those little tops and tight capris / I pretended to be readin' the National Probe / As I was watchin' her wax her skis'. While they are playing cards by an open fire, Dupree makes his move, pointing out that with his 'boyish charm and good looks', how can she resist him? The response is the ultimate put-down:

> She said maybe it's the skeevy look in your eyes
> Or that your mind has turned to applesauce,
> The dreary architecture of your soul,
> I said – 'but what is it exactly turns you off?'

The pace is relentless from the start with an upbeat bounce and key additions from Ted Baker's Fender Rhodes. Walter adds some sprightly soloing, and there's even a spot of whistling from Amy Helm, who went on to provide the same service on Fagen's cover of Al Green's 'Rhymes'. Despite being the biggest hit from the album, it has not been played live particularly often.

In 2006, a tongue-in-cheek post appeared on the Steely Dan website regarding how the premise for the Owen Wilson movie *You, Me, and Dupree* – about a house guest who outstays his welcome – was stolen from this song. Wilson responded in similar comic style: 'I have never heard the song "Cousin Dupree" and I don't even know who this gentleman, Mr Steely Dan, is. I hope this helps to clear things up and I can get back to concentrating on my new movie, *Hey 19*.'

'Negative Girl' (Becker / Fagen) (5:34)

On face value, a song about a compelling junkie girl, but this one is almost certainly about the drug itself – 'Deliciously toxic / The original classic thing', paraphrasing the old Coca-Cola strapline: 'She' is 'Coke', intoxicating, hard work, but fascinating, making the good times wonderful, and the bad times much worse. He knows that continuing will only lead to where it has previously; 'it's happening again ... I know she's ill, I'm cruising for a spill ... more of the same' – but he can't help himself.

The words have the clipped urgency of 'Green Earrings', after the first chorus she's crying on the phone – or is it a desperate call to his dealer, then 'I'm on the street again / Staggering out into the burn of the brain-dead dawn / To arrive in time to find her [the dealer] gone.' There's a reference to 'a doctor friend uptown' and 'maybe she gets to me when she comes back down'.

The song was recorded live on the second take, with no playing contributions from Becker or Fagen. It has an elusive quality and starts tentatively with Fagen singing in a high register. The backing is sparse but detailed, with key contributions from guitars, keyboards and drums, subtly provided by Vinnie Colaiuta this time. The chorus is a bit more focused, but the dream-like qualities return with the next verse. Dave Shank adds a delicious vibraphone solo, and after the final chorus there's some gorgeous jazzy ensemble playing with a superb fast picking guitar motif to the end fade.

'West of Hollywood' (Becker / Fagen) (8:21)

The longest studio recording In the Steely Dan catalogue, as a result of Chris Potter's four-minute sax solo at the end. The 'tick-tock' snare and bass drum rhythm from Sonny Emory continues right through, slide-rule perfect timekeeping.

Fagen said of the chorus: 'we started playing something and it reminded us of a chorus of a sort of reggae song we wrote in the eighties, and so we dug it up and we adapted it, you know, but we had to change a few things, but essentially we were able to use that idea fifteen years later', Becker pointing out 'We're very economical.'

Ted Baker's Fender Rhodes colours the intro, the opening lines setting the scene superbly: 'Brother in tears / Look at this chain of sorrows / Stretching all the way from here and now to hell and gone', going on to explain the characters, 'I was Kid Clean / She was Anne de Siecle / Just a thrill away from punching through to the cosmic wow', possibly on a wave of drug-induced euphoria. 'Anne' is a clever switch on the French 'fin de siecle', the end of the century, *Two Against Nature* appearing early in 2000.

Things started well for the two, 'But with a business like this / There's a gnarly downside' and 'the axis of pain/pleasure sheared the arc of desire'. It seems that as a result of an overdose Anne has gone: 'She reached out for my hand / While I watched myself lurch across the room / And I almost got there', another poignant and desperately sad image from Walter's life?

The story is told to a therapist, but the sessions don't work, 'You can't ask me to access the dreams I don't have now' and 'together we'll endure the tyranny of the disallowed', meaning the loss of his beloved, leading into the intriguing final verse:

Don't you love Port Blanc
When Hooterie is over
When the girls get easy and the crowds are gone
A weekend of bliss
Then the rainy season.

The balance is held between organ, Rhodes and acoustic piano, Becker adding distinctive guitar and a hard-edged solo. Potter's extended ending solo is unexpected but supported by some fine playing, particularly from Baker, the result is wonderful songwriting from a team at the peak of their powers.

Related Songs:

'Wet Side Story' (Becker / Fagen) [unreleased]
A regular in the set in 1996 for the 'Art Crimes' tour, but not played live since. It could easily have made the comeback album, it's groovy and confident, the backing singers do a great job and there's a sweet, laid-back solo from Walter.

'Cash Only Island' (Becker / Fagen) [unreleased]
Another number originally meant for *Two Against Nature* but not finished, again played a few times on the 'Art Crimes' tour. It's a compelling scratchy funk, courtesy of Wayne Krantz's guitar in the live version, and quite compelling, so a shame it wasn't completed.

'The Steely Dan Show' (Becker / Fagen) [unreleased]
Worth including here due to the shameless self-promotion. Played live in the early 2000s as the second-half intro after the intermission, without Becker and Fagen – 'So buy a program / And/or a hat / You don't pass up a deal like that'. The backing singers get a chance to shine with sax and guitar solos in the easy groove, encouraging the audience to 'Forget their troubles / In tasty riddum n' rime / So here you are / And now it's party time / Wrap your mind around this sound / And let the goodness ripple down. / Goodbye to Lonely Street / You're in the Catbird Seat / At THE STEELY DAN SHOW!'

Plush TV Jazz-Rock Party (2000)

Personnel:
Walter Becker: Guitar
Donald Fagen: Fender Rhodes, Lead Vocals
Ted Baker: Piano
Jon Herington: Guitar
Tom Barney: Bass
Cornelius Bumpus, Chris Potter: Saxophone
Michael Leonhart: Trumpet
Jim Pugh: Trombone
Ricky Lawson: Drums
Carolyn Leonhart, Cynthia Calhoun, Victoria Cave: Background Vocals
Director: Earle Sebastian
Producer: Joel Hinman
Recorded: Sony Studios (New York), Jan. 2000
Record Label: Image Entertainment
Released: 13 June 2000
Running Time: 102:00
Highest chart place: US –, UK –

The only other officially sanctioned live document of the band is *Plush TV Jazz-Rock Party*, a live video album recording for a PBS *In the Spotlight* special in 2000 at Sony Studios in New York, and subsequently released on DVD. It features fan favourites 'Green Earrings', 'Josie', 'FM', 'Bad Sneakers', 'Black Friday', 'Babylon Sisters', 'Kid Charlemagne', 'Peg' and '*Pretzel Logic*', plus five tracks from *Two Against Nature*, released shortly after this performance: 'Cousin Dupree', 'Janie Runaway', 'Gaslighting Abbie', 'Jack of Speed' and 'What a Shame About Me'. There's also additional documentary and interview footage, made more fun by having Donald and Walter asking questions of members of the band and others. It's a good record of the band playing live, albeit in a studio, well filmed and entertaining, the duo clearly more at home being recorded in a studio environment than in an actual full-blown stage performance, almost certainly driven by the quest for perfection and the requirement to show the songs in their best light.

Everything Must Go (2003)

Personnel:
Donald Fagen: Lead Vocals, Organ, Synthesizer, Piano, Hohner Clavinet, Fender Rhodes, Wurlitzer, Percussion
Walter Becker: Bass, Guitar, Lead Vocals, Percussion
Ted Baker: Piano, Fender Rhodes, Wurlitzer
Bill Charlap: Piano, Fender Rhodes
Jon Herington & Hugh McCracken: Guitars
Keith Carlock: Drums
Gordon Gottlieb: Percussion
Ken Hitchcock: Clarinet
Walt Weiskopf: Alto & Tenor Saxophone
Chris Potter: Tenor Saxophone
Roger Rosenberg: Baritone Saxophone
Tony Kadleck & Michael Leonhart: Trumpet
Jim Pugh: Trombone
Tawatha Agee, Ada Dyer, Michael Harvey, Carolyn Leonhart, Cindy Mizelle, Catherine Russell, Brenda White-King: Background Vocals
Producers: Walter Becker, Donald Fagen
Engineers: Tom Doherty, Roger Nichols, Dave Russell, Elliot Scheiner
Arrangers: Walter Becker, Donald Fagen
Record Label: Reprise Records
Recorded: Sear Sound; Skyline Studios; Bearsville Studio (all New York); Hyperbolic Sound (Hawaii), 2001 to 2003
Released: 10 June 2003
Running Time: 42:24
Highest chart place: US 9, UK 21

Following quickly on from *Two Against Nature*, Becker and Fagen returned to the studio to record *Everything Must Go*. Often derided as the worst Steely Dan album, I find this unfair. There's much to enjoy, and it has a charm of its own, another mature work that only struggles to compete because of the heights scaled by the rest of the catalogue. Fagen himself has commented that he considers it to be underrated. Ultimately, I think I like it in a different way to the other albums. It has more of a late-night vibe, at least to start with, more intimate than the widescreen vistas of their recorded past, and if anyone else had come up with this, it would be regarded more favourably. As always, the songs are great, every single note delivered with thought and consideration to get the best out of the material.

In contrast to their earlier work, the music was written to capture a live feel, no doubt inspired by the tours they'd clearly been enjoying in recent years. It is immediate, not as layered, yet still funky as hell with fewer session musicians than had become typical of Steely Dan albums: Becker played bass on every track and lead guitar on five, also singing a full lead vocal for the first time on a Dan studio album. Fagen added acoustic and electric piano, organ, synthesizers and percussion on top of his vocals, more instrumental work than at any time since the early days. Now regular guitarist Jon Herington is present and correct, as is Hugh McCracken and touring drummer Keith Carlock, all three playing on every track, Carlock having previously only appeared on the title track of *Two Against Nature*.

There was a different ethos for this album – rehearse the track all day and go for a take in the evening. Encouraged by engineer Elliot Scheiner they recorded it in 24-track analogue, which resulted in a very warm and, as you'd expect, immaculate sound.

Overall, the oblique and wilfully dense songs of the classic period are replaced with more obvious themes, the stories more clearly waymarked, but as with Donald's later solo albums, those stories are witty and well worthy of hearing, jazzed up with all the requisite Dan smarts. The band works as a whole, giving the jazziness or bluesiness of the songs, shape. Probably due to the faster than normal recording and vibe-based methodology, the songs may have a little less dynamic shift than previously, but when you have a band this good hitting the groove with pristine sound, it's a thing of beauty.

The cover image features a dodgy New York street salesman with a suitcase full of knock-off watches, more images of watches featuring throughout the artwork to underline the overriding theme that 'time's up'. The reverse holds images of Fagen and Becker, clutching keyboard and bass respectively, cut off at the neck, so one presumes it's them at least, with a standard portrait on the back of the CD booklet.

A two-disc CD and DVD edition was released, featuring the *Steely Dan Confessions* short film, 20 minutes of Donald and Walter riding around Las Vegas in the back of a taxi, promoting the album via conversation with driver Rita, in a special version of the HBO cable show *Taxicab Confessions*, picking up various young women along the way to continue the chat. It's fun if inconsequential but worth finding to have a look at.

In hindsight, *Everything Must Go* sounds like a full-stop album, bookended by songs relating to a once-successful business coming to the end of the road. It is unlikely that this was the intention, but as it has panned out, no further releases have appeared since. Sounding like it was telegraphing the end of their recording career, particularly in the words to the final song, that is what it ultimately proved to be. It does feel that this is the line from where Steely Dan moved to becoming a legacy act, rather than an artistic songwriting endeavour, with just the subsequent tours keeping still eager fans warm at night.

The Songs:

'The Last Mall' (Becker / Fagen) (3:36)
It's an upbeat blues, snappy as you like with walking bass and tasty laid-back guitar soloing from Becker. Fagen is immediately in good voice, and the bass sound is lovely, horns doing just what they need to, right up to the standard

blues ending of the missed last chord, completed by a vigorous drum roll from Carlock.

The words describe grabbing everything you need at the last minute in a pre-apocalyptic shopping splurge (''Cause in the morning – that gospel morning / You'll have to do for yourself when the going gets tough'). Don't wait, it'll be too late; 'You'll need the tools for survival / And the medicine for the blues / Sweet treats and surprises / For the little buckaroos' – the world's about to end, so make your final purchases, then 'Ride the ramp to the freeway / Beneath the blood orange sky'!

'Things I Miss the Most' (Becker / Fagen) (3:59)

Mournful horns and a bass pulse move into Carlock's snare. His kick-drum jabs you in the chest as the keys take a descending path and all is a little subdued as Donald tells us his least favourite things about being single after a recent split. He's alone and trying to make the best of it but missing the closeness and companionship. He has also been stiffed for a lot of the creature comforts, like the Audi TT, various salubrious properties, 'The comfy Eames chair / The good copper pans / The '54 Strat.' All is not lost, but there's irony in the fake enjoyment of his own company, cooking his 'sad cuisine' and 'curling up with a girlie magazine'. He's reduced to finding hobbies to occupy his time, learning to meditate and building a model of the *Andrea Doria*, a typically off the wall choice, being an Italian cruise liner that collided with a Swedish ship and sank in the North Atlantic in 1956, with the loss of 51 lives.

Occasionally wheeled out live, this song works a treat, it's typically funny, without being a comedy song, but at its heart, it's genuinely sad. Possibly based around Walter's divorce from Elinor in 1997, his beloved 1954 Stratocaster was also previously stolen. It's instrumentally lovely with momentum and a gorgeous chorus, all as beautifully arranged as you'd expect, particularly the horns, with the added small-group jazz of the rejuvenated band. Walter adds a great little guitar phrase to finish.

'Blues Beach' (Becker / Fagen) (4:29)

Not an easy song to get a handle on lyrically, there's a real spring in the step with an upbeat twang that drives it along very agreeably. Fagen's piano has a front-row seat and the bridge soars beautifully. Carlock is a human metronome, keeping the beat kicking to perfect time, Fagen locking vocals with Carolyn Leonhart in the fadeout.

The singer appears out of luck – and probably out of work – so heads, possibly metaphorically, to Blues Beach, where he can relax, 'Sizzlin' in the merciful rays' of the 'long sad Sunday of the early resigned.' Despite the upbeat nature, there's a bleak end, his luck doesn't appear to change and in the last chorus it becomes 'I'm dying / Freezin' in the merciful rays.'

I particularly enjoy the brilliantly out-there lines 'We could rent a paranymphic glider / My hypothetical friend / And we could sail / 'Til the bending end.' When asked about the paranymphic glider, Becker responded that it's 'an imaginary vehicle on which you would take an imaginary girl on an imaginary date.'

'Godwhacker' (Becker / Fagen) (4:57)

Hands down the best song on the album, it's one of my favourites in the catalogue. In Donald's book, *Eminent Hipsters*, he explained how the song developed from the anger he felt after his mother's death from Alzheimer's: 'It's about an elite squad of assassins whose sole assignment is to find a way into heaven and take out God. If the Deity actually existed, what sane person wouldn't consider this to be justifiable homicide?' Indeed, as all-encompassing and all-knowing, God was always going to be in the firing line; it would be hard to argue against him being guilty of some pretty heinous crimes against humanity, but we almost certainly deserve it.

Within a righteous Carlock groove, Becker adds driving bass and a whacking and light-fingered guitar solo, Fagen soloing on synth-harmonica. It's cutting in all departments, carried along on a repeated guitar phrase, right from the start with its *Book of Genesis* referencing 'In the beginning', but things have gone awry, from hangin' with God to putting a bounty on his face because of his bad attitude: 'For crimes beyond imagining / It's time to pay the price'.

The Godwhackers, aka 'The Rajahs of Erase', are on the case: 'We track your almighty ass / Through seven heaven-worlds / Me, Slinky Redfoot [the Devil] / And our trusty angel-girls', seeking their target (referenced as 'Daddy', 'Poppie' and 'Big Tiger' in the swinging lyric) – when they catch up with him it's going to be a case of 'Give the man some whackin' space / You know this might get messy'.

Whereas in 'The Last Mall' it's looking like the end of all things, 'Godwhacker' is 'the start of the end of history', possibly linking the two songs together, and tying in with the 'endings' theme. Becker and Fagen's regard for 'Godwhacker' is clear as it far outstrips the other songs from this album in terms of live performances over the last 15 years or so.

'Slang of Ages' (Becker / Fagen) (4:15)

From its sleazy intro, this song is as cringy as you can get, an older guy trying to pick up girls using the slang of yesteryear ('Tomorrow's for squares – tonight's for real'). Strangely, it doesn't work out for him. Walter puts on the character, gruffly speak-singing the words, suiting his limited range, and it's a strange diversion. Does it work? Well, yes and no. Fagen is the voice of Steely Dan, that was discovered early on, but I don't think he could have pulled this one off as well as Walter.

The bass is precise, the horns come in at just the right time, Walter supported by the backing singers in an expansive lift, Walt Weiskopf's jazzy tenor sax cutting through. The chorus is the complete antithesis of the awkwardness of the premise; it's a sublime uplifting lilt on a bubbling keyboard run. 'Drop me off in Groovetime' indeed.

'Green Book' (Becker / Fagen) (5:55)

After the slow-burn opening, there's a prowling slinkiness. It's a tricky one to decipher but Becker has said that 'We imagined a pornography beyond pornography – a pornography involving some sort of magical remote viewing. That flirts somewhere on the borderline between jealousy and intense arousal.' Fagen is at his most sleazy and it certainly has that fantasy element, the book seemingly being the catalyst to bringing various attractive parts together into a delicious 'Marilyn 4.0' package; in that way, it's a kind of precursor to virtual reality.

It's steamy and atmospheric, 'I tango down to the smoky lobby / My eyes adjust to the light', the new cashier taking him by surprise by looking like former Bond girl Jill St. John. It also seems to be a love song to NYC, 'this dirty city / This crazy grid of desire'.

One can only guess, but the comment regarding the music being 'anachronistic but nice' could possibly be self-deprecating. Carlock adds a sumptuous groove against Ted Baker's piano, bass providing an easy funk. Becker's guitar and Fagen's synth duet, and it is ensemble playing of the highest order.

'Pixeleen' (Becker / Fagen) (4:01)

There is just a great, a rolling drive to the rhythm, apeing the thrill of the chase, as our teen heroine Pixeleen, a Lara Croft-type heroine, evades the bad guys and fights wrongdoing. This is all in the head of her creator, who has to put up with her 'as-if boyfriend' Randall ('better keep it real – or whatever') and getting calls from her 'stupid' father telling her to be home by 10 – 'again'. Hearing Fagen do the teenage affectations is great fun.

It seems that a movie has been made of the character's heroic doings, as set out in discarded cartoon form by the real-life Pixeleen ('Dream deep my three-times perfect ultrateen'), but Don and Walt don't seem keen on the results: 'Soaked through on the floor of a noodle shop / Penned by a hack in the Palisades / Backed by some guys from Columbia / Shot all in digital video / For a million and change / ... / Pitched in a trailer in Burbank / Cast by a cool-enough yes-man / Screened at a festival in Utah.' Ouch!

This is a prime example of the scriptwriting, lyrical style of later work. The bass pumps things along with lovely featured vocals from Carolyn Leonhart and a tip-top chorus. There's also the understated piano by Bill Charlap and Walt Weiskopf's winning sax solo. The whole thing works like a dream, petering out to a beautiful finish.

'Lunch with Gina' (Becker / Fagen) (4:27)

On face value, it's about a stalker, a woman that won't take no for an answer, but 'Gina' is also slang for the recreational drug GHB, so this could well be a drug song, featuring such typical effects as paranoia, addiction, avoidance and physiological changes.

Looking at the more obvious interpretation, Gina is at the door...

That must be her again
She's leaning on my bell
That cold psychotic ring
The one I know so well.

How do you deal with that? 'I'm nailed to the floor in the no-option zone / There's about zero chance she'll give up and go home'. Gina is a psycho, but she's also very attractive, which is how he got involved in the first place: 'It started on the day I met her / Lunch with Gina is forever'. She's a bundle of energy, and on the next encounter he ducks into Nino's on the Upper East Side, knowing that she's barred, but when he leaves, thinking the coast is clear, she's there. He hides in his apartment, 'I crouch on the carpet / Not breathing just being'. It seems that the final verse is actually the start of their interaction.

It's another driving song, bass taking the strain and pushing things forward, with spot-on horn additions and a tasty synth solo from Fagen. The double-tracked chorus vocal is deliciously tight.

'Everything Must Go' (Becker / Fagen) (6:45)
The opening jamming section, led by Walt Weiskopf's mellifluous sax, is highly unusual in the Steely Dan catalogue, but here underlines the homogenous nature of the band, everyone together, playing at once, or so it would seem.

It settles down into a slow-paced song of resignation, of failure in business despite giving it your best shot. Rather than an announcement that the Dynamic Duo were about to re-hang their working capes back in the cupboard, it's a cynical dig at recklessness at the heart of big business, and the lack of any ethical view of the consequences. The 'store' is going out of business in the boom and bust as the dot.com bubble bursts, it's a song about losers who once rode high on the hog, complicit in fraud, false accounting, jobs for the boys and sexual misconduct (but there's still time for one more round with Miss Fugazy in the service elevator, particularly if Dave from Acquisitions has his Handicam with him), but now it's done and 'It's high time for a walk on the real side.'

It's a lovely bittersweet sound to end the album and the recording career of one of the most fascinating bands ever. The quality was always maintained, right from the start, all the way through to the final note. A more impressive body of work is surely impossible to find.

Morph the Cat (2006) (Donald Fagen Solo)

Personnel:
Donald Fagen: Lead & Background Vocals, Keyboards, Acoustic Bass (as 'Harlan Post, Jr.'), Vibraphone & Marimba (as 'Phonus Quaver'), Flute (as 'Illinois Elohainu')
Freddie Washington: Bass
Brian Montgomery: Remedial Bass
Keith Carlock: Drums
Gordon Gottlieb, Bashiri Johnson, Joe Pasaro: Percussion
Frank Vignola, Hugh McCracken, Wayne Krantz, Jon Herington, Ken Emerson, Ken Wessel: Guitars
Walt Weiskopf: Tenor & Alto Saxophone
Lawrence Feldman: Tenor Saxophone, Flute
Roger Rosenberg: Baritone Saxophone, Bass Clarinet
Marvin Stamm: Trumpet
Mark Patterson: Trombone
Ted Baker: Piano & Wurlitzer Electric Piano
Howard Levy: Harmonica
Jerry Barnes, Michael Harvey, Amy Helm, Carolyn Leonhart, Cindy Mizelle: Background Vocals
Camille Meza, Candice Predham, Eddie Jackson, Jennifer Battista: Handclaps
Producer: Donald Fagen
Recorded: Avatar Studios (New York), 2004 to 2005
Record Label: Reprise Records
Released: 7 March 2006
Running Time: 52:49
Highest chart place: US 26, UK 35

Fagen produced albums for Boz Scaggs and Phoebe Snow, but with some downtime after the *Everything Must Go* tour, he started work on the final part of a trilogy of solo albums. Where *The Nightfly* looked at adolescence and discovering a brave new world, *Kamakiriad* considered mid-life and the perils and fears common to that period, *Morph the Cat* is about getting old and, similarly to *Everything Must Go*, 'endings'. The writing process was shot through with trauma; the death of his mother in 2003, and the continuing fallout of New Yorkers dealing with the aftershocks of 9/11. Fagen has described it as his 'Death' album – 'It's about the death of culture, the death of politics, the beginning of the end of my life.'

Dedicated to Libby Titus, it's a sumptuous collection of varied songs, darkly political but also filled with the cheeky wit we've come to expect. The cover features a clearly-ill-at-ease Fagen in the workroom of his New York apartment. It looks comfortable, but I suspect he's more comfortable when he's there on his own with no one shoving a camera in his face.

As a change, Donald brought in harmonica for this album, but familiar faces abound, including drummer Keith Carlock, saxophonist Walt Weiskopf, bassist Freddie Washington, and guitarists Jon Herington, Wayne Krantz, and Hugh McCracken.

At the time of *Kamakiriad*, Fagen said he was losing his love of melody and getting more interested in rhythm, and that's obvious here; a big, stomping record, still with melody in spades, but rhythm is king. Fagen admitted to being more relaxed and comfortable musically, regaining energy and enthusiasm, this album being a beautifully produced treat for the ears.

Despite Donald and Walter contributing to some of each other's solo work previously, there was an uneasiness about work away from the band, Fagen saying 'We have this pseudo-manly thing where we don't want to play our solo stuff for each other. We work together so much, it's embarrassing playing something you've done yourself. It's like, "Sorry I wrote this without you."'

Morph the Cat was released on CD plus a CD/DVD-Audio 2-disc package, Elliot Scheiner winning a Grammy for the surround sound mix. Donald supported the album with his first solo tour, including a handful of Steely Dan songs in the set.

The Songs:

'Morph the Cat' (Fagen) (6:49)
The liner describes how 'a vast ghostly cat-thing descends on New York City, bestowing on its citizens a kind of rapture'. Morph's presence has an almost narcotic effect on the populace ('like an Arctic mindbath'), but are his intentions good? This is less than clear and, cats being what they are, there's probably mischief afoot. As Fagen put it: 'the cat is narcotizing the citizens. I observe it in people, this mind-death, these layers of brainwashing that's gone on for so many years. It's in the techniques of political machines, the unbelievable stupidity on television.'

So, is Morph an entity whose job it is to keep the people in line for the benefit of the powers that be? It does seem likely that the cat's name is a reference to Morpheus, the Greek god of dreams, keeping the populace sedated while the political elite go about their self-aggrandising business.

As Morph mysteriously envelopes the city (making time to enjoy a latte), the song is a journey through Manhattan, the horns almost replicating the sounds of traffic, Walt Weiskopf's sax soloing over the top as the noises of the city come together. There's a Christmassy feel ('without the chintzy stuff') within the uplifting harmonies that are warm and cosy, but it's all ultimately quite sinister. Described as a 'Rabelaisian puff of smoke', in reference to 16th Century French satirist Francois Rabelais, whose writing was known for its bawdiness, is Morph a cat of the people, an entertaining joy-bringer and rabble-rouser? Or is that just the public face as he distorts their reality...?

The last song written for the album, it's a great opener with thumping, steady as a rock bass from Freddie Washington and another superb Carlock groove. Donald is in fine voice towards the top of his range and the harmony backing vocals are beautifully tight. Jon Herington adds a sinuous solo before the final verse, brimming with restrained power, and overall this is a cracking start.

'H Gang' (Fagen) (5:15)

'The birth, life and death of a band in a nutshell. Let's hope The H Gang waxed some worthy sides as their story is ultimately mangled in one of the most hilariously bad films of all time.'

We don't know why Denise was serving an eight-month stretch, but prison time has offered the opportunity to plan her own rehabilitation via a musical juggernaut that will be 'slammin' out of Hinktown' to take the nation by storm. They mean business and won't be taking any nonsense: 'Get off the stage son / Unless you're ready for a kickfight.'

It's about recovery and how it's possible to pick yourself up and become a success – redemption through music again – although with a sting in the tail as the movie of the whole uplifting story turns out to be terrible. But it doesn't matter, Denise, the Gong Sisters et al get to blaze briefly but brightly and make people happy along the way, before fading back into the obscurity of 'normal life'. The first single from the album, it's big, bright and bouncy with an upbeat groove. From the lush introduction, Carlock's snare leads into some lovely wah-wah textures from Herington, piano punctuating the verses before the sumptuous close harmony chorus sweeps in, a thing of beauty. Donald delivers the tale in his inimitable style, and Weiskopf adds another soaring tenor sax solo. The bass has an unbelievable warmth throughout; the result is a finger-snapper that never falters, Herington returning to solo through the fade.

'What I Do' (Fagen) (6:01)

A tribute to one of Fagen's heroes: 'A conversation between some younger version of myself and the ghost of Ray Charles', but rather than quizzing Ray on his musical prowess, Donald is after tips from the great lothario on how to score with the fairer sex. The advice is simple: 'it's not what I know / What I think or say / It's what I do … It's what I major in', going on to say, 'I'm specially qualified / To keep them satisfied'. Thanks Ray, but that's not actually much help at all!

Ray does offer some comfort: 'Don, don't despair just take some time / You find your bad self, you're gonna do just fine.'

As always, the backing vocals are superb, and there's a bluesy soul stomp to proceedings, with room for an extended harmonica contribution from Howard Levy that keeps the down-home simplicity of it working. The Wurlitzer piano from Ted Baker is also excellent, with a nod to Ray's skills in that area, but Fagen doesn't contribute instrumentally.

It's a wonderful smouldering mood piece, right through the long fade-out, but possibly a strange choice for the album's second single.

'Brite Nitegown' (Fagen) (7:16)

From the crash intro and horror movie keys, it's a spooky affair with a superb contribution from the rhythm team. In fact, the snare shots are so sharp they could have somebody's eye out.

With a title derived from a favourite phrase of W.C. Fields, who referred to death as 'The Fellow in the Bright Nightgown', this is probably the best song on the album, a groove that really will not quit, with sparky additions from the horns and a typically unhinged guitar solo from Wayne Krantz. It has swing and drive. And it's about Death. What else could you want?

The chap in the titular bedroom attire appears in each verse, to spread a little love unto the unexpectedly soon to be deceased. The first is a case of natural causes from fever, the family saying a tearful goodbye as Big D lingers at the window. The second verse ramps things up as a guy is whacked while getting money from an ATM, murdered by a couple of crack heads who 'do the steal and leave me to deal / With the fella in the Brite Nitegown'. Finally, death by your own making, in this case, drugs: 'Ten milligrams of Chronax / Will whip you back through time / Past Hebrew kings – and furry things / To the birth of humankind. / I shared in all of nature's secrets / But when I finally came around / I'm sittin' on the rug gettin' a victory hug from…', yep, you got it.

You've got to go some time, but with a groove of this magnitude, it would be a hell of a send-off. Marvellous, a thing of wonder and darkly funny with it. The extended repetition at the end possibly goes on too long – but at least you can continue to groove. I defy anyone to stay still to this.

The odd little brass trills at the end are genius. There's so much going on that it should be too dense. It's not.

'The Great Pagoda of Funn' (Fagen) (7:39)
This is a strange one. On face value it's a dreamy song for lovers who 'attempt to shut out the harsh realities of life' – 'The stars are bright tonight / The air is sweet' – but it takes a turn to the macabre, inspired as it is by sabotaged oil pipelines and news broadcasts of beheadings in Iraq. This is a highly politicised album, probably more so than any other in the Becker and Fagen catalogue, a reflection of the post-9/11 world in which it was written.

'The Great Pagoda of Funn' (the spelling meant to be 'sort of bogus Oriental') sounds like a great place to be, but it's dark outside and it wouldn't take much to break the spell of the smitten: 'We're one thoughtless word away / From poison skies / And severed heads / And pain and lies'. The lovers have to keep things right in their own small world, to build a life together in the pagoda, because if they fail 'Then these walls will fall away / And we'll find we're in the realm / Of psycho-moms / And dying stars / And dirty bombs', all ending with a plaintive 'Please follow me and hold me tight'. We all need someone to hold on to in these very troubled times.

There's plenty of space, and the mix is warm and clear. A strong lead vocal from Fagen, he does strain a little here and there for the top notes, but there's no disputing the emotion he delivers. He's superbly supported by the horns and another wonderfully idiosyncratic solo from Wayne Krantz, with vibes from our old friend Phonus 'Fagen' Quaver. Marvin Stamm provides a beautifully dextrous and suitably embracing mute trumpet solo with Ted Baker's piano adding jazz textures. It's a lovely song, languid and calming, stylishly delivered but with a particularly disturbing message. Fagen's music always sounds sweet, but taking that as the whole picture does the man's words a disservice.

'Security Joan' (Fagen) (6:09)

We've all been there. Waiting around at the airport and trying it on with the gun-toting security personnel. Must happen a lot.

This breezy pop stomp is the antidote to the boredom and anxiety of departure lounges, a big bass and piano strut featuring 'A sweet interlude at Laguardia: travelling man and airport security babe "meet cute"'.

Let's bask in its wonderfulness: having set off the x-ray machine, Joan calls Don to step behind the screen – 'And when I felt the wand sweep over me / You know I never felt so clean'. With an aside of 'Search me now!' Don suggests that they 'won't find my name on your list / Honey you know I ain't no terrorist'. Having held back to deliberately miss his fight, Don's back at the checkpoint, 'Just one thing on my mind'. There's been a minor change of plan, 'I'll be stayin' for one more night'. Everything is, indeed, gonna be alright.

It's as beautifully delivered as you're going to expect, no one can tell a tall tale like Fagen; the detail, the quips, the delightful cheekiness. Again, Ted Baker's Wurlitzer piano is sublime, with a '60s Booker T edge, and there's a nice guitar solo from Ken Wessel. The breakdown during the fade-out is just great and I'd like to have heard more of it.

'The Night Belongs to Mona' (Fagen) (4:18)

A song for a reclusive and depressed insomniac 'concerning some morbid business on a high floor, perhaps our girl will find a reason to live (or an effective anti-depressant) before it's too late.'

This song is so well observed and eloquently set out: 'A child of the night / When she goes out / It's only for bare necessities.' High in her apartment, she comes alive after dark, 'When she's dancing all alone / Forty floors above the city / CDs spinnin' / AC hummin' / Feelin' pretty.' But what changed 'that sunny girl we used to know'? Was it 'the fire downtown' on 9/11, or being let down by some guy, or any number of other things? How is it going to end, 'Will she fall hard / Or float softly to the street?'

It's a bleak vision of life getting on top of someone and heading out of control, either from a catastrophic event or a seemingly never-ending run of smaller happenings. There doesn't seem to be anything that can be done, it's all dependent on Mona and the feelings in her head. Hopefully, it all ends well, but if this were real life...

The stilted guitar picking sets a tone, again harmonica from Howard Levy and trumpet from Marvin Stamm are prominent, but as with all these songs, it's the warmth of the ensemble playing that rules. There was never anything clinical about the search for perfection in Becker and Fagen's world.

'Mary Shut the Garden Door' (Fagen) (6:29)

The most sinister song on the album: 'Paranoia blooms when a thuggish cult gains control of the government', the 'cult' being the worst excesses of the Republican Party after they held their convention in strongly Democrat NYC. The atmosphere is reminiscent of George Orwell's *1984* – big brother is watching.

The arrangement is filled with foreboding. Freddie Washington's bass is deep and resonant, a warning of the perils ahead, over skittering beats. Fagen takes a Melodica solo to the close – his only one on the album – and it's unsettling in its simplicity, the reedy instrument set against immeasurable power and influence.

A dark end to what has been quite a bleak album in many ways. Now, where's that cat...?

'Morph the Cat (Reprise)' (Fagen) (2:53)

Watch out! He's back, stomping through NYC with his rich harmonies in a brief coda. Jon Herington and Frank Vignola trade guitar solos and it all ends perfectly with a plaintive trumpet phrase from 'I.G.Y.' – 'Blessed Yankees have an ally / When this feline comes to bat', and blessed are the good folk of NYC to have the erudite wit of Mr Fagen in their midst.

Related Tracks:

Bonus tracks, from *The Nightfly Trilogy MVI* Boxed Set:
'Rhymes' (Al Green / Mabon Hodges) (4:22)

Is that Donald whistling!? Sadly not, it's backing singer Amy Helm.

This is a fantastic version of the Al Green classic, produced by and featuring Todd Rundgren (on backing vocals and keyboards) in an almost note-perfect remake. Funky, sassy and fun with some wonderful Wayne Krantz guitar and Donald adding a rip-roaring vocal, clearly sung from the heart and with more grit than we're used to. The drums and keys intro hits the whistling section and it smoulders for a while before kicking off on a funky strut. The horn additions and backing vocals are spot-on, lifting it all to the stratosphere. Excellent.

'Hank's Pad' (Live)' (Henry Mancini / Fagen) (4:48)

A lovely big band jazz cover of Henry Mancini's 'Session at Pete's Pad', originally recorded for the *Peter Gunn* soundtrack in 1959. Fagen's version as a tribute to Mancini, adding a swinging lyric to the end, hence the writing credit, and re-christening it 'Hank's Pad'.

'Viva Viva Rock 'N' Roll (Live)' (Chuck Berry) (2:42)

A high-energy Chuck Berry cover, played as the finale of the live shows, Fagen is on fine form here, and the band is smoking, Wayne Krantz a force of nature as usual.

Circus Money (2008) (Walter Becker Solo)

Personnel:
Walter Becker: Vocals, Guitars, Bass
Keith Carlock: Drums & Percussion
Jon Herington, Dean Parks: Guitars
Ted Baker, Jim Beard, Henry Hey: Keyboards
Larry Goldings: Organ
Luciana Souza: Pandeiro, Background Vocals
Gordon Gottlieb: Percussion
Chris Potter: Tenor Saxophone
Roger Rosenberg: Horns
Larry Klein: Bass
Carolyn Leonhart-Escoffery, Kate Marokowitz, Cindy Mizelle, Windy Wagner,
Carmen Carter, Tawatha Agee, Sharon Bryant, Sweet Pea Atkinson, Sir Harry
Bowens, Terry Dexter, Franki Richard, Tiffany Wilson: Background Vocals
Producer: Larry Klein
Recorded: Avatar Studios (New York); Market Street (Santa Monica); B&C Studio,
2007 to 2008
Record Label: 5 Over 12 / Mailboat Records
Released: 10 June 2008
Running Time: 59:59
Highest chart place: US 20, UK –

Not one to take things too fast, it was 14 years before Walter completed his
second, and as it turned out final, solo album, Becker slyly noting the 'unique
career strategy'. In the intervening years, there had been two Steely Dan
albums and a solo from Fagen, plus a number of tours, so he hadn't been
completely out of it. From the mid-2000s, Walter's life changed again. He
divorced and moved back to New York, still returning to Hawaii now and then
to recharge. He now enjoyed live performance more, thanks to the improved
sound systems available. The 2006 'Steelyard "Sugartooth" McDan and The
Fab-Originees.com Tour' featured the likes of Jon Herington, Keith Carlock,
Roger Rosenberg, Carolyn Leonhart and Cindy Mizelle, who all appear on
Circus Money. The 'Heavy Rollers' tour followed in 2007 with dates in North
America, Europe, Japan, Australia and New Zealand, their widest-ranging tour
to date, with a scaled-back 'Think Fast Steely Dan' tour in 2008 before Becker
finally had time to release the album, produced by Larry Klein and inspired by
his love of Jamaican music.

With the exception of the title track, all the songs were co-written with Larry
Klein. Three years in the making, with the title coming from a skit on Gandhi
by American comedian Lord Buckley and cover depicting a traditional Alaskan
Yup'ik face mask, the sound is a move forward from *11 Tracks of Whack*.
Becker seems more comfortable with the singing, having sung live regularly
in recent years, and it is probably a more rounded album, idiosyncratic words

mixed with quite sparse structures, taking plenty of influence from jazz and reggae – 'I'm fascinated by that deep, spacious groove of dub that speaks very directly and profoundly to the nervous system.'

Klein was more than a little nervous about writing with Becker, but the results are a testament to both their skills, full of memorable songs with wonderful – and often cutting – lyrics. Klein encouraged Walter to play more bass and also to curb the volume of his singing, with pleasing results on both counts. Carlock and Herington turn up on every track, the backbone of the band alongside Walter's guitar and bass. Also present are saxophonist Chris Potter and Dean Parks, who adds guitar to three tracks. Becker briefly considered getting a live band together, but ultimately nothing came of it.

The Songs:

'Door Number Two' (Becker / Larry Klein) (4:34)
There's immediately a jazzier feel to this album when compared to *11 Tracks of Whack*, piano in the forefront with a sax solo from Chris Potter. The backing singers have a larger role, starting the vocals on this one, and Walter, sounding deliberately fragile, adds character to the words. The rhythm is basic with stabs of guitar for colouring. It takes in gambling, on fruit machines and cards, with a smoochy slinkiness that is quite appealing, although low-key for an album opener. Potter's sax gets to dance around in the fade.

'Downtown Canon' (Becker / Larry Klein) (5:38)
A twinkly dreaminess infiltrates the intro here, drifting into an easy reggae lilt with electric piano as Walter imparts real emotion into 'We found the loft on Greene Street, swept that bad boy out / Alsatian wine, playing records way past four / Making some crazy soulful love on the hardwood floor.' There's a reference to Dizzy Gillespie in the second verse, the tale of a lost idyll of love tangibly heartfelt as 'You met that half-crazed painter fool in some damn bar / Cocaine dreams and chiba-chiba nights / You had to share his world in shades of black and white.' The 'Downtown Canon' of the title appears to be the law of the streets ('Keep it real, it'll be OK'), the parting shot of 'I'm leaving with all I need but less than I deserve' particularly cutting, set against the warmth of the song, with its beautiful backing vocals and instrumentation. Walter puts in a great vocal, accenting the bitterness of his regret.

'Bob Is Not Your Uncle Anymore' (Becker / Larry Klein) (4:46)
More dub in the reggae on this one, it's the swaying rhythm that's important and it's no pastiche, Carlock locking in with Becker's bass, the deep echoes giving an otherworldly edge. The keys and guitar are understated and it's all about the rhythm. The imagery of 'there's an ocean full of midnight rolling right up to the door' is almost breathtaking, and lines like 'Before Bob was

not your uncle anymore' throw you sideways, trying to decide where in the timeline we currently lie.

It seems that things aren't what they were, now that Bob has gone, this deceptively simple song carrying much weight in the sparseness of the arrangement. Has the prodigal son returned years later, 'Uncle' Bob, who created the problem in the first place, now out of the picture?

'Upside Looking Down' (Becker / Larry Klein) (4:09)

From the odd rhythmic start, which continues through the track, there's a laid-back ache as a former success finds himself down on his luck, the chickens of his former misdemeanours coming home to roost. The falsetto chorus is unexpected as Walter croons 'And O, the hero in disguise / Believing his own alibis / You run so scared, you're standing still.' There's a lovely Dean Parks solo with a country tinge that adds to the subdued atmosphere. The backing singers make another important contribution and the arrangement is lovely, particularly the electric piano at the end.

'Paging Audrey' (Becker / Larry Klein) (6:49)

Electric piano ticks like a clock counting out time, it's a sultry night-time look for more lost love. Hurtful words were said, and Audrey is gone: 'Can I stand right here? Call them back and say / Those were never meant to be heard that way / Let the heavens crack, let the day go black / I'd give anything.'

The pace is relaxed and steady until Chris Potter adds a couple of jazzy solos, almost out of place but working well in the framework of the song. Walter is very good at songs like this, the world-weary voice maintaining dignity and holding the passion within, only hinting at the true depths of his despair.

The song itself was almost a self-imposed challenge by Becker that took more than 30 years to realise. His girlfriend in the early '70s, Audrey Thaler, had noted the lack of songs about Audreys; Becker finally delivered.

'Circus Money' (Becker) (4:16)

With a militaristic beat, Carlock is at the centre of this one, getting louder towards the end, with additional keys and guitar setting the scene for Walter's more forthright vocal. Again, it's a beautifully arranged but almost fragile song, plenty of air and room to breathe, Chris Potter soloing after the second verse. The jazzy vibe is there but held in check.

It seems to be a childhood reminiscence of a visit to the circus with his father, the child trying to keep up with the walking pace ('Little Walter's got a ways to go'). In typical Walter fashion there's 'You watch some hobo take a nasty spill / Laugh like a bastard oh you know you will', but towards the end it all seems somewhat darker somehow, and overall it is something of a metaphor for life itself.

An instrumental dub version was released as part of the 'Somebody's Saturday Night' single package.

'Selfish Gene' (Becker / Larry Klein) (4:39)

Selfish gene – Gigolo or biological building block? You decide!

A self-obsessed sexual chancer tries it on wherever he can to see what he can get ('Hey, pretty baby, let's have a little fun / The Pinot is flowing and the night's still young'). He has the gift of the gab but only in the pursuit of his self-serving needs ('what a prize you are? / Honey don't you scratch my new car'). As the evening ends, Gene's real nature hovers into view as he says 'so long' to his short term companion – 'Take a dollar from the drawer / Daddy's got a whole lot more', the following chorus tying the liaison up tightly ('Selfish Gene needs clarity and closure / This is his house and that's your cab'). Becker likened Gene to Jive Miguel from *Gaucho*'s 'Glamour Profession'.

With the title coming from Richard Dawkins' 1976 book on evolution, the biological side seems to come in with '(Why) must every time I turn my ship around? / Some bastard come and knock my skyline down?', an angsty Walter complaining about the vagaries of his selfish genes. Perhaps.

It's cheeky stuff, bouncing along on an easy beat. Coming in on a strange little fairground rhythm, the reggae struts along as Gene goes about his business, female voices take the chorus as Walter fills the verses with colour, adding tasteful guitar accents and a funky solo in the second half. The drums are rock steady with keyboard stabs and chords taking it forward. The middle-eight is a lovely diversion, and overall it works a treat.

'Do You Remember the Name' (Becker / Larry Klein) (4:15)

The verses spell out questions over four lines, building in additional information as it goes 'Do you remember the scene … The scene of the crime of a love?' The next verse considers the time, it was spring; 'The year was the spring of our ruin.' There seems to have been an affair, but it's not clear who was involved, although the suggestion is of a woman who uses her men and casts them off without a thought.

Swept in on a wave of Carlock drums, and a snare that just rings throughout, it's an easy rolling rhythm with dub keys, drums and guitar. Carolyn Leonhart shares the chorus vocals with Walter, Jon Herington adding a wicked echoed slide before a multi-tracked female vocal choir. Very nice.

'Somebody's Saturday Night' (Becker / Larry Klein) (4:30)

Goings on in a pick-up joint, hints of the salacious details therein and the great line 'She looked good in the available light', but things go awry, and it seems that no one is quite getting it the way they like it. The reggae is back with this one, skanking along nicely with Becker's energetic vocal, it slides into a sweet chorus with backing female harmonies. Ted Baker adds some jazzy asides on his keyboards and Walter takes a jaunty solo. Fun and bouncy.

'Darkling Down' (Becker / Larry Klein) (5:05)

Spooky keys lead into this one, and it's a strange but beautiful song with some wonderfully obtuse lines: 'Well, there's a coffee shop right 'round the corner /

The proprietor knows my name / Cup of Joe and a Vicks inhaler / Now you're ready for the big boy game.'

> Who will feast on this buzzard's banquet?
> Who will render my heroic bust?
> Who will choke on my lachrymose musings?
> Who will eat my zero dust?

The reggae vibe remains, and it's a compelling groove, opening out into a great chorus, with support from keys and the female vocals. Larry Goldings' organ makes itself known in the second half and through to the fade, the arrangement for this song again exemplary, with Becker in fine voice and showing his literary smarts, should that be necessary, by lifting the title from Samuel Johnson's *The Vanity of Human Wishes*, published in 1749.

'God's Eye View' (Becker / Larry Klein) (6:03)
Bubbling keys lead into a ska beat, the call and response vocals between the backing singers (all nine of 'em) and Becker are very effective. Things stretch out in the chorus, and it's a great little skank with unexpected bass clarinet from Roger Rosenberg. Herington is on point to keep everything moving on Carlock's clinical snare, and the keys from Ted Baker and Jim Beard are particularly good.

Lyrically, there are a lot of words in this one, and a great listen they are too, Walter playing off the pithy statements from the crowd vocals with two lines of detail in an overview (the 'God's eye view') of a failing relationship. When you're in the trenches you can't see all the detail on the map, but with a wider frame of view the ultimate (and grim) destination is all too clear:

> (Bad luck)
> There are no surprises
> When the best laid plans go bust
> (Deal with it)
> In the glaring absence
> Of anything you could trust.

But the best lines are probably '(Mind meld) / Like a permanent picture / Of your pussy print in cement', which I would never have thought of!

Walter's love of chess returns with 'It's the God's eye view / Baby, it's the queen and the rook / Chasing one lonely pawn', and it all ends badly with:

> (He says)
> Me and her went walking
> By the river on Friday night
> (He says)
> And we started talking

And she says you know it don't seem right
(She says)
After all that's happened
And I end up with a prick like you
(Too bad)
Well, it's too bad darlin'
And there's nothing for a man to do.'

I love it, this is a fantastic song that clearly shows the powerful writing that Walter always brought to the Steely Dan table, each couplet picked for maximum impact, and underlining what a superb album *Circus Money* is.

'Three Picture Deal' (Becker / Larry Klein) (5:28)

Another Dan-related movie song and the piano intro is pure Hollywood, as a musician uses his actress girlfriend to access some lucrative soundtrack action: 'Now a man like me should never be / Where a man like me does not belong / But I know they're gonna need a soundtrack / I know they're gonna need a song.' As usual, the words live and breathe: 'Here she stands in the doorway / Her face is framed in golden light / With creamy thighs and bedroom eyes / Call it, "Urchin with an appetite."'

The keyboards again feature centrally, Herington's guitar just working the rhythm, until a very brief solo. Roger Rosenberg is back with his bass horn, and it gives a smoochy sophistication.

If anything, the chorus lets it down slightly, it's too repetitive and not quirky enough, but it's well-delivered with strong and smooth backing, and the rest of the song works fine. Ultimately, it's an OK way to finish the album, but certainly not the best one here, although the piano and organ in the fadeout are lovely.

Related Tracks:

'Dark Horse Dub' (Becker / Larry Klein) (6:46)

The bonus track for the international release is a strange one, starting with echoing dub sounds and sinister guitar chords. Walter shares the vocal with Carolyn Leonhart. Keith Carlock adds skittering reggae patterns and the brass section has plenty of space with fine hook phrases.

It has a smouldering aura, and lyrically it's very sparse, revolving around Chalk Miller and Jimmy Fish gambling on horse racing. Unusually, most of the printed lyric is unsung, the remainder giving the barest framework upon which to hang the story in your head. The brass hook almost has a Celtic feel and Roger Rosenberg's bass horns lock in with Jim Pugh's trombone to really make an impression, the music weighing down on the listener like a glowering cloud. It seems that no one will be a winner in this one.

Sunken Condos (2012) (Donald Fagen Solo)

Personnel:
Donald Fagen: Lead & Background Vocals, Piano, Keyboards, Synth Bass (as Harlan Post), Rhythm, Vocal & Horn Arrangements
Michael Leonhart: Trumpet, Flugelhorn, Keyboards, Vibraphone, Percussion, Accordion, Background Vocals, Drums (as Earl Cooke Jr.), Vocal & Horn Arrangements
Jon Herington: Acoustic Bass, Lead, Rhythm & 12-string Guitars
Walt Weiskopf: Alto & Tenor Saxophones, Clarinet
Charlie Pillow: Tenor Saxophone, Clarinet, Bass Clarinet, Bass Flute
Roger Rosenberg: Baritone Saxophone, Bass Clarinet
Jim Pugh: Trombone
Carolyn Leonhart, Jamie Leonhart, Catherine Russell, Cindy Mizelle: Background Vocals
Lincoln Schleifer, Freddie Washington: Bass
Joe Martin, Jay Leonhart: Acoustic Bass
William Galison: Harmonicas
Gary Sieger, Larry Campbell, Kurt Rosenwinkel: Guitars
Antoine Silverman: Violin
Aaron Heicke: Bass Flute
Producers: Michael Leonhart & Donald Fagen
Engineers: Michael Leonhart, Charles Martinez
Recorded: Candyland; Hirsch Studios; Sar Sound; Avatar; Audio Paint; Stratosphere; Pat Dillett's Studio, 2010 to 2012
Record Label: Reprise Records
Released: 16 Oct. 2012
Running Time: 44:07
Highest Chart Place: US 12, UK 23

Fagen contributed keyboards to Martha Wainwright's *I Know You're Married but I've Got Feelings Too* in 2008, and in 2009 Steely Dan embarked on the 'Left Bank Holiday and Rent Party' tour of Europe and America. Stand-alone dates were interspersed with multi-night theatre shows where performances covered full albums in their entirety, including *The Royal Scam*, *Aja* and *Gaucho*. 2010 saw Fagen tour with the Dukes of September (a reworking of the New York Rock and Soul Revue), featuring Michael McDonald, Boz Scaggs and members of Steely Dan's live band, covering songs from the repertoire of each of the principals. The project continued until 2012, interspersed with Steely Dan's 2011 'Shuffle Diplomacy' tour, which saw dates in Australia and New Zealand.

On 10 April 2011, Roger Nichols died of pancreatic cancer at the age of 66. Having worked on every Steely Dan album, his contribution to the band over the years, and particularly during the classic era, had been immense, and it is almost certain that they wouldn't have reached the heights that they did without him. He had lectured and written prose and articles for audio magazines for many years, eventually completing a textbook on recording techniques, which was published posthumously.

Sunken Condos, Fagen's fourth solo release, the first outside the *Nightfly* trilogy, was released in 2012, its name coming from a subversion of the title of a favourite Debussy piece, 'The Sunken Cathedral'. As of 2019 it's the last Steely Dan related release, and it's a wonderful collection of stand-alone songs that shows that Donald still has the skills and willingness to pull together incredibly crafted music and skewed tales. He takes in regular themes, like older guys dating younger women and the perils of being with a free-spirited and often irrational partner, plus unexpected diversions, including a tender song about bowling with a tragic denouement, mobster violence, depression and even collecting memorabilia from nuclear test sites and now vaporised tropical islands. It's quite a ride – typically odd and typically Donald, delivered with immaculate precision, one of my favourite collections in the catalogue, a mature masterwork and not to be overlooked.

Again, no Walter here, but Donald utilises later period Dan stalwarts Jon Herington and Michael Leonhart to fantastic effect. In fact, Leonhart is pivotal to this record, co-producing and adding keys and vocals, as well as his trademark trumpet, but it is the drum work, under the pseudonym 'Earle Cooke Jr.', that takes the biscuit – wonderful stuff with a dancey groove.

Donald is in good voice throughout and widens his instrumental palette a little with string bass and violin making appearances, plus harmonica for the second album in a row. The arrangements are fabulous, the harmonies as tight as expected, and the songs, especially when you really dig into them, well worthy of repeated attention.

Fagen later considered his worldview in *Eminent Hipsters*, which followed *Sunken Condos* in 2013: 'I guess I'm someone for whom youth still seems more real than the present or the half-century in between. And why not? I'm deeply underwhelmed by most contemporary art, literature, music, films, TV, the heinous little phones, money talk, real estate talk, all that stuff. The Internet, which at first seemed so fascinating, appears to be evolving into something even worse than TV, but we'll see.'

The Songs:

'Slinky Thing' (Fagen) (5:12)

Featuring twangy acoustic bass, courtesy of Joe Martin, 'Slinky Thing' is indeed slinky, by name and nature. This is another song that pairs older gentlemen with desirable younger women. Unlike 'Hey Nineteen' where the guy knows that they have nothing in common, here he draws his elixir of youth from her energy – 'She smile (There's a sun in my sky) / She laugh (That's my power supply)'.

Each verse features a different chapter of their relationship – and at each stage a passerby is warning him that he needs to 'Hold on to that slinky thing'. The guy eventually worries whether she does indeed need someone her own age, but ultimately deciding that he needs to try and keep hold of her, even though he knows it can't last for long.

It's a slinky funk start to finish and an engagingly slithery way to start the album, Michael Leonhart's drums keeping everything tight. Vibraphone highlights add to the lighter than air feel, and there's a deliciously gorgeous guitar solo from Jon Herington after the second verse that teeters delicately.

The repeated phrase 'More Light!' from the backing singers in the bridge comes from the German poet Goethe, who supposedly uttered the words on his deathbed – the last words of a dying old man.

'I'm Not the Same Without You' (Fagen) (4:31)

There's a pumping energy to this one, the flip side of the opening track, the protagonist feeling released and rejuvenated once out of a relationship. After the horn fanfare intro, Harlan 'Fagen' Post's beautifully thumping synthetic bass keeps the momentum going amid Leonhart/Cooke's spectacular groove, Don realising that 'I'm evolving at a really astounding rate of speed / Into something way cooler than what I was before'. He's stronger, his mind is sharper, he's even grown an inch and the shape of his face is changing – 'What in the world is going on? Please tell me...' He delights in the fact he can now hold his breath for 'a really long time' and has '...eyes to see / Some other destiny / A futurescape of brighter dreams / In which I bring off heroic escapades.'

William Galison's harmonica solo, with oh so Dan horns behind, adds colour to the second half in an unusual way. The horn arrangements are lovely, sparingly delivered with pinpoint accuracy whenever they have the most impact. Donald's piano is even more sparse but, as usual, the clarity keeps it in focus.

'Memorabilia' (Fagen) (4:14)

This is an odd one – a sunny tropical sway with a dark centre, reminiscing the early days of Cold War nuclear weapons testing, namechecking the Ivy King test from 1952 (the US's largest pure fission bomb) and Castle Bravo at Bikini Atoll in 1954 (their biggest thermonuclear device). Note the lyrics, 'There WAS an island...'

Louis Dakine seems to have been in the services and stationed on the islands in question at the time of the tests, the memorabilia being his collection of photos and relics from those days ('Souvenirs of perfect doom'), probably common for many of those who bore witness. The gas centrifuge is not something that crops up in lyrics very often, so savour its presence. Could Louis be related to Bobby Dakine, mentioned in 'What A Shame About Me' from *Two Against Nature*?

Michael Leonhart's muffled trumpet has a mournful tone throughout, beautifully supported by the other horns and Gary Sieger's guitar, the spacey organ sounds giving a subtle '50s sci-fi feel.

'Weather in My Head' (Fagen) (5:29)
A pure blues, and rendered with astonishing clarity, that cleverly equates
weather variations as a result of climate change with depression – 'the weather
in my head' – namechecking Hurricane Katrina and Al Gore's environmental
stance, climate shift ultimately being what will sink the beachfront condos of
the album's title. The words mention 'Four old hippies drivin' in the rain',
possibly a reference to the Four Horsemen of the Apocalypse who will no
doubt be on hand at the time of ultimate global disaster.

Donald is highly skilled at singing the blues, his in-built sense of rhythm
working a treat in this kind of song. The horns ebb and flow but Jon Herington
rules on this one, peeling off solos all over the place and ringing out emotion.

'The New Breed' (Fagen) (4:35)
Another Old Dude/Young Chick song, but this time Donald loses out to the 'new
breed', maybe it's a follow on to 'Slinky Thing'? It seems that the newcomer has
been upgrading her tech (!) and they hit it off, the song featuring fragments of
a conversation and the incumbent's thoughts as realisation dawns that he's lost
her to the younger man ('are you trying to hide that special glow?'). It's over: 'I
get it, you look at me and think, he's ready for Jurassic Park. / He's sweet, but it's
time to find a keener spark' and he becomes resigned to the situation ('I guess
that you're what she wants now / You're young and strong, and you own the
night / Good luck to you both, I'll get along somehow'), but with a sting as he
leaves her to her 'new dot-com-slash life' with the tech guy.

String bass, this time from Jay Leonhart, and harmonica reappear in a light
stepper with lots of space for things like horns to swing in and out. It's upbeat
despite the overall sadness of the situation for our hero.

'Out of the Ghetto' (Isaac Hayes) (4:54)
An unexpected – and pretty straight – cover of Isaac Hayes' 1977 strutter, it
works a treat here as an uptempo kick after the last number. Set a step higher
than the original and running a bit shorter, it's big and funky yet delivered
with knowing jazz in the way only Donald can. Michael Leonhart and Freddie
Washington lock into the groove, with unusual textures coming in from
Antoine Silverman's scratching violin, also adding some Eastern European
Jewish vibes at the end, and the lugubrious solo lines of Charlie Pillow's
clarinet, alongside organ stabs and Herington's edgy guitar.

Giving the song an interracial spin, the blatant 'I took you out of the ghetto /
But I could not get that ghetto out of you' sees Donald addressing an African-
American woman that he lusts after. However, once she's had a drink she
loses her graces and reverts to her roots – and he kind of likes it ('don't you
change... stay the same').

'Miss Marlene' (Fagen) (4:43)
This is a lovely song – and one of the few you're going to hear about bowling.
Starting with a gorgeous and suitably rolling electric piano before the groove

kicks in with a deep bass. There are bowling references aplenty, Miss Marlene clearly being a prodigy of the sport, able to roll with the pros 'whether straight or hammered', and at her best when the stakes are high ('The ball would ride a moonbeam / Down the inside line').

Herington again adds a bluesy air with his sparing guitar and the backing vocals and horns shine. As is common in Dan related songs where things appear to be going right, one night Marlene is upset by a boyfriend and runs into the path of a speeding taxi, which proves fatal, as confirmed by Fagen: 'Well, because when someone dies young, they're preserved for all time in their youthful state. She was a sensitive girl, she was unlucky in love, and she kind of lost it there and there was a terrible taxicab accident, and, you know, shit happens, right?'

The bowling continues without her, but her buddies clearly miss her company at the lanes 'every Saturday night', but with an air of the film Ghost, after she's gone 'Sometimes on a league night / I catch her scent again / Her hand guiding my hand / We drop the seven-ten.'

This being the wacky world of Steely Dan, alternative theories suggest this song as being a metaphor for either oral sex or drug-taking. Bowling. It's about bowling. Probably…

'Good Stuff' (Fagen) (4:54)

This is a slow-burning firecracker: a fantastic escapist romp through prohibition-era mob violence against a pumping rhythm. Peppered with slang, the lyric to this is wonderful, the music matching it slug for slug – quite literally at times.

The lead character arrives at the boss' office, 'tired and tight' after a night of fighting with his girlfriend. He's late but there's a 'beef with a small concern we must liquidate'. The gang cab it down there, the targets are 'all loungin' in the lobby, and we do what we come to do'.

It's a bloody spectacle – 'Lotsy goes down easy, Moe takes it in the face, Weinburg brothers run for cover, squirting metal all over the place', but the work gets done and 'there's a special satisfaction when a job comes off so right'.

There's an authentic '20s feel to it all: his girlfriend is in chorus at the Ziegfeld Follies, but she's running hot and cold, so it's good to get your orders and hijack a liqueur convoy, delivering the gains to the illicit speakeasies, 'All that bubble, no trouble, whole crew gets to dip their beaks'.

But after a hard night doing his boss's bidding, when he gets home she's with 'that punk Johnny Rome'. Not a wise thing to do: 'So I popped the both, and I ankled downtown / To a hop-house in the Tenderloin, need to kick that gong around'.

It's a breathless caper, shot through with darkness, sinister piano stabs and wah-wah guitar setting the atmosphere. The groove is superb, and Fagen knows instinctively how to work the words into it, he's a master at this kind of thing. Vibraphone and harmonica again make distinctive appearances.

'Planet D'Rhonda' (Fagen) (5:35)

A wild free spirit who's hot to handle – but he just loves getting burned. She's unpredictable and craves attention, the irrational side driving him to distraction, but like 'Slinky Thing', she's his energy, his 'vitamin xyz'. She loves to dance, 'when she does the Philly Dog – I gotta have CPR!'

Rhonda wears unusual clothes ('She put on a dress last night made of plastic wrap / It was off the hook – crazy sweet') and this good-time party girl is on her own in her own world where 'you got to be a mind reader just to guess her mood'. She's not the sort to take home to Mom, 'but when you need big lovin' / She never stops / Yes it's Monkey Time – twenty-four-seven', so no major complaints there then!

It's another slinky strut to end the album, exuding the confidence that Rhonda has in spades, the individualistic feel reflected in Kurt Rosenwinkel's unusual and very effective bubbling guitar solo.

Live 2013 – 2017, Becker's Death & Beyond

Donald has said, 'It's great to know that our old stuff still sounds good to our fans, just as it's wonderful to think that we've turned a few people on to jazz over the years', and the live dates continued with the 'Mood Swings: 8 Miles to Pancake Day' tour in 2013. This included an eight-night run at the Beacon Theatre in New York. The 'Jamalot Ever After' US tour of July to September 2014 was followed in 2015 by the 'Rockabye Gollie Angel' tour, with Elvis Costello as the opening act. 'The Dan Who Knew Too Much' tour in 2016 saw them tour with Steve Winwood, and Steely Dan appeared at The Hollywood Bowl in Los Angeles with an orchestra.

Through this period Walter showed a reluctance to go back into the studio so the duo never quite got around to any serious writing for a follow-up to *Everything Must Go*, the seeming finality of that release possibly becoming more appealing to them as time passed.

The 'Reelin' In the Chips' tour saw a 12-date residency in Las Vegas in April 2017. Around this time Fagen co-wrote and sang on the anti-Donald Trump 'Tin Foil Hat' from Todd Rundgren's *White Knight* album. Becker's final show with Steely Dan was on 27 May 2017 at the Greenwich Town Party in Connecticut. He pulled out of the Classics East and West concerts in July, at Dodger Stadium, Los Angeles, and Citifield, New York, with the Eagles and the Doobie Brothers, replaced by Larry Carlton for the shows. Fagen embarked on a tour that summer with a new backing band, The Nightflyers, comprising up and coming young musicians.

On 3 September 2017, Walter Becker died of complications from oesophageal cancer. In a press statement, Fagen eulogised his friend and partner, promising to 'keep the music we created together alive as long as I can with the Steely Dan band.' He honoured prior commitments to perform dates in October, in the US and three shows in the UK and Ireland as part of the Bluesfest double bill with the Doobie Brothers, a mic stand left empty in Becker's place in tribute, the band performing his solo song 'Book of Liars' with Fagen singing lead vocals.

Walter's contribution to Steely Dan cannot be underestimated. The songs would never have come out the same, in fact, they would never have come out at all without him. As a duo, he and Fagen complemented each other beautifully while working from the same page, having plenty in common but bringing different things to the table. On stage, he was usually one of the band, Donald upfront singing these crazy little songs, but off-stage he was the more confident of the two, more comfortable in interviews and happy to talk, adding an easy flow of sardonic lines. His death put a final nail into many fans' hopes that another studio recording would appear, but at least we're left with what is, in my view, an unparalleled catalogue of songs, in terms of quality control, attention to detail, delivery and pure enjoyment. The irony is that this most cynical of bands refused to fleece their fans with substandard material, unlike just about every other major band you could name. When you consider that *Gaucho* was their contractual obligation album, it speaks volumes.

Walter's estate has subsequently released a number of previously unavailable solo recordings and videos for fans of his work to enjoy (via www. walterbeckermedia.com), but shortly after Becker's death, in a very sad turn, his widow and estate sued Fagen, arguing that they should control 50% of the band's shares. Fagen filed a countersuit, arguing that the band had drawn up plans in 1972 stating that band members leaving or dying relinquish shares of the band's output to the surviving members, a case that he finally won.

In December 2017, Fagen said that he would rather have retired the Steely Dan name after Becker's death and toured under a different name, but he was persuaded not to for commercial reasons, and again, having turned 70, he took the band out on the road in 2018 for the 'Summer of Living Dangerously' tour.

Postscript

It's a quite warm Thursday night for February, and I'm in Manchester to finally get to see Steely Dan in the flesh. It's an emotional evening, Walter now gone, but having been unable to get to any of the band's previous trips to the UK, this could be a one-shot deal. With excellent support from Steve Winwood and his band, the MEN might not be crammed full, but is certainly well-attended, the audience vocal and up for a good time. The Steely Dan Band do not disappoint, Donald leading an eleven-piece outfit through a set comprising entirely '70s material, hitting a number of home runs in the process. This is a crack band in anyone's language, and they deliver this wonderful music with aplomb amid an excellent sound, Fagen conducting from the front. His voice may not be what it was, but he is the still-beating heart of these songs, and we can forgive that, the trio of backing singers filling in the gaps and supporting sensitively where required.

Bookended by covers, it really is a great performance. The band is electrifying, and by describing them as the 'Steely Dan Band', Fagen legitimises the possibility of an official entity playing these wonderful songs after he decides that touring is no longer for him. But for the moment he's still here, allowing all of the band space in the limelight – and what a band it is. Keith Carlock nothing short of amazing, start to finish, Jon Herington putting his own spin on the classic solos, the bass, the horn section, the backing singers and Jim Beard's keys.

A wonderful evening made all the more poignant by the lonely mic stand where Walter Becker should have been.

Appendices

Becker & Fagen's Early Recordings: 1968-1971

Early demos started appearing in the '80s after Kenny Vance licensed an album of them to Aero Records, much to Becker and Fagen's annoyance as they were never intended to be heard publically, noting that the releases came about via 'some greedy little record people'.

However, despite the basic nature of many of the songs, there's gold for the serious Dan fan, the quality of the songs shining through and underpinning the high levels of writing attained throughout their career. These songs feature the likes of Denny Dias and Kenny Vance, with singer Keith Thomas, from Dias' band Demians (which Becker and Fagen took over and subverted to their own ends) and drummers John Discepolo (from Jay and the Americans) and John Mazzi, plus an early appearance from Elliott Randall.

There are 28 tracks available, some in alternative versions, and a number of unofficial releases cover these songs. The *Catalyst and Legends Collection* (which purports to be a Steely Dan 'best of') albums have all 28 tracks (*Catalyst* with an additional version of 'Sun Mountain'), *Android Warehouse (The Early Years)* and *The Collection* cover 22 songs, *Art Crimes* eighteen, *The Origins and The Root of Steely Dan* seventeen, *Sun Mountain* sixteen, *Beat the Bootleggers, Beginnings* and *Berry Town* fourteen each, and several albums with fewer. It is worth noting that the *Roaring of the Lamb* compilation of seventeen songs features additional instrumentation, supposedly recorded in a German studio in 1978 by persons unknown, so are not completely original recordings, drums, bass, guitar, piano and even background vocals added.

There will almost certainly be other tracks out there somewhere, but here is a run-through of the ones that I am aware of, in alphabetical order.

'A Horse in Town' (Becker / Fagen)
A bitter song about someone reluctantly putting an end to an unhealthy relationship, bringing in New York lowlife environs familiar from later songs. It's not the best quality but you can tell that the song itself is more than worthy. There's a soulful blues feel as it moves along at a fair clip, with decent harmonies and a country-esque guitar solo that suggests Jeff Baxter but is, in fact, Denny Dias. Keith Thomas takes the lead vocal and John Discepolo drums.

'A Little with Sugar' (Becker / Fagen)
A simple solo piano piece with Fagen's already impressive vocals, augmented by Becker and Kenny Vance in the straightforward but well-rendered choruses, where Fagen gets the chance to freestyle. It's jaunty and upbeat, displaying a sophistication that points to later work, seeming to be a fictionalised reminiscence of Becker's memory of his family (with particular reference to his mother) – 'Years ago I tried to tell her / What was in my heart / But she was part of the city',

dissipated from a viewpoint years down the line ('As if it mattered anymore').

The verses are where hints of the future emerge, descriptive passages such as 'I recall her tailored jersey / And the flowers that she wore' in the first and the enigmatic tone of the second ('All the years that she was with us / You could count them on one hand / I was taken with her showboat style / But too young to understand / She was all alone / Ahead of her time'). Whatever the interpretation of the second part of the song, it's a powerful piece driven by Donald's voice and a quality melody.

'Android Warehouse' (Becker / Fagen)

A tale of pure science fiction, again piano-led, but more driving this time on a simple drum track (from Kenny Vance). The assured vocal stands out. Again, the second half is enigmatic, 'Did you really gobble up / The things they claimed you ate? / Were you fit to swallow it / Or scared to clean your plate?' Walter again helps with the choruses, the repeated high pitched 'That you're alive' bits are a little odd, and slightly wobbly, but this is a demo after all.

'Any World (That I'm Welcome To)' (original version) (Becker / Fagen)

This later turned up on *Katy Lied* in 1975. The instrumentation is very basic, tinny-sounding organ to the fore with bass, mainly from the keyboard. It's sung by Donald with some different lyrics, which gives it a different spin. Similar in structure to the finished version, this is a good way of hearing the stripped-back approach without the bells and whistles added in the studio. The little yelps are a bit strange though!

'Barrytown' (original version) (Becker / Fagen)

Before appearing on *Pretzel Logic* in 1974, this original demo sees Donald in full Bob Dylan mode, supporting himself on piano. It's nice, if a little wayward in the vocal department, and certainly doesn't have the impact of the finished version, but the piano playing is great, and it's a fine song none the less.

'Brain Tap Shuffle' (Becker / Fagen)

A slightly tongue in cheek introduction to a prospective new dance craze which will help you 'Lose your mind / You'll see the oceans part / You'll think your goin' blind', so there might be a hint of recreational lubricant in the vicinity, Fagen's *Eminent Hipsters* semi-autobiography suggesting that there was some LSD experimentation going on around this time.

It's a great slice of early Becker and Fagen, a nice band piece with twangy electric guitar (from Dias), steady rhythm, and good harmony vocals, smacking of late '60s hippy hedonism. There's a rather nifty instrumental break too, and an early stab at commercialism and the capitalist mindset in 'If making money doesn't soothe your mind / We've got something here, here for you'. The lead vocal is shared between Fagen, Becker and Keith Thomas, with John Discepolo on drums.

'Brooklyn' (original version) (Becker / Fagen)
Piano supported by organ with simple electric guitar, drums (from Discepolo) and bass support, Donald's voice gives it a different spin from the completed *Can't Buy a Thrill* version that David Palmer sings. The quality of the song is apparent even in the demo, plaintive and melancholy with a stately melody. There's a very nice guitar solo too, from Elliott Randall, and overall this is a lovely version, performed with taste and care.

'Charlie Freak' (original version) (Becker / Fagen)
This one is strange, almost a barrelhouse piano boogie to start. The structure is similar, but the chords are different, and it lacks the power of the masterful final version from *Pretzel Logic*. It's a little wayward vocally, Walter's contributions limited, but there's still something about this song and I'm glad they dug it out of the briefcase for one more turn around the block in 1974.

'Come Back Baby' (Becker / Fagen)
The early material features more traditional songs of romance than became the norm, including this one which has a typical late '60s sound with a funk edge, particularly to the guitar. There's a full band and the sound points towards future developments, with very nice harmony vocals and a lovely chorus that gets under your skin. The more sardonic elements are starting to creep in too; 'I can't say thank you for a kick in the head / But I need you just the same.'

John Mazzi plays drums, and there's some tasty guitar soloing from Denny Dias, in keeping with the rest of the song. It seems to have been recorded towards the end of the New York period and is a lot closer to later work than some of the other demos and would probably have been a more worthy introductory single for Steely Dan than 'Dallas'.

'Don't Let Me In' (Becker / Fagen)
The strutty blues-funk of later work appears here, sliding into a smooth verse. Piano is again at the front, but it's a full band arrangement with good vocals. There's a rolling quality, the rising scale at the end of the chorus a nice addition. It's relatively simple but a real toe-tapper that is hard not to like, with drums again from John Mazzi. There's another extended guitar solo from Dias, and it swings along nicely, relating a relationship gone bad.

'I Can't Function' (Becker / Fagen)
Saxophone makes an appearance on this soulful jazz number, including a solo in the second half, and the vocal harmonies, from Becker and Vance, are very good. With Dias' guitar and Mazzi on drums, it's another song where the guy's girl done gone left him, and he knows that he needs to sort himself out. The melody is very agreeable, and this would have been a no-brainer to release in other, less exacting hands. The 'Drinking dinner from a paper sack' line later reappeared in 'Daddy Don't Live In that New York City No More' from *Katy Lied*.

141

'Ida Lee' (Becker / Fagen)

Bass-heavy with a lovely rolling guitar figure, its typical '60s motif feels familiar. The arrangement is stripped back; guitar, bass and drums from Vance, with Donald often speaking the words. It appears to be Walter providing both guitar and bass, all very steady and not deviating much. There are elements of 'Josie' about this one, a party being thrown for Ida with 'The hooters and the hats', but it gets a lot steamier towards the end. There's also 'The man from the skyway', an early reference to themes of 'Trans-Island Skyway' from *Kamakiriad*?

'Let George Do It' (Becker / Fagen)

The *Faciat Georgius* ('Let George Do It') was an ironic unofficial medal awarded to members of the US Marine Corp on Guadalcanal during World War II. The design was a hand extended from a Navy uniform sleeve dropping a hot potato to an entrenched Marine, the reverse showing the rear-end of a cow with an electric fan blowing across it, symbolising shit hitting the fan.

Keith Thomas takes the lead vocal (with Fagen backing him) in this sneery, swaggering song, bemoaning the amount of crap being dished out to this particular individual. Walter plays bass with Dias on guitar and Discepolo's drums.

'Mock Turtle Song' (Becker / Fagen / Lewis Carroll)

When asked in a late '80s interview whether they ever wrote a complete lyric and then set it to music, Walter commented, 'The only time I remember doing that was back in the Sixties when we set a Lewis Carroll poem ['Lobster Quadrille'] to music. But even then, we didn't have a melody. It was kind of an improvised melody.'

It reeks of psychedelia, from the undulating marimba-like percussion and guitar figure, and the harmony vocals – this could only have been put together in the '60s! It's an anomaly, even within the early demos. The guitar solo is cool though, sounds a little Becker, but is actually Dias, who also adds percussion. Walter sings the lead with Fagen and Keith Thomas joining him for the chorus. With Discepolo on drums, it's a fun toe-tapper from an unusual source.

'More to Come' (Becker / Fagen)

With Fagen at the piano and singing lead, Walter sings back-up alongside the higher-pitched contribution from Kenny Vance, who also provided the basic drums. It's a jaunty little number, upbeat, but with an unusual melody line and an enigmatic lyric – 'The kids have torn a yellow packet apart / Ain't that enough to break a rich man's heart / I see the rats have found the cradle again / I'll let you know if I remember when.'

'Oh Wow, It's You Again' (Becker / Fagen)

An introspective and sad song of lost love, a relationship that has ended painfully, but the ex-lovers unexpectedly bump into each other: 'Oh Wow, it's you again / You haunt me / You taunt me / Why don't you disappear?'

This is lovely, stripped back with just Fagen's piano and subtly basic drums from Vance, Walter singing back-up. Donald sings in a higher than usual register, heartfelt and sad, it would have been great to hear a finished version.

'Old Regime' (Becker / Fagen)
A commentary on the turbulent political situation of the late '60s. The strident drums (from Disceplo) and bass opening leads into a light and airy guitar solo from Dias with a jazzy edge. Keith Thomas' vocal also has a jazz feel, Fagen joining him for the chorus – and that's when it sounds more like a Dan song. Unusually, there's almost a vocal fugue later, the whole thing upbeat and full of energy with some lovely chording from Fagen's piano.

The choice of wording is very strange, pointing to the style of later work. Some examples: 'I saw their eyes, their chests, their secret smiles', 'Overrun the great placenta' and 'There in the breadbox / Cheese in the mouths of babes is fine with me.' There seems to be unrest in the streets and looting is suggested in 'Who got the bottles? / Who got the ladies' fashions and the tray? / Did you get the radio? / Did you get the princess' collar?' I particularly enjoy Thomas' pronunciation of the title line, which often sounds like 'The Aubergine'!

'Parker's Band' (original version) (Becker / Fagen)
Another basic and stripped-down version of what would later become a popular album track, Kenny Vance on drums, Fagen's rolling piano and excellent lead vocal with Becker backing him. The structure of the final version is all there, and it's amazing how they can still deliver the song in this basic setting, no sign of Fagen's reluctance to sing and he already has the distinctive quality that sets Steely Dan songs apart – great stuff.

'Roaring of The Lamb' (Becker / Fagen)
There's a portentous opening, and the chorus is successfully epic. Vance drums, Fagen leads on piano and echoed vocals, Becker again backing him. The organ addition on the 1978 studio reworking by persons unknown is very sympathetic and works well to fill the track out, but the original has a power of its own, mainly coming from Fagen's vocal performance.

The words are again quirky and filled with strange characters and unusual phrases: 'There's a fight reported in the wash-dry / Smart Eugene refused to share his moon-pie' and 'Red Kimono torn and soaked in salt spray' is a lovely line.

'Soul Ram' (Becker / Fagen)
The light and airy feel breezily ignores the inherent meaning here. Becker and Fagen remained tight-lipped about most of their cryptic and often unsettling lyrics, this one being a case in point, but from the words, it wouldn't be a stretch to make it about 'pegging' – anal sex in reverse where the woman uses a strap-on to penetrate the man. This interpretation is backed up by the duo's first use of the words 'Steely Dan', of course, taken from William S. Burroughs'

dildo in *Naked Lunch*, the book also containing a depiction of pegging. It's bright and fun, riding on Discepolo's drums, Fagen's piano upfront with lead vocals from Keith Thomas.

'Stone Piano' (Becker / Fagen)
A rolling groove with an unorthodox melody, the harmonies are a bit wayward and would have been further developed no doubt, but the basic song is an easy listen, Fagen putting in a laid-back vocal, the music piano-focused with basic drums from Vance, backing vocals again from Becker. The verses are neat, and the chorus is catchy, but I've no idea what the significance of the stone piano is.

'Sun Mountain' (Becker / Fagen)
The meaning revolves around addiction, being 'Strung out and downhearted', but the mood is joyous. There are two versions of this song, one with just Fagen's piano and vocals, the other with Vance on lead, Fagen, Becker and Keith Thomas backing him, with Discepolo's drums and Becker's bass. It's stately and laid-back, but with real beauty and it would have made a gorgeous finished item.

There's a deep sense of happiness within, a warm and welcoming enlightenment upon finding Sun Mountain, but there's also a sadness, which gets right to the heart of what addiction actually is: 'No eyes of my own / That could take me through the nighttime / No moonlight to guide me / No shadow to hide me'. Mystical and optimistic.

'Take It Out on Me' (Becker / Fagen)
Just Fagen's piano and vocals, showing great touch with both. The chorus is lovely and it's a plaintive and fragile song. It seems that one of the parties in a relationship is having a hard time, the other absorbing the punishment so that they can both get to the other side together. That could make it another drug song, the junkie getting relief from his habit via a cold-turkey intervention. A moving song and another gem among the early demos.

'The Caves of Altamira' (original version) (Becker / Fagen)
Just piano and voice, with some echo, it's sparse, but the bones of the finished version from *The Royal Scam* shine through, a different intonation seeping in at the end of some of the lines, Walter joining in for the chorus. There's an additional verse where the secret location is discovered and devalued as a tourist attraction, this song more than the other re-recorded numbers showing how pieces developed from their humble beginnings into sophisticated later works.

'This Seat's Been Taken' (Becker / Fagen)
Another early song with a traditionally romantic outlook, or is it? The future may not be rosy: will she be waiting at the next station, ready to take her seat next to him, or has she gone for good? Alas, we'll never know.

Fagen sings and plays piano, with Vance on drums and Walter playing guitar this time. The vocals are a little off, and the song is quite lightweight compared to some of the others.

'Undecided' (Becker / Fagen)

Sung by Keith Thomas, it's an attempt at a 3-minute pop song, the protagonist in a love/hate relationship and unsure which way to go: 'I love you / Go away / I hate you / No please stay / I want you / I'm so undecided.'

There is more of a band feel to this one, featuring Discepolo on drums with Dias' guitar, Fagen's piano, Becker's bass and excellent harmony vocals filling out the sound. It's mid-paced with a definite '60s sound, particularly from the duelling guitar lines, there's also a bit of acoustic in there.

'Yellow Peril' (Becker / Fagen)

Some early Eastern inspiration, but the title and 'finer minor from China' lines are wincingly cringy, and it's all a bit clumsy. The song features Josie, as the at-home sweetheart of our exploring hero Ambrose – the same Josie who got a song of her own on *Aja*?

'On an island of gleaming rock / Jutting up from the blue lagoon' Ambrose finds a ceremonial music box, 'And from it flowed, a bright new mode / That made our hero swoon.' He returns home to civil unrest, but the sounds from the musical box enchant the warring parties and bring peace.

With some Beatles influence in the verse, Kenny Vance drums and Becker plays guitar, with a nice touch, while Fagen provides piano and lead vocals, although he struggles for some of the falsetto.

'You Go Where I Go' (Becker / Fagen)

Another pretty straight forward song of love. There's positivity in lines like 'I can't complain about the pain and the heartache', but hurt and 'tears when your kisses disguise the lies.' Ultimately, he needs her and 'My eyes don't see / And what do I need to know / As long as you go where I go.' There's a sadness at the heart of this song, in a bare arrangement of just Fagen's tinny keyboards and slightly wayward voice, with Becker's bass supporting.

You've Got to Walk It Like You Talk It or You'll Lose That Beat (OST) (1971)

Produced by Kenny Vance and released on Spark Records, this soundtrack is a prototype for the recognisable Steely Dan sound that would later develop, featuring Fagen's keyboards and vocals (on three tracks) and Becker's bass alongside guitar (and percussion) from Denny Dias, drummer John Discepolo and some lead vocals by Vance. The film itself involves a young hippie and his search for the meaning of life in Central Park. Upon the film's release, on 19 September 1971, a review in the New York Times didn't mention the music but considered the film as 'the latest example of youthful, charming iconoclasm that appears to be losing some of its charm', concluding that it 'projects lots of walking and talking but precious little heartfelt beat.'

The Songs:

'You Gotta Walk It Like You Talk It (Or You'll Lose That Beat)' (Becker / Fagen / Peter Locke) (2:47)
Co-written with writer/director/producer Peter Locke, the title song is sung by Donald, in a very odd Randy Newman-esque style, with his electric piano, Discepolo's drums, Becker on bass and Dias' twangy guitar. It's catchy and funky, strange but fun. Not the best of the early songs, but the chorus is great, all ending in a garbled conversation over a piano and guitar vamp.

'Flotsam and Jetsam' (Becker / Fagen / Vance) (3:25)
A jazzy instrumental jam, it sounds a bit like 'Chest Fever' from The Band's *Music from Big Pink* – only tinnier, with Fagen on organ, Dias' guitar and the rhythm section of Becker and Discepolo.

'War and Peace' (Discepolo) (1:33)
This instrumental is a brief drum solo written by John Discepolo with dissonant piano chord accompaniment.

'Roll Back the Meaning' (Fagen / Becker / Dorothy White) (3:39)
Sung by Kenny Vance, this is a great song, upbeat and with purpose. Denny Dias adds a lovely electric guitar figure before the harmony vocals and Fagen's electric piano come in. The rhythm is steady, and the harmonies nailed. This is a smashing toe-tapper with a hippy vibe. Fagen's girlfriend Dorothy White has a writing credit for helping with the words.

'You Gotta Walk It Like You Talk It (Reprise)' (Becker / Fagen / Peter Locke) (0:37)

A brief reprise of the title song, as you might expect, but with added twangy mouth harp and tomato splat at the end!

'Dog Eat Dog' (Fagen / Becker) (3:36)

Nicely rocking with an R'n'B vibe, Fagen sings strongly alongside his electric piano. Dias' guitar rips it up while Discepolo and Becker attempt to keep it nailed down. The chorus harmonies are again very good, and it's a nice number that kicks along pleasantly. Dias gets a solo which he delivers with plenty of confidence and overall, it's a song that should be more widely-heard.

'Red Giant/White Dwarf' (Becker / Fagen / Kenny Vance) (7:47)

Piano opens into a stately guitar and organ section in a very good 7-minute instrumental with a strong melody and good work from Walter. Co-written with Kenny Vance, Dias is in fine form, with Fagen, Becker and Discepolo supporting well. A mature work delivered at an early stage, supporting its length nicely.

'If It Rains' (Fagen / Becker) (6:52)

Vance sings this one – and very well too – a slow-burning semi-epic with a bit of country and a hint of Crosby Stills Nash & Young that builds to some nice crescendos. Fagen's piano, supported by synth and electric piano, is to the fore with sterling work from Discepolo's drums.

Official Compilations

Greatest Hits
Record Label: ABC Records
Date of Release: 30 Nov. 1978
Highest Chart Place: 30 US, 41 UK
The first hits collection, and it's a good one. A double vinyl album of 18 tracks from the first six albums, up to and including *Aja*, plus the previously unreleased 'Here at the Western World'. A handy collection of most of the obvious hits.

Steely Dan
Record Label: ABC Records / Nippon Columbia
Date of Release: 1978
Released in Japan, only seven tracks (so rather pointless) and not chronological, but notable as the only album release to feature both sides of the 1972 debut single 'Dallas' and 'Sail the Waterway', although in mono as they were sourced from a copy of the original single.

Gold
Record Label: MCA Records
Date of Release: 1982
Highest Chart Placing: 115 US, 44 UK
Effectively a 'Vol. 2' of the 1978 compilation, containing tracks not included on that and covering *Gaucho*, plus the 'FM' single, the original eight track album originally came with an additional 12" single with 4 additional tracks. The album was reissued in 1991 with extra tracks, oddly including 'Here at the Western World' that had previously appeared on the 1978 *Greatest Hits*, the 1974 live take of 'Bodhisattva' and Fagen's 'Century's End' and 'True Companion' solo tracks. The version of 'FM' was also changed from the original to the one with saxophone solo ending.

A Decade of Steely Dan
Record Label: MCA Records
Date of Release: 1 Jan 1985
Highest Chart Placing: 122 US, 100 UK
The first compilation for the CD era, it covers all of the band's Top 40 singles to that point, with the exceptions of 'Josie' and 'Time Out of Mind', so is a pretty good overview of the obvious tracks. The version of 'FM' is original from the soundtrack.

The Very Best of Steely Dan: Reelin' In the Years
Record Label: MCA Records
Date of Release: 1985 / 1987

Highest Chart Placing: – US, 43 UK
There are actually two versions of this album – same name and cover, different track listings, but all pretty obvious choices with plenty of crossover. The 1985 double LP has 18 tracks, with 14 on the 1987 CD.

Remastered: The Best of Steely Dan – Then and Now
Record Label: MCA Records
Date of Release: Nov. 1993
Highest Chart Placing: – US, 42 UK
A good 16 track CD overview, the obvious tracks with no surprises.

Citizen Steely Dan
Record Label: MCA Records
Date of Release: 14 Dec. 1993
Released for the Christmas market in December 1993, the entire '70s album catalogue in a handy 4CD box, plus non-album tracks 'Here at the Western World', 'FM' and 'Bodhisattva (live)' and one unreleased track, the 1971 demo of 'Everyone's Gone to the Movies', but no place for 'Dallas'/'Sail The Waterway'. It's a great shame that no other unreleased material appeared as the quality of the outtakes are better than most artists' finished work. It's a great way to scoop up the released riches of the band's first run but is ultimately a missed opportunity for dyed in the wool fans. Becker and Fagen insisted on a clause in their MCA contract that nothing could be released without their consent, and, being the perfectionists they are, it seems unlikely that the outtakes will ever get an official release.

Showbiz Kids: The Steely Dan Story, 1972–1980
Record Label: MCA Records / Universal Music TV
Date of Release: 14 Nov. 2000
Highest Chart Placing: – (US), 53 (UK)
An in-depth 2CD 33 track overview, again with only a remix of 'FM' and 'Here at the Western World' as non-album tracks.

Steely Dan: The Definitive Collection
Record Label: Geffen Records
Date of Release: 1 Aug. 2006
Highest Chart Placing: – 92 (US), – (UK)
16 tracks from all eras, therefore the first to cover the later tracks, including 'Cousin Dupree' and 'Things I Miss the Most'.

20th Century Masters – The Millennium Collection: The Best of Steely Dan
Record Label: Geffen Records
Date of Release: 12 June 2007
A chronological 10 track trawl through the '70s with no surprises.

20 Dan Deep Cuts

Heard the hits but don't know where to go next? Here are some good options…

'Kings' (*Can't Buy a Thrill*, 1972) – Donald proves early on that he is The Man.

Only a Fool Would Say That (*Can't Buy a Thrill*, 1972) – Funky, odd and groovy, a classic of early Dan.

Fire in the Hole (*Can't Buy a Thrill*, 1972) – Who said the Dan don't do emotion?

The Boston Rag (*Countdown to Ecstasy*, 1973) – Intense, smouldering and enigmatic.

King of the World (*Countdown to Ecstasy*, 1973) – Leave the hole where the marigolds grew, not in your collection.

Charlie Freak (*Pretzel Logic*, 1974) – An object lesson in brilliant efficiency.

Chain Lightning (*Pretzel Logic*, 1972) – Expect the unexpected…

Mister Sam (unreleased, 1975) – Unreleased? Seriously!?

Don't Take Me Alive (*The Royal Scam*, 1976) – Storytelling with an edge.

Everything You Did (*The Royal Scam*, 1976) – Smooth and filthy.

Deacon Blues (*Aja*, 1977) – Heartfelt authenticity.

I Got the News (*Aja*, 1977) – Funk, disco and oral sex in one handy package.

The Bear (unreleased, 1977) – Do you got The Bear?

Gaucho (*Gaucho*, 1980) – If only all arguments could be like this.

Time Out of Mind (*Gaucho*, 1980) – When love isn't all you need.

Kulee Baba (unreleased, 1980) – Energetic mysticism.

Gaslighting Abbie (*Two Against Nature*, 2000) – A scheme to provoke insanity and death has never been so delightful.

Almost Gothic (*Two Against Nature*, 2000) – For when you're tied up with nothing else to do.

Godwhacker (*Everything Must Go*, 2003) – Some people deserve it, no matter how important.

Pixeleen (*Everything Must Go*, 2003) – So much more than a flash of spectacular thigh.

Bibliography & References

Billboard Magazine, vol.95, no.5 – 5 Feb 1983
Fagen, D., *Eminent Hipsters* (Vintage Books, 2013)
Hoskyns, B., *Major Dudes: A Steely Dan Companion* (Constable, 2017)
Sweet, B., *Steely Dan: Reelin' in the Years* (Omnibus Press, third edition, 2008)

Online References
Album Liner Notes – *albumlinernotes.com*
All Music – *www.allmusic.com*
A-Z Lyrics – *www.azlyrics.com*
Genius – *genius.com*
Lyric interpretations – *www.lyricinterpretations.com*
Lyric Wiki – *lyrics.wikia.com*
Rate Your Music – *rateyourmusic.com*
SetlistFM – *www.setlist.fm*
Song Meanings – *songmeanings.com*
Steely Dan Dictionary – *steelydandictionary.com*
Steely Dan Official – *steelydanofficial.com*
Steely Dan Song Database – *www.steelydan.nl*
The Steely Dan Reader – *steelydanreader.com*
Unmask Us – *www.unmask.us*
Walter Becker Media – *www.walterbeckermedia.com*
Walter Becker Official – *walterbecker.com*
Wikiquote – *en.wikiquote.org*

The Beatles - *on track*
an A-Z guide to every song

Andrew Wild
Paperback
336 pages
978-1-78952-009-5
UK £20.00
USD 26.95

Completely unique, this book is the ultimate reference guide to the Beatles, analyzing every song they recorded or performed.

The Beatles - on track analyzes every single song that the Beatles recorded or performed - whether live or in the studio - from the most famous, to the most obscure. The songs that the Beatles performed mirror the history of rock and roll. From the hard-won reputation as the thrilling live act in the Cavern and Hamburg, through to their own classic early songs, the Beatles developed as performers and songwriters of rare distinction. They were always one step ahead of their competition. And then, they mastered the studio. In 1965 and 1966 they increasingly pushed the boundaries of what a pop band could achieve, before breaking down the walls for *Sgt Pepper's Lonely Hearts Club Band*.

Writer and music collector Andrew Wild has gathered together every known Beatles song and every known performance – every studio take, every live recording, every release, every session. In this book, the full breadth of available Beatles music has been collected, catalogued, listened to and analysed, then presented in a format that's easy to read. There are almost 1,000 songs, from the very famous to the very obscure, from the dazzling to the dire. They produced over 1000 recorded versions, over 300 different songs performed in concert, nearly 600 different songs recorded, close to 400 different songs released. If you're a Beatles collector, you need this book.

The Solo Beatles 1969 to 1980 - *on track*
every album, every song

Andrew Wild
Paperback
176 pages
35 color photographs
978-1-78952-030-9
UK £14.99
USD 21.95

Every track recorded by John Lennon, Paul McCartney, George Harrison and Ringo Starr during the ten years after the end of The Beatles.

The Beatles, as a band, released over 200 songs in the eight years between 1962 and 1970. After they split, each commenced a solo career to varying degrees of commercial and critical success. All four of the Beatles achieved number one solo singles in the US between 1970 and 1974. These included great, half-forgotten songs such as 'Give Me Love (Give Me Peace on Earth)', 'My Love', 'Photograph' and 'Whatever Gets You Thru the Night'. Three of the four had UK number one solo singles between 1970 and 1980 in the UK, too, with only Ringo missing out.

Between them, Lennon (and Ono), McCartney (and Wings), Harrison and Starr had twenty-two top ten albums in the US and twenty-five in the UK between 1969 and 1980. They were nothing if not productive. But who but the most committed fans listen today to *Ringo's Rotogravure* (Starr), *Thirty-three and a Third* (Harrison), *Some Time in New York City* (Lennon) or *Wild Life* (McCartney)? It is surely time to re-evaluate the Beatles solo work in the period to 1980. This book examines every solo Beatles album from 1969 to 1980, track by track. It includes the classics, the lost gems, the turkeys, the collaborations, the backbiting, the hits and the misses.

Seinfeld - Seasons 1 to 5 - *on screen*
an episode guide

Stephen Lambe
Paperback
160pages
978-1-78952-012-5
UK £14.99
USD 19.95

A guide to all 84 episodes of the first five seasons of this classic situation comedy series produced between 1990 and 1994.

When the final episode of *Seinfeld* aired on 14 May 1998, an amazing 76.3 million Americans tuned in, making it the most popular situation comedy is US television history. Co-created by Larry David, this 'comedy about nothing' made celebrities of its four stars: stand up comedian Jerry Seinfeld; comedian and actor Michael Richards who played eccentric neighbour Kramer; Julia Louis-Dreyfus who played Jerry's former girlfriend Elaine and Jason Alexander as his volatile, insecure best friend George. Completely unique in its outlook and execution, the success of the series lay in its early years, able to develop its own style below the radar as a minor network hit, before reaching a mass public with its fourth season in 1992. Classic episodes discussed here include: 'The Junior Mint', 'The Chinese Restaurant', 'The Puffy Shirt' and the ground-breaking 'The Contest'.

Much analyzed during its time on screen, the show has not been re-evaluated for many years. Now, over twenty years since the series finished, Stephen Lambe's timely and superbly-crafted new book examines Seinfeld's first five seasons episode by episode, tracing the development of every character, catchphrase and quirk, from the series' embryonic pilot episode in 1989, to its status as an Emmy award-winning show by the time that season five wrapped in 1994. While the show was a huge success in the USA, it was also a cult hit across the globe and its legacy continues into the new millennium.

Frank Zappa 1966 to 1979 - *on track*
every album, every song

Eric Benac
Paperback
176 pages
35 color photographs
978-1-78952-033-0
£14.99
USD 21.95

Every track recorded by Frank Zappa during the most commercially-successful period of his career.

Frank Zappa is, one of the few rock and roll musicians who can truly be labelled a genius. With a career that spanned four decades before his untimely death in 1993, Zappa broke all the rules of composition and production and did things his way. No other rock musician could compose in as many idioms or write music of such sublime complexity and profound beauty.

In this in-depth album guide, the most crucial part of Zappa's discography will be examined in-depth to provide readers with the ultimate guide to the man's recorded work. Each album will be discussed in detail, including the historical context behind the record, an examination of each song on the album, and full details of the musicians who played on it. The book will begin with Zappa's 60s albums with The Mothers of Invention, before delving into his prolific 70s solo career, typified by *Hot Rats, Apostroph*e and *Sheik Yerbouti*. Throughout this period, his albums remained complex musically while the subject matter was often satirical and controversial.

Fans of Zappa's 60s and 70s work will appreciate the level of detail, research, and depth provided in each review, making this the most comprehensive guide to this enigmatic musician's music yet written.

Elton John 1969 to 1979 - *on track*
every album, every song

Peter Kearns
Paperback
144 pages
35 color photographs
978-1-78952-034-7
£14.99
USD 21.95

Every track recorded by music legend Elton John during the 1970s, arguably his most creative and most commercial successful period.

In 1970, Elton John, formerly Reginald Kenneth Dwight, stepped from the obscurity of suburban Pinner, Middlesex, England, into a pop culture reeling from post-Beatles fallout, to become one of the biggest-selling recording artists in the world. To date he has sold over 300 million records from a discography of 30 studio albums, four live albums, over 100 singles, and a multitude of compilations, soundtracks and collaborations. He is the recipient of six Grammys and ten Ivor Novello awards, was inducted into the Rock and Roll Hall of Fame in 1994, appointed a Commander of the Order of the British Empire in 1995 and knighted in 1998. In 2018 he embarked on what is intended to be his swansong world tour, *Farewell Yellow Brick Road*.

This book covers the period from Elton's earliest 1960s releases to his final 1970s album, *Victim of Love*. It is a critical overview of every track on the thirteen studio albums released in an era when Elton was at his most successful and that many fans consider to be the musical high-point of his career. Also included are the two live albums *17-11-70* and *Here and There*, and the trove of album-worthy B-sides that augmented the discography along the way.

Toto - *on track*
every album, every song

Jacob Holm-Lupo
Paperback
176 pages
35 color photographs
978-1-78952-019-4
£14.99
USD 21.95

**Every track recorded
by USA rock legends
Toto throughout their
40 year career.**

Turn on the radio anytime, anywhere in the world, and sooner or later you will hear 'Africa'. Along with just a handful of songs by artists and groups like Michael Jackson and The Beatles, Toto's 'Africa' is one of the most ubiquitous musical works of our time. It was written by a group of session musicians who grew up together in Los Angeles' San Fernando valley. Together they helped define the sound of the late 70s and 80s, appearing on numerous hit records by Michael Jackson, Boz Scaggs and Steely Dan. But it was together, as Toto, that they found their true form, fashioning a fine blend of funk, hard rock, pop and progressive rock that has enamoured millions of record buyers

since their debut in 1978.

'Hold the Line', 'Rosanna' and 'Stop Loving You' are just a few of their other iconic hits. At the same time, their success came at a price. From the early days, Toto were a target for the music press, who disdained their anti-image, their slick chops and polished sound – all at odds with the post-punk and new wave aesthetics prevalent at the time. Yet Toto have always persevered, driven by their love for the music – and their fans' love for them. Lately Toto has been riding a renewed wave of popularity, not to mention a belated restitution from the rock media.

On Track series

Queen – Andrew Wild 978-1-78952-003-3

Emerson Lake and Palmer – Mike Goode 978-1-78952-000-2

Deep Purple and Rainbow 1968-79 – Steve Pilkington 978-1-78952-002-6

Yes – Stephen Lambe 978-1-78952-001-9

Blue Oyster Cult – Jacob Holm-Lupo 978-1-78952-007-1

The Beatles – Andrew Wild 978-1-78952-009-5

Roy Wood and the Move – James R Turner 978-1-78952-008-8

Genesis – Stuart MacFarlane 978-1-78952-005-7

JethroTull – Jordan Blum 978-1-78952-016-3

The Rolling Stones 1963-80 – Steve Pilkington 978-1-78952-017-0

Judas Priest – John Tucker 978-1-78952-018-7

Toto – Jacob Holm-Lupo 978-1-78952-019-4

Van Der Graaf Generator – Dan Coffey 978-1-78952-031-6

Frank Zappa 1966 to 1979 – Eric Benac 978-1-78952-033-0

Elton John in the 1970s – Peter Kearns 978-1-78952-034-7

The Moody Blues – Geoffrey Feakes 978-1-78952-042-2

The Beatles Solo 1969-1980 – Andrew Wild 978-1-78952-030-9

Steely Dan – Jez Rowden 978-1-78952-043-9

Hawkwind – Duncan Harris 978-1-78952-052-1

Fairport Convention – Kevan Furbank 978-1-78952-051-4

Iron Maiden – Steve Pilkington 978-1-78952-061-3

Dream Theater – Jordan Blum 978-1-78952-050-7

10CC – Peter Kearns 978-1-78952-054-5

Gentle Giant – Gary Steel 978-1-78952-058-3

Kansas – Kevin Cummings 978-1-78952-057-6

Mike Oldfield – Ryan Yard 978-1-78952-060-6

The Who – Geoffrey Feakes 978-1-78952-076-7

On Screen series

Carry On... – Stephen Lambe 978-1-78952-004-0

Powell and Pressburger – Sam Proctor 978-1-78952-013-2

Seinfeld Seasons 1 to 5 – Stephen Lambe 978-1-78952-012-5

Francis Ford Coppola – Cam Cobb and Stephen Lambe 978-1-78952-022-4

Monty Python – Steve Pilkington 978-1-78952-047-7

Doctor Who: The David Tennant Years – Jamie Hailstone 978-1-78952-066-8

James Bond – Andrew Wild 978-1-78952-010-1

Other Books

Not As Good As The Book – Andy Tillison 978-1-78952-021-7

The Voice. Frank Sinatra in the 1940s – Stephen Lambe 978-1-78952-032-3

Maximum Darkness – Deke Leonard 978-1-78952-048-4

The Twang Dynasty – Deke Leonard 978-1-78952-049-1

Maybe I Should've Stayed In Bed – Deke Leonard 978-1-78952-053-8

Tommy Bolin: In and Out of Deep Purple – Laura Shenton 978-1-78952-070-5

Jon Anderson and the Warriors - the road to Yes – David Watkinson 978-1-78952-059-0

and many more to come!

Would you like to write for Sonicbond Publishing?

At Sonicbond Publishing we are always on the look-out for authors, particularly for our two main series:

On Track. Mixing fact with in depth analysis, the On Track series examines the work of a particular musical artist or group. All genres are considered from easy listening and jazz to 60s soul to 90s pop, via rock and metal.

On Screen. This series looks at the world of film and television. Subjects considered include directors, actors and writers, as well as entire television and film series. As with the On Track series, we balance fact with analysis.

While professional writing experience would, of course, be an advantage the most important qualification is to have real enthusiasm and knowledge of your subject. First-time authors are welcomed, but the ability to write well in English is essential.

Sonicbond Publishing has distribution throughout Europe and North America, and all books are also published in E-book form. Authors will be paid a royalty based on sales of their book.

Further details are available from www.sonicbondpublishing.co.uk. To contact us, complete the contact form there or email info@sonicbondpublishing.co.uk